SUBMARINES
The History and Evolution of Underwater Fighting Vessels

Antony Preston

Illustrated by John Batchelor

OCTOPUS

in association with
Phoebus

First published 1975 by
Octopus Books Limited
59 Grosvenor Street, London W1

ISBN 0 7064 0429 7

This book has been produced from previously published material
by Phoebus Publishing Company in cooperation with Octopus Books Limited

Produced by Mandarin Publishers Limited
22a Westlands Road, Quarry Bay, Hong Kong
Printed in Hong Kong

Acknowledgment
Front of Jacket: USS Tautog (SSN639)
(U.S. Naval Photographic Centre)

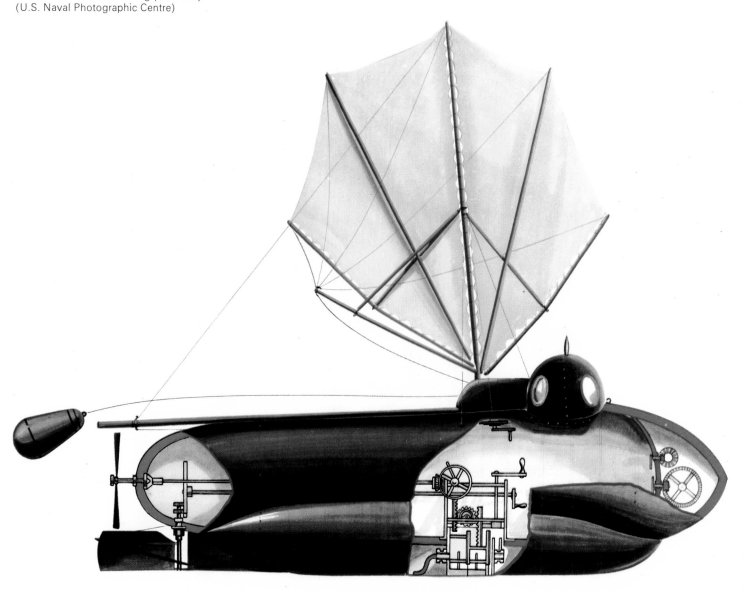

Contents

THE EVOLUTION OF SUBMARINES

The First Submarines

Two of Man's most illogical ambitions are to be able to fly like a bird and to be able to live underwater like a fish. He has no natural aptitude for either, but these two ideas have held Man's imagination for thousands of years. Now, human ingenuity has achieved what Nature clearly did not intend; flight has progressed to space travel and nuclear propulsion has given us the 'true submarine', almost independent of the atmosphere.

Like an aircraft, the submarine owes its startling achievements to the needs of war. However pacific the sentiments of inventors the chief purpose of submarines has been destructive. German U-Boats twice came close to a victory which would have altered the course of history, while a Polaris submarine can unleash missiles with more destructive power than all the bombs dropped in the Second World War.

The first recorded instance of a sub-marine, as opposed to apparatus for diving and working underwater, comes as late as 1578, when the Englishman William Bourne wrote in *Inventions and Devices* about his 'submersible boat'. Unlike later submarines, Bourne's boat actually was shaped like a boat, but its bilges were fitted with leather ballast tanks which admitted seawater through holes below the waterline. The boat would then sink, but buoyancy could be restored by screw presses which squeezed the leather tanks and forced the water out again. While below the surface, the operator could

draw air through a hollow mast, but later experience with hand-operated sub-marines suggests that the exertions would have soon exhausted him. There was a further practical drawback to Bourne's device; it had no means of propulsion and so we must conclude that Bourne was merely anxious to prove that a boat *could* be made to submerge.

Scarcely 40 years later a Dutch emigré, Cornelius van Drebbel, took Bourne's idea a stage further by devising an oar-propelled submersible. Van Drebbel, however, relied on his rowers to force the boat partially below the surface – in nautical parlance, it was only running awash, and since he had no means of altering the displacement it would have been impossible to actually propel under water. However, Drebbel had a flair for publicity which Bourne lacked, for when

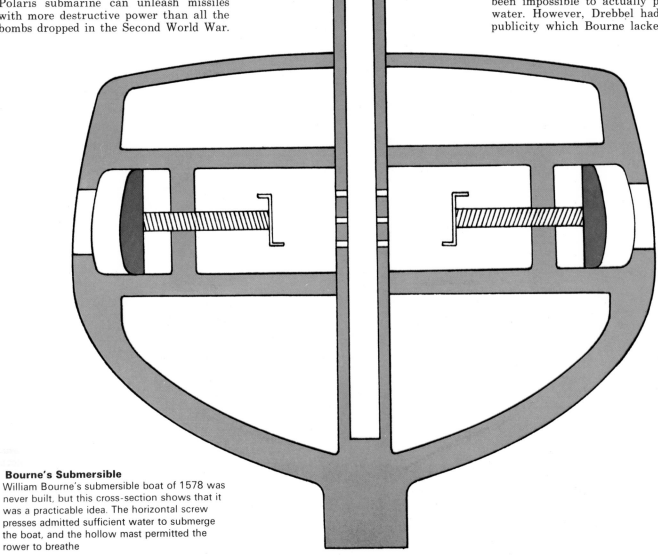

Bourne's Submersible
William Bourne's submersible boat of 1578 was never built, but this cross-section shows that it was a practicable idea. The horizontal screw presses admitted sufficient water to submerge the boat, and the hollow mast permitted the rower to breathe

he built two boats of different sizes and tested them on the Thames, he attracted great interest. He is reputed to have induced that intrepid monarch James I to travel in his boat, but when we read that it travelled from Westminster to Greenwich and was rowed at a depth of twelve or fifteen feet for several hours we can see the hand of some Jacobean public relations expert at work.

Ahead of their time
What is most interesting about both these early experimenters is that they were some 250 years ahead of their time; Bourne's principle of varying the displacement to obtain submergence is essential to the design of modern submarines, while some of the Confederate submersibles used in the American Civil War revived Van Drebbel's idea of forcing themselves below the surface by oar-power. No detailed description of Van Drebbel's submarine has survived, apart from the fact that it was wooden, and covered with greased leather.

Not until 1653 is there any indication that a submarine could be used to destroy ships, when a Frenchman, de Son, built a boat at Rotterdam which 'doeth undertake in one day to destroy a hondered Ships'. Its other qualities were no less modest, for it was to have the speed of a bird and 'no fire, nor Storme, nor Bullets can hinder her, unless it please God'.

M. de Son is immortalised as the inventor of the first mechanically powered submarine, for his craft was propelled by an internal paddle-wheel, but as it was driven by clockwork it is hardly surprising that it was too weak to move. Which was a pity, for this 72-ft craft embodied sound principles, and because of her size could

British warships, and he applied his inventive mind to the problem. The first priority was strength, and the hull was made in the form of two tortoise shells, hence the name *Turtle*; this naturally strong structure was stiffened by a baulk of timber which also served as a seat for the operator. His head came level with a cylindrical brass top, which was fitted with an access hatch and illuminated by glass windows.

The *Turtle* was a most advanced machine which could travel awash, and then ballast down for the final attack. While travelling awash, air was provided for the operator through two brass pipes in the hatch cover, fitted with a simple stop valve like a swimmer's snorkel-tube. A foot-operated valve admitted water when submerging, and there were two hand-pumps to expel water ballast for surfacing. The boat was propelled horizontally and vertically by separate propellers; the horizontal propeller was operated by hand or foot-crank, but the vertical one was only hand-cranked.

In the past, submarine-designers had avoided the most important problem, namely how to sink a ship, but Bushnell was a thorough man. He devised a detachable explosive charge which could be left beneath the hull of a ship by means of

a line attached to a screw driven into its keel. In essence this is very close to the method used in the Second World War by 'human torpedoes', and to complete the modern touch about everything done by Bushnell, he also provided a compass and depth-gauge for navigation.

Ideally, the next step should have been a successful attack on the British Fleet, but here the submarine story met another problem – a minor one, but enough to relegate the submarine to a mere nautical curiosity again. The first experiments in Long Island Sound were promising, but to avoid premature discovery the *Turtle* was removed to the Hudson River. Bushnell's brother had been operating her in these tests, and when he fell ill, possibly from the effects of carbon dioxide poisoning, General Parsons was asked to provide three 'volunteers' from the Army.

Whatever inducements were offered to the trio, one of them, Sergeant Ezra Lee, must have been an exceptionally brave man. On the night of 6 September 1776 he climbed into the *Turtle* and was towed down river to attack the British blockading squadron anchored off Plateau Island. When within a few miles of New York harbour, the two rowing boats slipped their tow and left the tide to carry her downstream. The tide was too strong, and swept the little submarine past the anchorage, so Lee had to work for some two hours, cranking the *Turtle* back into a position where he could reach the 64-gun

hold enough air to keep a man alive for three hours. The lack of any suitable power unit was to hold back the development of submarines throughout the 17th and 18th centuries, although progress was made with diving bells as Man continued in his battle to find a way of surviving underwater. For this reason the next successful step in submarine development reverted to human motive power when, in 1776, the American David Bushnell produced his one-man *Turtle*.

After the outbreak of the American War of Independence, British warships had blockaded the Atlantic coast and, as a young patriot, Bushnell was keenly aware of the need for the colonies to break the British stranglehold. With no large navy to match the Royal Navy, Bushnell reasoned that an underwater boat might cause sufficient damage to drive away the

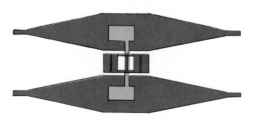

De Son's Submersible
De Son's submersible catamaran of 1653 was 72 ft long, and was the first mechanically propelled design. Unfortunately, the clockwork engine was not strong enough to move the hull, so she never had a chance to live up to any of her inventor's extravagant claims

Eagle, flagship of Lord Howe, which was lying off Governor's Island.

He manoeuvred carefully under the massive hull, and proceeded to work the screw for attaching the explosive charge, but to his dismay he found that the screw could not penetrate. English warships were now being coppered and sheathed against shipworm, and this was thought to be the reason, though Bushnell felt that Lee had probably encountered iron bracing near the keel. It is now known that HMS *Eagle* had no coppering on her hull, which means that Bushnell's theory may have been correct. If not, Lee could have been suffering from his prolonged submergence, and could have been too easily discouraged. At any rate he decided to abandon the attempt as it was nearly daylight.

Fortunately, the tide was now in his favour, and he made good progress. A guard-boat gave chase, and Lee was able to discourage it and gain speed by jettisoning the 150-lb charge, but not before he set the clockwork fuse; the fact that the charge exploded indicates that Lord Howe's flagship might have been sunk or disabled with only a little more luck.

Although further attacks are said to have been made with the *Turtle*, and a copy may have been built for an attack on HMS *Ramillies* in the War of 1812, Bushnell's contribution to the submarine story was over. His fellow-countryman, Robert Fulton, claimed to have worked out his own ideas quite separately, and although he seems to have discussed them with Bushnell, he was certainly the first of the pacifist submarine-inventors, for unlike Bushnell, he wanted to perfect a machine to destroy *all* warships. He felt that the inevitable growth of the United States Navy would contaminate her spirit of republicanism and destroy its power for good.

Like other ardent republicans he regarded the French Revolution as the apotheosis of democracy, and he emigrated to France in 1797 to be able to put his inventive genius at the service of the Directory. After working on a number of engineering projects with some success, Fulton wrote to the Directory in December 1797 to offer them a 'mechanical engine' for the destruction of the Royal Navy, which was then blockading the coast of France with conspicuous effectiveness. Fulton offered to manufacture at his own expense a submarine to be called the *Nautilus*, on condition that the French Government

Extracts from David Bushnell's letter to Thomas Jefferson, 1787.

General Principles and Construction of a Sub-marine Vessel, communicated by D. Bushnell of Connecticut, the inventor, in a letter of October, 1787, to Thomas Jefferson then Minister Plenipotentiary of the United States at Paris.

The external shape of the sub-marine vessel bore some resemblance to two upper tortoise shells of equal size, joined together; the place of entrance into the vessel being represented by the opening made by the swell of the shells, at the head of the animal. The inside was capable of containing the operator, and air, sufficient to support him thirty minutes without receiving fresh air. At the bottom opposite to the entrance was fixed a quantity of lead for ballast. At one edge which was directly before the operator, who sat upright, was an oar for rowing forward or backward. At the other edge, was a rudder for steering. An aperture, at the bottom, with its valve, was designed to admit water, for the purpose of descending; and two brass forcing-pumps served to eject the water within, when necessary for ascending. At the top, there was likewise an oar, for ascending or descending, or continuing at any particular depth — A water-gauge or barometer, determined the depth of descent, a compass directed the course, and a ventilator within, supplied the vessel with fresh air, when on the surface.

When the operator would descend, he placed his foot upon the top of a brass valve, depressing it, by which he opened a large aperture in the bottom of the vessel, through which the water entered at his pleasure; when he had admitted a sufficient quantity, he descended very gradually; if he admitted too much, he ejected as much as was necessary to obtain an equilibrium, by the two brass forcing pumps, which were placed at each hand. Whenever the vessel leaked, or he would ascend to the surface, he also made use of these forcing pumps. When the skilful operator had obtained an equilibrium, he could row upward, or downward, or continue at any particular depth, with an oar, placed near the top of the vessel, forming upon the principle of the screw, the axis of the oar entering the vessel; by turning the oar one way he raised the vessel, by turning it the other way he depressed it.

Description of a magazine and its appendages, designed to be conveyed by the sub-marine vessel to the bottom of a ship.

In the forepart of the brim of the crown of the sub-marine vessel, was a socket, and an iron tube, passing through the socket; the tube stood upright, and could slide up and down in the socket, six inches: at the top of the tube, was a wood-screw (A) fixed by means of a rod, which passed through the tube, and screwed the wood-screw fast upon the top of the tube; by pushing the wood-screw up against the bottom of a ship, and turning it at the same time, it would enter the planks; driving would also answer the same purpose; when the wood-screw was firmly fixed, it would be cast off by unscrewing the rod, which fastened it upon the top of the tube.

Behind the sub-marine vessel, was a place, above the rudder, for carrying a large powder magazine, this was made of two pieces of oak timber, large enough when hollowed out to contain one hundred and fifty pounds of powder, with the apparatus used in firing it, and was secured in its place by a screw, turned by the operator. A strong piece of rope extended from the magazine to the wood-screw (A) above mentioned, and was fastened to both. When the wood-screw was fixed, and to be cast off from its tube, the magazine was to be cast off likewise by unscrewing it, leaving it hanging to the wood-screw; it was lighter than the water, that it might rise up against the object, to which the wood-screw and itself were fastened.

Experiments made to prove the nature and use of a sub-marine vessel.

The first experiment I made, was with about two ounces of gun powder, which I exploded 4 feet under water, to prove to some of the first personages in Connecticut, that powder would take fire under water.

The second experiment was made with two pounds of powder, enclosed in a wooden bottle, and fixed under a hogshead, with a two-inch oak plank between the hogshead and the powder; the hogshead was loaded with stones as deep as it could swim; a wooden pipe descending through the lower head of the hogshead, and through the plank, into the powder contained in the bottle, was primed with powder. A match put to the priming, exploded the powder, which produced a very great effect, rending the plank into pieces; demolishing the hogshead; and casting the stones and the ruins of the hogshead, with a body of water, many feet into the air, to the astonishment of the spectators. This experiment was likewise made for the satisfaction of the gentlemen above mentioned.

I afterwards made many experiments of a similar nature, some of them with large quantities of powder; they all produced very violent explosions, much more than sufficient for any purpose I had in view.

KEY

1 Ventilation pipes with simple self-sealing valves to prevent water entering boat
2 One vent pipe stayed shut as shown so that foul air could escape through top of dome
3 Skylights in brass dome
4 Port holes on either side and in front of dome. These could be opened to admit air during surface running
5 Brass hinge allowed brass dome to tip sideways to admit crew. This could be screwed down from inside or out
6 Screw for attaching 'bomb' to underside of target ship. After screw was firmly attached to bottom planks, the boat was submerged even further to release screw, rope and bomb
7 Ascent and descent propeller
8 Bomb. Made from two pieces of oak hollowed to take 150 lb of black powder. Inside an 'apparatus' (most probably clockwork) was made to run up to twelve hours, when it would release a sear allowing a flintlock to fire and explode the main charge. When released, the bomb, which was lighter than the water it displaced, would float up against the target to give better performance
9 Bomb release screw
10 Depth gauge. A glass tube, its open end at the bottom, allowed outside water pressure to float a phosphorus-covered cork up and down according to depth. The light of the phosphorus allowed the operator to see the position of the cork and measure his depth against a graduated line on the glass
11 Propeller. Could move forward or astern
12 Propeller operating crank. A removable handle could be used for hand operation
13 Foot pedals for operating propeller cranks
14 Major transverse beam and operator's seat
15 Compass
16 Two brass forcing pumps for pumping out leaks and ballast water
17 Forcing pump operating handles
18 Rudder bar: down for port and up for starboard
19 Rudder bar crank
20 Rudder
21 Ventilation pump, to force fresh air in and foul air out at 2
22 Completely sealed down, the operator had enough air for about 30 minutes. This valve ensured that no water was admitted
23 Ballast reel
24 Tackle for lifting emergency ballast
25 Below deck, 200 lb of lead ballast could be released on 50 ft of line in an emergency, and recovered if and when the operator was able to continue his mission
26 Ballast water inlet valve operated by right foot. Perforated cover prevented weeds etc. entering and blocking pumps or valve
27 Although not mentioned, it is fairly certain that the operator would carry some means of 'repelling boarders' in the event of being forced to surface
28 Internal lead ballast which could be added according to the weight of the operator

would pay 4,000 francs per gun for every British warship carrying more than forty guns, and 2,000 francs per gun for smaller ships. (At this rate he would have been richer by 400,000 francs if he had sunk HMS *Victory* – in modern terms at least four million pounds.) He also stipulated, among other things, that his weapon would not be used against his own countrymen unless they used it first against France.

The impoverished Directory cut the amount of money and, on the advice of

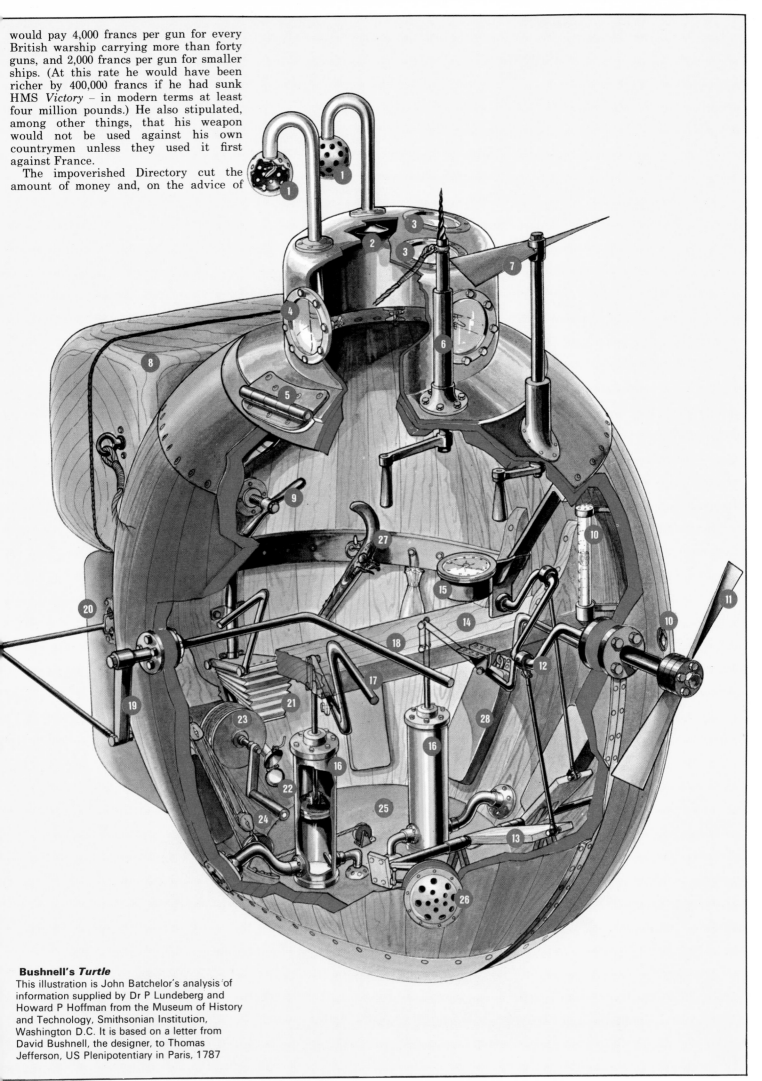

Bushnell's *Turtle*
This illustration is John Batchelor's analysis of information supplied by Dr P Lundeberg and Howard P Hoffman from the Museum of History and Technology, Smithsonian Institution, Washington D.C. It is based on a letter from David Bushnell, the designer, to Thomas Jefferson, US Plenipotentiary in Paris, 1787

the Minister of Marine, refused to grant commissions to any future crew-members of the *Nautilus*, thus ensuring that the English could hang them as pirates. After further haggling, the disappointed inventor took his designs to Holland only to be rejected. Three years later, however, when Napoleon Bonaparte had replaced the Directory with the title of First Consul of the French Republic, Fulton was given a more friendly reception. A grant of 10,000 francs was made to allow him to build the *Nautilus*, and she was completed in Paris in about five months.

The *Nautilus* was far bigger than the *Turtle* and was closer to the modern submarine in having a conning tower, diving planes, flooding valves and space for three men. The hull was built of copper and strengthened with iron frames, and although its designed diving depth was only 25 ft this was more than enough. Without periscopes, the only way to navigate such a craft was by taking frequent sights at the surface, and for this purpose the *Nautilus* had a hemispherical conning tower fitted with lookout scuttles of thick glass.

As Bushnell's experience had shown, a submarine was useless without an efficient ship-killing weapon, and in this respect Fulton was no more successful. The *Nautilus* had a heavy hollow spike projecting through the top of her conning tower, and this was intended to be driven into the botton of the target ship. The submarine then drew free, and pulled in a line which was towing a buoyant explosive charge; a percussion lock would fire the charge as soon as it struck the target. As before, the main motive power came from a hand-operated screw, but there was also a kite-like sail which would be used to make 2 – 3 knots and take the strain off the operator in favourable conditions.

In the spring of 1800 some startled Frenchmen saw Fulton take his boat down to 25 ft in the muddy waters of the Seine, and while the trials indicated that the lack of motive power was still the most limiting factor, he was encouraged to continue. Although Fulton was not

Fulton's *Nautilus*

Robert Fulton's *Nautilus* was built in 1800 to help the French Navy to break the British naval blockade. The sail was to reduce the strain on her three-man crew, and the explosive charge can be seen on the end of its trailing line. Although this submarine proved workable, it lacked a suitable weapon for sinking ships, and never had a chance to prove itself

allowed to use the dockyard at Brest for his experiments, the officers' were instructed to give him any assistance needed. In September 1800 he claimed to have attacked two English brigs off the Normandy coast, but said that in each case the vessels had weighed anchor before he could approach them. It was also reported that the *Nautilus* had managed to remain submerged for an hour at a depth of about 20 ft, and some sources claim that the addition of a compressed air reservoir made a five-hour dive possible, though the French archives suggest that Fulton fitted an air-tube to extend the endurance.

Too convincing

In August 1801 an old shallop was successfully blown up in a demonstration by the *Nautilus*, but when it was suggested that she should attack an English warship lying off Brest it was clear that the forces of orthodoxy were, if anything, too well convinced. The officers at Brest, particularly Admirals Villaret de Joyeuse and Latouche-Treville, made no secret of their dislike of Fulton's infernal machine, and as Bonaparte was trying to negotiate the Peace of Amiens with the British he was anxious not to encourage such anti-British activities.

When a final rejection came in February 1804, Fulton was so disheartened that he was able to compromise with his conscience, and went to London to present his idea to the British. One explanation of this startling abandonment of Fulton's well-known pacifist ideals is

that the British, being well aware of the *Nautilus*, had made him a secret offer; some French officials were certain that he had been suborned by their enemies, and the rejection of Fulton's plans may have been caused by these fears.

Whatever the background to Fulton's change of allegiance, the Government of William Pitt showed as much interest in the *Nautilus* as Napoleon's had in 1801. A high-powered committee, including the gifted inventor of military rockets, Major Congreve, was appointed, and a target-brig was blown up off Walmer. But an invention which inspired revulsion in French naval officers was hardly likely to appeal to the world's largest navy, and Lord St Vincent pronounced sentence: "Pitt was the greatest fool that ever existed to encourage a mode of warfare, which those who command the seas did not want and which, if successful, would deprive them of it".

The British have been ridiculed for adopting this negative attitude, but it is hard to see what else they should have done. The *Nautilus* was ingenious, but she was conceived when there was no practical alternative to hand-propulsion and no reliable means of sinking ships from under water. A light steam engine was still some fifty years away, as was the fish torpedo, and until these became practical a submarine had as little chance of reaching a target in the open sea as she had of sinking it. Added to which, these very small submarines had such limited visibility that navigation was extremely difficult.

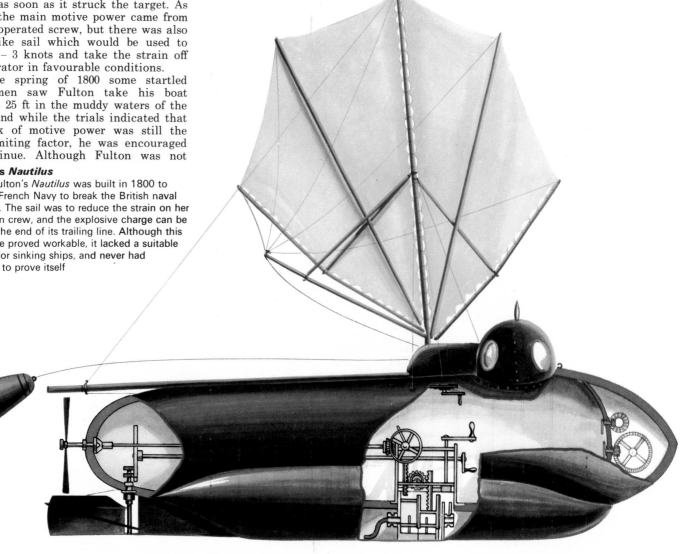

The Next Step

The next step forward was in 1850, when a Bavarian NCO named Wilhelm Bauer produced a submarine called *Le Plongeur Marin*, the Sea Diver. The Danish fleet was blockading the German coast, and with the backing of several influential citizens of Kiel, a boat was laid down in a private shipyard. *Le Plongeur Marin* had some features in common with Fulton's design, but she was built of sheet iron, and resembled a large oblong tank. Water was admitted into a double bottom to ballast the boat down, but when awash a heavy weight was moved backwards and forwards to produce a series of dips.

Despite her limitations, the boat was successful in making the Danish ships keep a more respectful distance, but in February 1851 Bauer achieved unenviable fame when his submarine's hull plating buckled under pressure, and he found himself on the bottom of Kiel harbour. By sheer force of personality Bauer persuaded his two panic-stricken seamen to do the one thing which could save them: admit more water to the boat until the pressure was equalised. Eventually they listened

to him, and when the pressure was right the two hatches burst open and all three men shot to the surface. Not until 1887 was the *Plongeur* rediscovered during dredging operations, and she was subsequently exhibited at the Naval School in Kiel.

Bauer's friends seem to have deserted him, and as he lacked sufficient funds to continue he was forced to offer his services to the Austrian Government. After getting involved in a political squabble which quickly obscured any of the merits of his invention, Bauer decided to try his luck in England, but despite getting the attention of Prince Albert he had little success. There is a story that the celebrated naval architect Scott Russell sacked Bauer, and then adapted his ideas and offered a submarine to the Admiralty during the Crimean War, but little evidence of this has survived.

However, Bauer was able to persuade the Russians to listen to him, and he was allowed to build *Le Diable Marin*. As the Russians were as secretive in 1856 as they

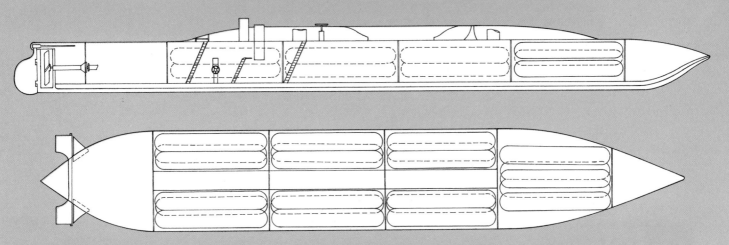

Bauer's *Plongeur Marin* (top)
Wilhelm Bauer's *Plongeur Marin* of 1850 looked like an iron tank, but proved that she could submerge. The big wheel moved a weight to and fro to make her dive in a succession of dips. She was also noteworthy as the first submarine from which anyone escaped after an accident

French *Plongeur*
The French *Plongeur* of 1863 was the first submarine to look anything like the modern ones. Although most of the hull was filled with reservoirs for compressed air she lacked sufficient pressure to blow her ballast tanks. The spar torpedo provided was a virtual suicide weapon, which was a further discouragement

are now, very little is known except that Bauer took his submarine below the surface of Kronstadt harbour with several musicians during the coronation of Tsar Alexander II, and during the royal salute the band struck up 'God Preserve the Tsar'. *Le Diable Marin* was later sunk, and thereafter Bauer drifted into obscurity, although he is now regarded as a man of great talent and perseverance who furthered the design of the submarine more than any of his predecessors.

The Anglo-French alliance during the Crimean War itself lasted only a short while, and one of the reasons for the tension between the two nations was the French discovery that they were enjoying a temporary lead over the British in ship-design. They had been able to offer the plans of their armoured batteries to the British, and when Dupuy de Lôme produced his plans for the ironclad frigate *Gloire* it seemed that France might be able to beat the British by sheer ingenuity.

It is against this background of revolution and innovation that a French officer, Captain Bourgois, suggested that a submarine propelled by compressed air would be a sound investment as a coast-defence weapon against ironclads. His ideas were put forward in 1858, the year in which the *Gloire* was ordered, and a year later the Minister of Marine called on various designers to produce detailed designs. The plans of M. Brun were accepted, and in 1863 the *Plongeur* was launched at Rochefort.

As a contemporary model has survived we are rather better informed about this boat than others. She was large, 140 ft long and 10 ft. in internal diameter from deck to keel, and had a spar torpedo. The boat's hull had an elliptical cross-section and the upper deck was flat, which gave her a marked resemblance to 20th century French submarines. Internally she had 23 reservoirs for compressed air at 180 lb/sq in, driving a four-cylinder engine sited right aft. Ballast tanks allowed the boat to be trimmed down, and regulating pistons gave a final adjustment of displacement, but the *Plongeur* differed radically from earlier boats in her ability to empty her ballast tanks by blowing the water out with compressed air. The low pressure in the reservoirs meant that this was a slow process, and as she proved difficult to handle with only a pair of hydroplanes aft, she was far too clumsy to be an effective weapon of war. With the suicidal properties of the spar torpedo to discourage them further, the French authorities discontinued their experiments, but they had made a big contribution to progress.

Seven years after Bauer's success in Russia, another naval blockade provided the stimulus for fresh progress. This time it was the American Civil War which was the focus for heroism and brilliant improvisation. As the Confederate forces were faced by a large fleet they saw themselves as giant-killers and the 'submersible torpedo-boats' produced by their designers were soon called 'Davids'.

The first type of 'David' was a totally new departure, for she was powered by a steam engine, and thus overcame one of the main limitations of earlier boats. She was not, however, a true submarine, for like Van Drebbel's boat she could only be trimmed down until she was awash. A small narrow superstructure containing the hatchway and the funnel remained above water, and as it was only ten feet long it could be mistaken for a baulk of timber at night. A suitable

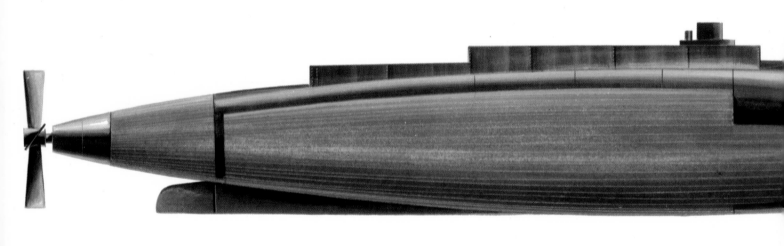

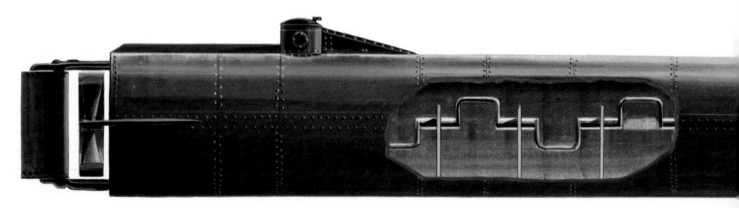

weapon was still lacking, however. All that a 'David' could bring to bear was a spar torpedo, a long pole tipped with a 134-lb canister of gunpowder fitted with a series of seven chemical impact fuses. Neither Bushnell nor Fulton would have thought much of such a kamikaze weapon, for nothing short of a miracle would prevent the 'David' from being swamped by the shock wave from the explosion of her 'torpedo', as she was never more than 20 ft away.

Nor was this the only danger – the very first 'David' was swamped during her trials by the wash of a passing steamer. But volunteers came forward to man her after she had been raised, and on 5 October 1863 she carried out an attack on Federal warships off Charleston, South Carolina. Under Lt Glassell the little craft headed towards the Federal ironclad *New Ironsides*, and when challenged by the watch she was close enough to disconcert her large adversary by firing a volley of rifle fire from her hatchway, killing an officer on board. Shortly afterwards came a powerful explosion which shook the *New Ironsides* and blew a hole in her side. Inevitably the little 'David' was swamped,

and only two crew members and Glassell were able to escape. Despite their efforts the Federal ironclad was only damaged, and this gave rise to a certain over-confidence among Federal officers. Just over four months later their complacency was shaken when an improved 'David', known from its inventor as the *Hunley*, attacked the new Federal steam sloop *Housatonic* off Charleston.

Although given the generic term 'David', this latest example was radically different to the steam-driven submersibles which had been used the year before. She was actually the third boat in a series built by a group headed by Horace L Hunley, the first two having been unsuccessful prototypes. The third boat was built at Mobile, Alabama, and sent by rail to Charleston, where she sank during trials on 15 October 1863, killing Hunley.

A new crew was assembled and trained to man the submarine when she was salvaged, and as a compliment to her late designer and commander she was named CSS *H L Hunley*. She was propelled by hand, but in order to provide sufficient power, an eight-man team

worked a pump handle arrangement to drive a single screw, while the commander conned the boat from forward. She was closed down, and had a pair of hydroplanes forward to keep her below the surface; the air supply was considered sufficient to last for two or three hours. On 17 February 1864, *H L Hunley* successfully sank the *Housatonic*, but nothing further was seen of her or Lt George E Dixon (actually a volunteer from the 21st Alabama Infantry Regiment) and his men. Some years later, divers examining the wreck of the *Housatonic* found a cylindrical hull alongside the sunken sloop, with nine skeletons aboard.

Another type of 'David' was used to attack the *Minnesota* off Newport News in April 1864. This was a picket-boat fitted with ballast tanks, and having a bullet-proof turtle-back deck fitted to make her silhouette as insignificant as possible. She was unusual in that she carried out a successful attack and escaped to tell the tale. The only other recorded attack was made in the North Edisto River at about the same time, but the target's propeller broke the spar torpedo, and the 'David' escaped.

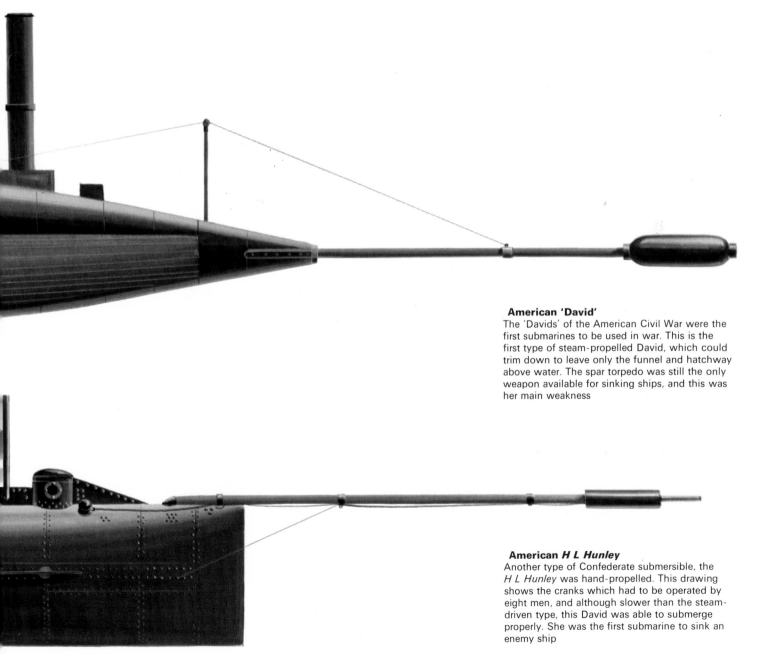

American 'David'
The 'Davids' of the American Civil War were the first submarines to be used in war. This is the first type of steam-propelled David, which could trim down to leave only the funnel and hatchway above water. The spar torpedo was still the only weapon available for sinking ships, and this was her main weakness

American *H L Hunley*
Another type of Confederate submersible, the *H L Hunley* was hand-propelled. This drawing shows the cranks which had to be operated by eight men, and although slower than the steam-driven type, this David was able to submerge properly. She was the first submarine to sink an enemy ship

Torpedoes: The Ideal Weapon

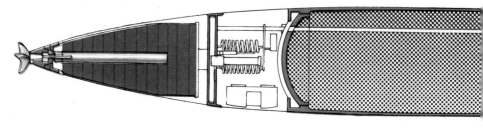

Guncotton warhead   Depth-keeping mechanism

The next noteworthy submarine design came from a Liverpool clergyman, the Rev. George Garrett, and it led in turn to the first commercially-built submarines. Technology was at last coming to the aid of designers, particularly with the perfection of the electric motor and the lead-acid storage battery, but a whole swarm of contrivances were investigated by 19th century inventors in an effort to store power under water. In 1878 Garrett built a small submarine out of steel plates, which submerged by the proven method of admitting water to alter the displacement of the boat. Like so many before it, this little egg-shaped boat was propelled by a hand-screw, and seems to have been sufficiently successful for Garrett to embark on a more ambitious project a year later.

American *Intelligent Whale*

The *Intelligent Whale* was the Yankee North's answer to the Confederate Davids. She was hand-propelled like the *Hunley*, but proved hard to manoeuvre and lacked a suitable weapon. Furthermore, the end of the Civil War robbed her of targets, so she was never used

The *Resurgam*

This was based on the original design in that the five-foot diameter was retained, but the hull was increased from 15 to 45 ft, and the ends were pointed. The second boat, christened the *Resurgam*, was steam-powered on the surface, and while running on the surface a full head of steam was raised to provide latent heat for heating water stored in special tanks. This system was already in use in Lamm's fireless locomotive to avoid making smoke on London's underground railways, and was good enough to drive the *Resurgam* at 2–3 knots for ten miles. Unfortunately Garrett's limited resources meant that he had to restrict the boat's size, and the boiler and pressurised tank took up so much room that the three-man crew had to crawl through 12- or 14-in spaces. Garrett had no qualms about using his ten-year-old son as a deckhand, presumably because the boy could squeeze through such spaces more easily, and the lad recorded years later that he had to lie on his back and pull himself along.

The experiment faced failure when the *Resurgam* was wrecked while carrying out sea trials off the Welsh coast, but Garrett

Whitehead Torpedo

The Whitehead torpedo, which was perfected in 1868, was the armament which the submarine needed before its potential as an effective and deadly weapon of war could be realised. It allowed the submarine to attack targets from a safe distance, and its speed made evasion difficult

was fortunate enough to attract the attention of the famous Swedish industrialist and inventor Thorsten Nordenfelt. As a supplier of arms to the world Nordenfelt could see the advantages of a workable submarine, and he willingly provided capital for a prototype to be built under Garrett's supervision at Stockholm in 1882.

By this time the Whitehead 'fish' or locomotive torpedo had come into service in many navies, and so another major obstacle to submarine progress had been eliminated. But the problem of propulsion remained, and Garrett's method of using latent heat from hot water tanks was retained. Vertical propellers were provided to take the boat below the surface, once she had been trimmed down to run awash, and a pair of bow hydroplanes assisted in depth-keeping. She was cigar-shaped,

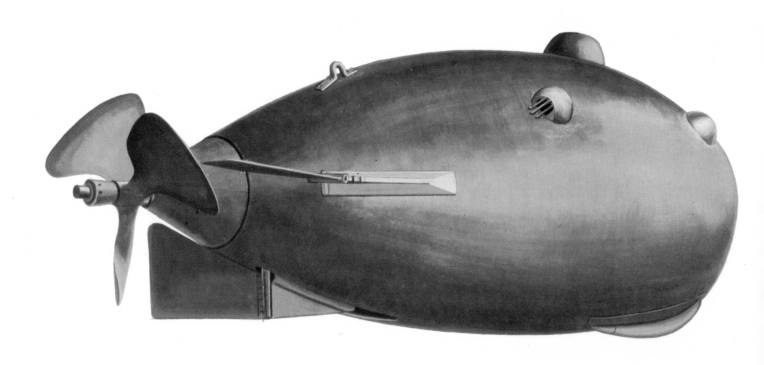

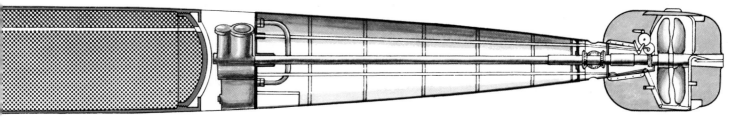

Air reservoir   Compressed air motor   Rudders and propellers

but without the conning tower of Garrett's *Resurgam*, and was the first submarine to have a surface armament, a 1-in Nordenfelt machine-gun. The Whitehead torpedo was fired from a bow tube placed in an external casing over the bow.

Trials took place at Landskrona in September 1885, and although moderately successful they proved that the submarine was not yet reliable enough. Although the steam engine gave a theoretical range of 15 miles underwater at four knots, the boat (known as *Nordenfelt No. 1*) proved unable to stay dived for more than three minutes and had great difficulty in keeping a constant depth-line. She proved quite successful while running awash on the surface, though, and this would have been of considerable value for an attack against the defences of the period. The air-supply was sufficient for six hours, but the slightest leakage from the furnaces or smoke-boxes produced carbon-monoxide poisoning. A contemporary account records the sinister fact that some men became drowsy, and cheerfully adds that any crew member badly affected needed to rest for 'several days'. Garrett himself was poisoned and this meant that he

was unfit for duty for three weeks.

Despite these problems, *Nordenfelt No. 1* was sold to Greece for £9,000 in 1886, and the firm started work a year later on two improved submarines for the Turkish Government. These were built in England, near Chertsey, and were to be known as the *Abdul Mejid* and *Abdul Hamid*. Despite the relative failure of the prototype, the Turks were anxious to keep abreast of submarine development, both on account of their dislike of the Greeks and on account of their fear of Russian ideas. In 1879 the Russians had ordered fifty small pedal-operated boats of the type designed by Drzewiecki, and although they proved to be quite useless their existence made the Turks apprehensive.

No volunteers
The two boats were shipped out to Turkey in sections, and re-erected at the government yard at the Golden Horn. Garrett received a commission as an Ottoman officer and, as no Turkish volunteers could be found, an English crew was provided. As with the prototype the biggest problem was securing a steady depth-line; the vertical screws proved to

have little effect, and the large ballast tanks did nothing to help, since the water tended to surge backwards and forwards. On the only recorded occasion on which a torpedo was fired, the bow leapt up violently and the boat plunged backwards to the bottom. The motion must have been unpleasant at the best of times, for she was described as being hardly ever on an even keel for more than a few seconds at a time.

The Turks were unable to recruit even the six men required to man one submarine, and the second boat was never finished. This was never announced, however, and for years the world thought that Turkey had two operational submarines. In 1914 the Germans found their remains in a dockyard shed, and tried to recondition them, but by that time they were beyond repair.

British *Resurgam*
The *Resurgam* was designed by the Reverend George Garrett and built in Liverpool in 1879. She overcame the propulsion problem by using a steam engine, but had no weapons of any kind. She was bad at depth-keeping because of her large ballast tanks and the absence of any diving planes

Like all arms-suppliers, Nordenfelt found himself supplying rival customers with counters to his own equipment, and it was not long before the Russians showed interest in the newest Nordenfelt submarine. This had begun as a speculative venture in 1887, and was considerably larger than the previous boats, being 125 ft long and 12 ft. in diameter. Her hull was made of 5/16-in plate, and the topside was 1 in thick as protection against light shells and machine-gun bullets. She differed in shape from the others in having a hull which was fuller throughout its length, with a blunt bow enclosing two torpedo-tubes, one above the other. The new shape was adopted to improve the underwater stability, and the vertical propellers were placed much further apart for the same reason. Two funnels were positioned close together amidships, and there were two small conning towers, one forward and one aft. She reached 14 knots on the surface, and was reported to be capable of 5 knots underwater, with a range of 20 miles.

As the first submarine to be seen publicly in England since the 17th century, she attracted a lot of attention,

and after trials she made her début at the 1887 Naval Review held to celebrate Queen Victoria's Golden Jubilee. Being painted a dull neutral grey she proved very hard to see. She seems to have been the first warship to adopt this serviceable colour-scheme. Despite the efforts of Garrett and Nordenfelt's designers the inherent problems were not solved, and the boat continued to be unreliable in depth-keeping. The ballast and hot water tanks were still too large, and surges exaggerated any movement. Neither of the inventors were able to design an adequate form of compensation for the change of weight caused by discharging a torpedo, and the heat in the engine room reached a staggering 150°F.

In spite of the submarine's inability to meet the claims of its designers the Russian Government offered to buy it, presumably to match the Turkish and Greek submarines, and having failed to find the answer in its own Drzewiecki boats. They did stipulate, however, that she should be capable of repeating her specified performance at Kronstadt in deep water, a wise precaution in view of what happened. *Nordenfelt No. 2* went out

to the Baltic in tow of Garrett's yacht, the *Lodestar*, but due to an error of navigation ran aground off the coast of Denmark. Although refloated two weeks later she was not accepted by the Russians, and she was written off as a total loss; the hull was subsequently scrapped by the salvage company. This brought an end to any collaboration between Garrett and Nordenfelt, and Garrett emigrated to the United States.

Nordenfelt persevered, and was able to sell his designs to the Germans in 1890. Two boats, called *W1* and *W2*, were built at Kiel and Danzig respectively, followed by an improved type built by Howaldt's yard at Kiel, but none of these proved successful in service. It is clear that Garrett-Nordenfelt designs were fundamentally unsound, in that they lacked a fixed centre of gravity, had only rudimentary depth-control, and were underpowered. Had the two inventors worked out the stability problems before rushing on to submarines four times as big as the prototype they might have contributed more. The ideal submarine weapon had arrived, but the propulsion problem still held up development.

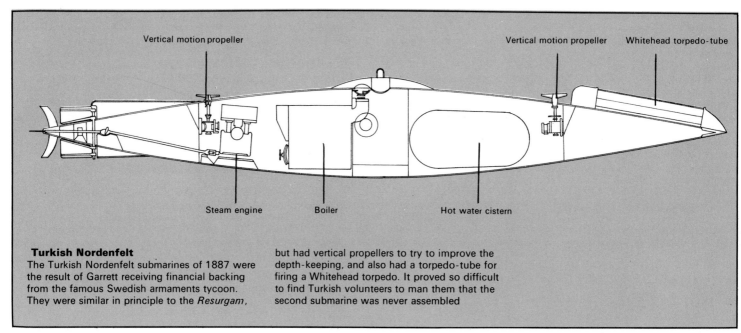

Vertical motion propeller   Vertical motion propeller   Whitehead torpedo-tube

Steam engine   Boiler   Hot water cistern

Turkish Nordenfelt
The Turkish Nordenfelt submarines of 1887 were the result of Garrett receiving financial backing from the famous Swedish armaments tycoon. They were similar in principle to the *Resurgam*, but had vertical propellers to try to improve the depth-keeping, and also had a torpedo-tube for firing a Whitehead torpedo. It proved so difficult to find Turkish volunteers to man them that the second submarine was never assembled

German Nordenfelt
Two German Nordenfelts were built in Germany in 1890, but they proved no more successful than their predecessors. Very little is known about these submarines, but the 'snout' appears to be the torpedo-tube

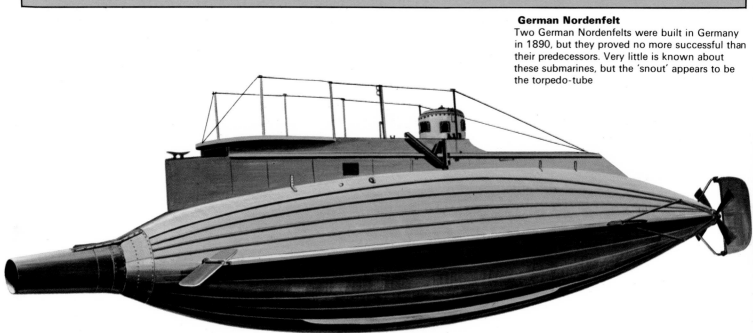

The Propulsion Problem

The propulsion problem was being
tackled, for at the time that Garrett and
Nordenfelt were pushing ahead with their
designs, a young Spanish naval officer,
Lieutenant Isaac Peral, was working on
an electric submarine. It is a strange
quirk of fortune that a small, under-
developed country like Spain should have
produced the first modern submarine,
when the leading naval and shipbuilding
power, Great Britain, was still unable to
find a suitable method of propulsion.
Peral was not the first Spaniard to build a
submarine (an engineer called Montjuriol
had built a copy of Bauer's boat called
El Ictineo in 1860), but his boat was
the first to use an underwater propulsion
system totally independent of the atmosphere. She was powered by 420 electric
accumulators (batteries) driving two
30 hp main motors, and three 5 hp
auxiliary motors for pumping out ballast
tanks. The vertical screws of the Nordenfelt boats were copied, and there was a
single tube for firing a Schwarzkopf
(German) torpedo.

Peral's ideas were generally sound,
and had he been allowed to develop them
it is probable that he would have cured
the depth-keeping problems which

inevitably plagued his submarine. But
the Spanish naval authorities ordered a
long-winded enquiry into the design,
harping on its drawbacks and Peral's lack
of experience. Peral was naturally in-
dignant when he tried without success to
get permission to build an improved
submarine. The idea was finally killed off
in 1890 in a long series of windy arguments
and official verdicts, and it was not until
the Spanish-American War of 1898 that
the Spanish Government realised the value
of submarines. The American Navy
admitted that the existence of only two
Peral submarines at Manila would have
made their squadron far more cautious,
and might have prevented it from destroying the Spanish cruisers with such
impunity.

France in the lead
The accumulator battery and the
electric motor were the keys to underwater
navigation, for they offered a reasonable
power-to-weight ratio and needed no
oxygen. The country which had made
most progress in the design of electric

motors was France, and it is surprising
that a Frenchman did not stumble on the
idea of a battery-driven submarine before
a Spaniard. The French civil engineer
Claude Goubet produced a very small
two-man boat in 1887, but as he failed to
provide a means of keeping longitudinal
stability it had little value. But the
French Navy, influenced by the doctrines
of the 'Jeune Ecole' which stressed the
need for cheap forms of indirect attack,
showed enough interest to make it worth
Goubet's while to design a larger boat.

Goubet II was built at Cherbourg in
1886–1889, and had a 26-ft bronze hull.
Her two operators could bring her to an
awash condition by flooding the ballast
tanks, and then they admitted more
water to destroy her reserve of buoyancy.
But the lack of any diving planes made
this boat just as hard to control as her
prototype, and she eventually finished up

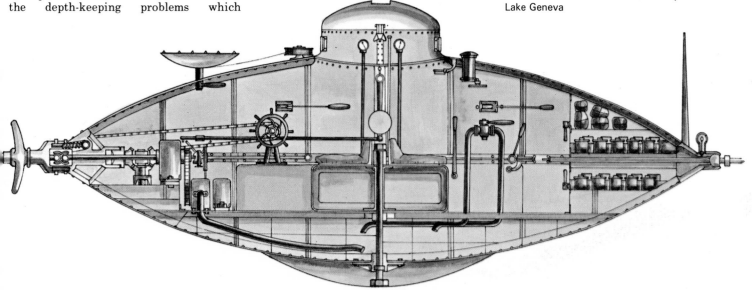

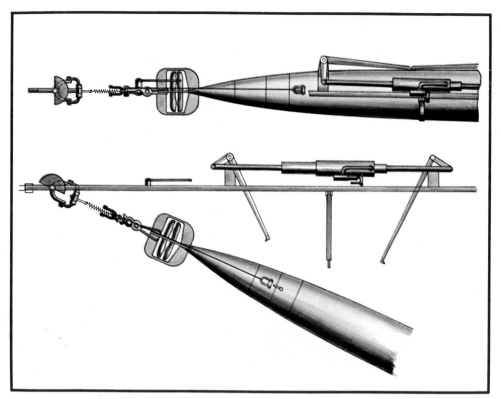

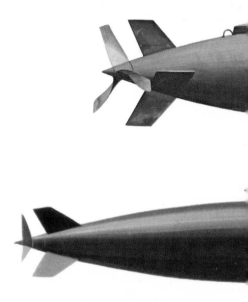

as the property of an amusement park on Lake Geneva. Goubet, like so many others, spent the rest of his life trying to promote his ideas without success, and died a bitter man.

His frustration must have been inflamed when the great naval architect Dupuy de Lôme started work on his own design for a submersible. Although de Lôme died in 1885 his disciple, Gustave Zedé, carried on where he had left off, and the plans of the first modern submarine were sent to the Minister of Marine, Admiral Aube, in January 1886. Approval followed and an order was placed with the *Société des Forges et Chantiers de la Mediterranée* at Toulon on 22 November 1886.

A giant step
As the details of this giant step forward had not been fully worked out it was April 1887 before the hull could be laid down, and more than a year before it could be launched. The new boat was 60 ft long, built of sheet steel, with a circular cross-section and a cigar-shaped form. The diameter of the hull was approximately 5 ft 10 in and it had a displacement of 30 metric tons on the surface (31 tons submerged). Great attention was paid to hull strength, and the frames were only some 20 in apart. The original electric motors developed 55 ehp for an estimated surface speed of 6.5 knots, but this proved unrealistic in practice as the motor was too light. A more efficient type was later installed, giving only 33 ehp, but the accumulator batteries gave a lot of trouble. This was one drawback to electric propulsion, for the 564 accumulators needed to produce 33 ehp weighed over 2,000 lb, and the motor itself weighed twice as much.

The little boat was named *Gymnote* ('Eel') when launched, and she immediately began an intensive programme of trials in Toulon harbour in September 1888. Depth-keeping was bad, as she had been fitted with two of the vertical propellers which proved so useless in the Garrett-Nordenfelt designs, and also

because only one diving rudder was fitted. In 1892 two sets of hydroplanes were added, a pair forward and a pair amidships, and the conning tower was raised to improve safety while travelling on the surface.

At this time the *Gymnote* was armed with a single tube for firing a 14-in White-head torpedo fitted in her bow, but later opinion in French circles hardened against the hull-mounted torpedo-tube for submarines, and when the *Gymnote* was rebuilt in 1898 she was given a pair of 'drop-collars' for a 14-in torpedo on either side of the conning tower. This device was the invention of the Russian designer Drzewiecki, and comprised a sling which held the torpedo at any desired angle before launching. Its main advantage was that it reduced the problem of compensating for the loss of weight, the torpedo forming a big percentage of total displacement in the small submarines of the period, and its advocates also pointed out that the choice of angles made it easier to hit the target.

But in practice the drop-collars were

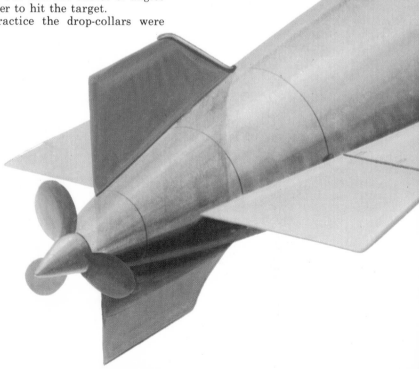

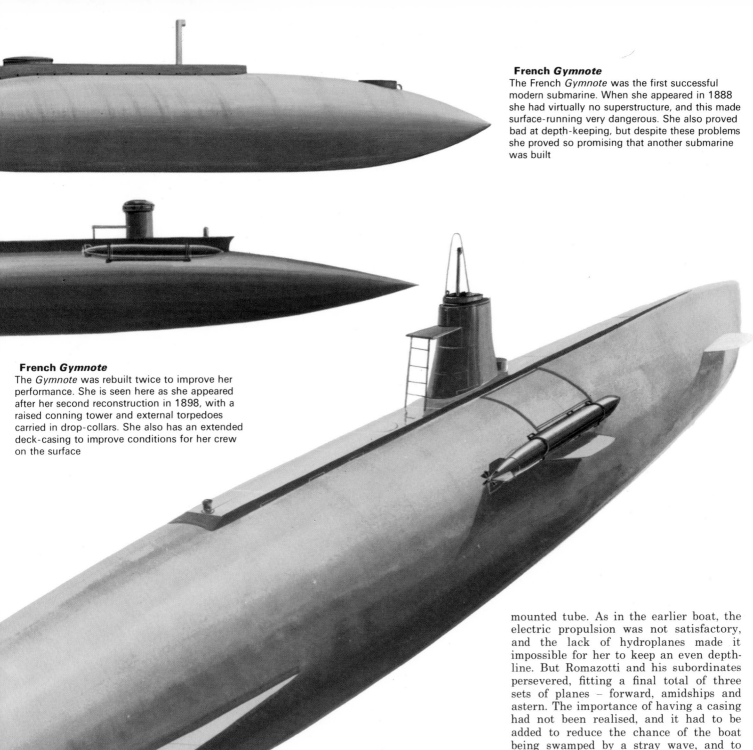

French *Gymnote*
The *Gymnote* was rebuilt twice to improve her performance. She is seen here as she appeared after her second reconstruction in 1898, with a raised conning tower and external torpedoes carried in drop-collars. She also has an extended deck-casing to improve conditions for her crew on the surface

liable to damage from seaweed and flotsam, and the angling mechanism proved very uncertain in its operation. A contemporary account says, 'When the gear is in working order it appears very neat, and to see a torpedo move itself off when one is looking through a scuttle ten feet under water possesses great fascination for a torpedo man; the suspense as to whether it will release at the exact angle it is set for, adds zest to the experience.'

The *Gymnote*, although she was a credit to her designers, was too small and rudimentary to be more than an experi-mental boat, and in October 1890 plans were finalised for a much larger boat to be called the *Sirène*, which would be able to develop the virtues of the proto-type. Gustave Zedé was a sick man, and the design work was left to his deputy Romazotti; when Zedé died the Minister of Marine ordered the name of the new boat to be changed to *Gustave Zedé* to commemorate his achievement. She was launched at the Mourillon yard in Toulon in June 1893, but like the *Gymnote* she needed an enormous amount of patient trial and error before she could be described as a success.

Problems of size
Everything about the *Gustave Zedé* was bigger, probably the reason why she had so many snags. The hull was 159 ft in length and 10 ft 5 in. in diameter; the electric motors developed 208 ehp and no fewer than three 17.7-in torpedoes were carried, for firing from a similar bow-mounted tube. As in the earlier boat, the electric propulsion was not satisfactory, and the lack of hydroplanes made it impossible for her to keep an even depth-line. But Romazotti and his subordinates persevered, fitting a final total of three sets of planes – forward, amidships and astern. The importance of having a casing had not been realised, and it had to be added to reduce the chance of the boat being swamped by a stray wave, and to give the crew somewhere to stand. The final solution was to raise the conning tower and provide a light 'flying bridge' extension.

Romazotti was obviously dubious about the big jump in size, and he had prepared another set of plans for a smaller submarine. As soon as the *Gustave Zedé* finished her lengthy trials, six years after her launch, the third boat was begun and was named *Morse* at her launch. She resembled the *Gustave Zedé* in many ways, but she introduced the periscope as an aid to navigation, and had Drzewiecki drop-collars for two torpedoes in addition to her internal tube. The *Morse* proved to be a greater success than her predecessors, but another submarine was building at Cherbourg at the same time, and this one caused such a sensation that the *Morse* was rather put in the shade.

The new Minister of Marine, M. Lockroy, had in 1896 proposed an open competition for a 200-ton submarine with a range of 100 miles on the surface and 10 miles submerged. Twenty-nine designs were submitted from all over the world, but the winner was a Frenchman, Maxime Laubeuf, with a truly remarkable boat, the *Narval*. What made Laubeuf's design different was the provision of separate propulsion systems for surface and submerged operation, and a double

of the deck-casing. The problem of coal storage was overcome by using oil fuel, and this was stored in the double hull. Laubeuf emphasised strength of construction, with $\frac{1}{4}$-in plating on the outer hull, and $\frac{1}{2}$-in plating on the inner, and the *Narval* proved the value of this when she survived a collision with a naval tug – it was the tug that sank.

As with aviation, the French embraced the submarine concept with enthusiasm, and submarines multiplied. The *Narval* came into service in June 1900, and by the end of 1903 there were four more of very similar type, two improved versions of

Basic Submarine Types

Above are shown the basic types of submarine hulls. *Left to right:* Single hull with saddle tanks; double hull with internal saddle tanks; modern double hull without deck-casing

French *Narval*

The French *Narval* of 1899 is the true parent of the modern submarine with her double hull and dual propulsion system. Note the funnel for her steam engine, the broad deck-casing for running on the surface, and the four Drzewiecki drop-collars

hull to accommodate water ballast and fuel.

The surface system was a single-shaft triple-expansion reciprocating steam engine, developing 220 ihp; the speed realised was just under 10 knots, but this failure to meet the original specification was overlooked. An 80 ehp motor drove the boat at 5.3 knots below the surface, but the effectiveness of the *Narval* was increased because she could recharge the accumulators from a dynamo running off the steam engine. For this reason she was christened a 'submersible' to distinguish her from the all-electric 'sousmarins' like the *Morse*. This has caused considerable confusion because it is so inappropriate; today diesel-electric boats are called submersibles to distinguish them from nuclear submarines, in the sense that the 'conventional' boats can spend so much less time fully submerged.

The *Narval* resembled later submarines in having a flat deck-casing to give her better handling on the surface. The need to shut down the boiler meant that she took some 15 minutes to dive, and this was undoubtedly her chief drawback. She had no torpedo-tubes, being armed with four drop-collars, two forward of the conning tower and two aft, in recesses at the edge

the *Morse*, and three of a new class designed at Rochefort by M. Maugas, all in service. A further 33 boats of various types were either building or on order, giving the French almost as many submarines as the rest of the world put together: the United States had 8, Great Britain 9, Germany 4, Russia 9, Italy 6 and Spain 1, for a total of 37.

WORLD WAR I

The Build-up

Above: The French submarine *Espadon* under construction in 1900. The early years of the 20th century saw a tremendous upsurge in interest in the submarine, and many nations, particularly the French, began a spate of submarine building. By 1903, the French had almost as many submarines as the rest of the world put together

The only country to show the same initial degree of interest in the submarine was the United States. As early as 1893 the Ordnance Bureau of the US Navy had appropriated $200,000 for building a submarine, with a view to stimulating private designers. With the exploits of Bushnell, Fulton, Hunley and others behind them, the Americans had always shown an interest in submarines, and three inventors produced material of sufficient credibility to arouse the interest of the Navy. Of these, Baker's boat soon dropped out, leaving John P Holland and Simon Lake as the contenders for the prize. Holland was an Irish-American who had been designing submarines in secret to destroy the British, from about the time of Garrett's experiments in England. His first effort was virtually a piloted

torpedo, reminiscent of German and Japanese ideas of the Second World War, and the design submitted in 1893 to the Bureau was his seventh. Lake, by comparison, only built his prototype *after* his design had been rejected by the Bureau.

Although Holland won the competition there was a long way to go. After several administrative delays a contract for construction was signed in March 1895, and the boat was launched as the *Plunger* in 1897. There were so many changes in

design during the building that Holland washed his hands of the whole venture, and the trials of the wretched *Plunger* were never completed. Holland and his company, the Holland Boat Company, decided to build *Holland No. 8* as a speculative venture to prove the soundness of the basic design. His faith was rewarded with the undisputed success of the second boat, and when he offered her to the United States Navy she was bought for $120,000, on 11 April 1900.

She had a fat cigar-shaped hull just under 54 ft long and 10 ft 3 in. in diameter, and her electric motor could drive her at 5 knots for about four hours. Like the French *Narval* she had a separate surface propulsion system, but she used an Otto petroleum engine, which, with its good power/weight ratio and ease of stopping and starting, proved better suited for quick diving. She did not have the double hull of the *Narval*, and this excellent feature of Laubeuf's design was not accepted in British and American circles for another 15 years.

One reason for the great difference in size between French submarines and the American newcomer was the relative lightness of the Otto gasoline engine, which could deliver more power for less weight than the French boats' steam engine or all-electric drive. Below the surface all three prototypes could make speeds of 5–6 knots, but electric power on the surface demanded so much weight that submarines of any reasonable size would clearly have to have a dual propulsion system. The French ordered a large class of electric-powered submarines of the *Naïade* class in 1901, but during construction they were given a benzol motor to increase their radius of action.

Submarines with wheels

Holland's rival, Simon Lake, continued his studies after losing the US Navy contract. In 1894/5 he built a tiny 14-ft prototype of yellow pine, lined with felt and coated with tar. She was fitted with wheels driven by hand with a chain and sprocket, for Lake wanted his submersible boat to travel about on the seabed. He also provided a diving chamber to allow a diver to leave the hull, for he thought that the submarine's greatest value was for cutting underwater cables and destroying defensive minefields. Here lay the cause of Lake's failure, for although he modified his ideas subsequently he never seemed to grasp fully the submarine's potential as a ship-destroyer on the high seas. Even when he received enough backing to build the *Argonaut I* he still insisted on giving her large wheels, as he did with the much larger *Protector* in 1901.

This boat was built to compete with *Holland No. 8*, and had many advantages to recommend her, such as a better hull-form for running on the surface, and three torpedo-tubes as against the single tube and two quite useless Zahlinski dynamite guns fitted in the Holland boat. Not only was the *Protector* very strongly built but her diving was smoother than the Holland's, yet those wheels seem to have annoyed the US Navy to the point where they turned her down. This was not the end of Lake's story, for he sold her to the Russians and subsequently received orders for four more. All five were sent to

French *Naïade*
In 1901 the French began a class of 20 small electric submersibles, the *Naïade* Class. When the Italian Navy wanted to build midget submarines for harbour defence in 1915 they asked the French for details of these 70-ton submarines

US Holland
The first Holland submarines built for the US Navy were the Plunger type, later renamed the 'A' Class. The first British submarines, called simply *Holland 1* to *5*, were almost identical. A feature of all early Holland designs was the 'fat cigar' shape, with a very small deck-casing and conning tower. Armament: one 18-in torpedo tube; Speed: 8 knots (surfaced) 7 knots (submerged)

Comparison of French and American designs			
	Gustave Zedé	*Narval*	*Holland No. 8*
Displacement (tonnes)* surface/submerged	261/270	117/202	64/74
Length overall (ft)	159	111.5	55.75
Diameter (ft)	10.4	12.5	10.3
Draught (surface) (ft)	10.6	6.1	8.5
Power (surface)	208 ehp	250 shp	45 ihp
Power (submerged)	208 ehp	80 ehp	50 ehp
Speed (knots) surface/submerged	9.22/6.5	9.88/5.3	8/5
*1 tonne = 0.9842064 long tons			

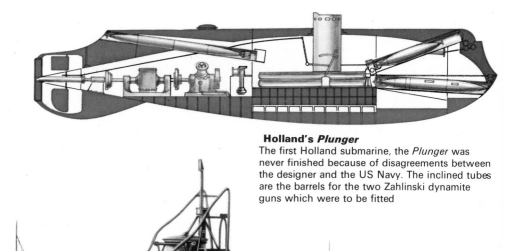

Holland's *Plunger*
The first Holland submarine, the *Plunger* was never finished because of disagreements between the designer and the US Navy. The inclined tubes are the barrels for the two Zahlinski dynamite guns which were to be fitted

Vladivostok in sections, and were assembled in time for the Russo-Japanese War. Neither side achieved much with their submarines in that conflict, though the existence of the Lake submarines is said to have made the Japanese defer an attack on Vladivostok.

Up to this point the British had maintained a position of masterly inactivity, as if they hoped that the rash of submarine building and designing would simply go away. Taking their cue from Lord St Vincent in 1801 they preferred to say that the submarine was only of use to a weaker navy, and as late as 1900 the official policy was to show no interest whatsoever. But it is now quite obvious that the Admiralty had been showing signs of life as far back as 1895, and the Director of Naval Construction had been instructed to draw up contingency plans for building submarines. However, with so little knowledge and so many claims being made by designers, the British decided to wait and see which designs showed most promise. The result was an announcement in 1901 that the Admiralty had ordered five submarine boats of the Holland type, with the intention of using them for experiments and training.

The boats which were ordered were very similar to the seven 'Improved Hollands' ordered by the US Navy in 1900, and were built by Vickers Sons & Maxim at Barrow from drawings bought from the Holland Company. This alone indicates how casually the USN took the submarine, for it is inconceivable that the French would have supplied drawings of the *Narval* to the British. The five British boats, named simply *Holland Nos. 1, 2, 3, 4* and *5*, were completed in 1901/2, and proved as successful as their American counterparts. An improved version was immediately put in hand by Vickers and became the 'A' class, the first British-designed submarine since Garrett's *Resurgam*.

Britain moves in

The British, having been so slow to move into the submarine field, now showed much more interest in their new toys than the Americans. After launching the seven *Plunger* Class or 'Improved Holland' type, the US Navy launched only two in 1906, two more in 1907 and six in 1909, during which time the British launched or completed 58 boats to their own designs. The French had not stopped at the *Narval* either, and had launched almost as many as the British. The Germans, however, had only built *U1* in 1906, and by the end of 1909 had added only three more boats.

With Bauer's efforts to inspire them, the Germans had not been as slow as they seemed. In 1890, as we have seen, two Nordenfelts had been built, one at Kiel and the other at Danzig, but they suffered from the faults inherent in the design. In 1902 an electrically-driven submersible of improved design was built by Howaldt's yard at Kiel, and although she was tried in Eckenfürth Bay she does not appear to have been a success either, and disappeared from the scene very quickly.

An indication of the growing suspicion of German intentions can be seen in the next development, which was an accusation by French newspapers that the Germans had stolen the plans of a new French submarine, the *Aigrette*, and had secretly constructed a submarine at Kiel. Like most rumours, this one had a grain of truth, in that a French inventor, M. d'Equevilley, after failing to interest the French Ministry of Marine, had sold his ideas to Krupps. The boat was never taken into German service, as she was bought by the Russians, along with two sisters, as part of the frantic efforts to make good the losses of the Russo-Japanese War. A fourth boat of similar design was launched in August 1906 at the Germania Yard at Kiel as *U1*, the Imperial German Navy's first submarine.

With a length of 101 ft 3 in, she was slightly smaller than the *Narval*, and nearly twice the size of the Holland prototypes. She had a double hull like the *Narval*, but instead of steam she used a Körting heavy oil engine, which gave her a surface speed of 10.8 knots. Like the French boat, she had a flat deck-casing and a hull-form which was more suited to surface running than the bluff bow and whaleback hull favoured by Holland. If we know a lot about *U1* it is because she survives as a museum exhibit in Munich. Her builders recovered her in 1919 after she had been laid up for scrapping. Although damaged by bombing during the Second World War, she was restored and is now in the Deutsches Museum.

Thus by 1906 the submarine had arrived, and was not only proving workable but reliable as well. It was clear now that a

dual propulsion system was essential in order to compensate for the limited endurance of accumulators, but opinion was divided as to the best method of propulsion on the surface. The French were still happy to use steam as late as 1905, in the 12 *Pluviôse* type, while the British clung to the gasoline engine until 1907. There were obvious disadvantages to steam operation, of which the worst were the time taken to dive and the heat generated inside the boat; the main drawback of using gasoline was the danger from gasoline vapour, which could easily explode from an electric spark. The solution lay in a new variant of the internal combustion engine which used a less volatile fuel. This was the Diesel engine, which soon displaced the gasoline engine in the world's submarines. The following list gives the launch dates of the first diesel-engined submarines in each major navy:

Aigrette (French)......23 January 1904
Minoga (Russian)......c.1906
D2 (British)...........25 May 1910
Skipjack (American)...27 May 1911
U19 (German).........10 October 1912

Although Russia could claim that Peter II had ordered a submarine to be built as far back as 1729, their first serious efforts date from Bauer's *tour de force* during Alexander II's coronation in 1856. Thereafter they showed great interest in the Nordenfelt boats, as we have seen, and built 30 small pedal-driven boats to Drzewiecki's design as a counter to the imaginary threat from Turkey's submarines.

At the turn of the century the *Peter Kochka* was begun at the Baltic Works, St Petersburg. She was a small boat, displacing only 60 tons on the surface, and was armed with two Drzewiecki drop-collars. A similar boat, the *Forel*, was sent in sections to Vladivostok via the Trans-Siberian Railway to provide defence for the harbour, but she was apparently never fully assembled.

War with Japan

The first Russian submarine in service was the *Delfin*, begun in 1902 and completed in 1904. She was 77 ft long, and had a Panhard gasoline engine for surface running; her armament was the same as the earlier prototypes, two torpedoes in drop-collars. Meanwhile, the tension between Russia and Japan was clearly leading to war, and in a frantic effort to reinforce the fleet in the Far East the Russians bought the *Protector* from Simon Lake. Subsequently, four more were ordered, the *Sig, Kefal, Paltus* and *Buichok*, and six of the Holland type, *Som, Peskar, Sterljad, Beluga, Schuka, Lossos* and *Schudak*. Only one of the Hollands, the *Som*, appears to have been built in the

Lake's *Protector*

Lake's submarine *Protector*, showing the wheels stowed within the hull. These were to allow the submarine to move on the sea bed, because Lake intended his submarine to send out divers to cut submarine cables or demolish harbour defences. His designs were overshadowed by Holland's, but they proved successful in service

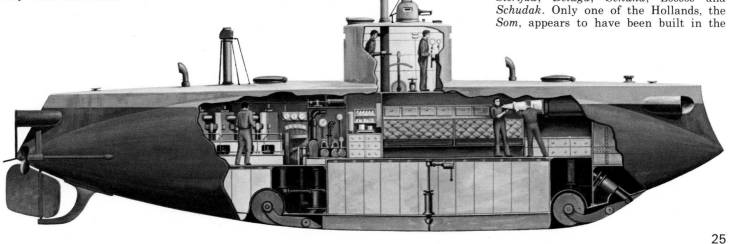

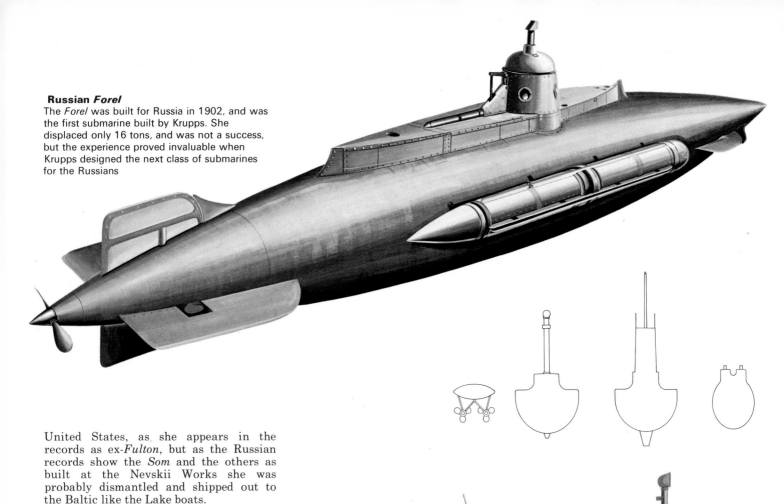

Russian *Forel*
The *Forel* was built for Russia in 1902, and was the first submarine built by Krupps. She displaced only 16 tons, and was not a success, but the experience proved invaluable when Krupps designed the next class of submarines for the Russians

United States, as she appears in the records as ex-*Fulton*, but as the Russian records show the *Som* and the others as built at the Nevskii Works she was probably dismantled and shipped out to the Baltic like the Lake boats.

The next class was a Russian design by Professor Bubnov, and comprised six *Kasatka* class, armed with four torpedoes in drop-collars. In 1904 the Germans built a prototype for the Baltic fleet named *Forel,* and then three of the *Kambala* type to the d'Equevilley design, for the Black Sea Fleet, which were delivered in 1907. Four more boats were built to a Lake design, the *Alligator* class, which were 134 ft 5 in long, and displaced 409 tons on the surface. They had an extremely heavy torpedo armament, two torpedo-tubes in the hull, a twin rotating tube in the deck-casing, and two drop-collars, but the class proved unreliable in service, and needed constant repair. Despite this, the *Drakon* carried out more patrols than any other Russian submarine during the First World War.

The next two submarines mark a big step forward in Russian submarine design. The *Minoga* of 1906 was the first Russian submarine to be driven by a diesel engine, but she did not prove very successful. The *Akula,* on the other hand, was considered to be the most successful of the pre-war designs, and had a heavy armament of two bow torpedo-tubes, two stern tubes and four drop-collars. These two boats were built in the Baltic, but a third interesting boat, the *Krab,* was begun in 1908 at Nikolaiev in the Black Sea. She was intended as a submarine minelayer, the first in the world, but as she was not completed until 1915 her achievement was overshadowed by German and British developments.

Europe was moving inexorably towards war, as each nation sought to insure itself against the possibility of aggression from its neighbours. In the last few years of peace the rate of submarine building was stepped up.

Russian *Minoga*
The *Minoga* (1906) was the first Russian submarine to have diesel propulsion. She carried two torpedoes in drop-collars and had a surface speed of 11 knots on a displacement of 122 tons. The diesels were not reliable, and in any case she was too small to be successful. The *Minoga's* diesel engine is shown, right

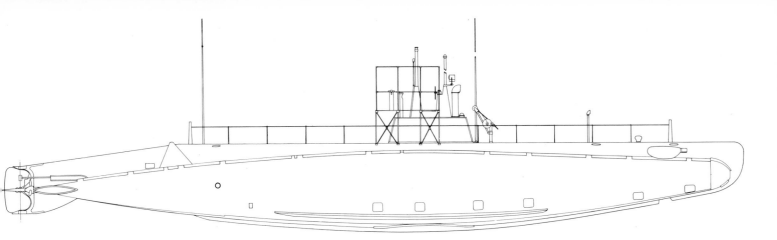

USS *Skipjack*

The *Skipjack*, launched in 1911, was the first US Navy submarine to be driven by diesel engines. She was 135 ft 3 in long, and was armed with four 18-in torpedoes. She and her sister entered service as *E1* and *E2* to conform with the USN policy of abolishing the old fish names

Russian Submarine Specifications 1908–1914			
	Minoga	*Akula*	*Krab*
Displacement (tonnes) surface/submerged	123/152	370/468	560/740
Length (ft)	106	187	174
Beam (ft)	9	12	14
Draught (surface) (ft)	9	11	13
Machinery (surface)	2×120 bhp	3×300 bhp	4×300 bhp
Machinery (submerged)	70 ehp	300 ehp	2×330 ehp
Speed (knots) surface/submerged	11/5	10.65/6.39	11/7.5
Armament	2 bow TT	2 bow TT 2 stern TT 4 ext. TT	2 bow TT 2 ext. TT 60 mines

German *U1*

U1 was the first submarine built for the German Navy, and was based on three earlier submarines built by Krupps for the Russian Navy to a French design. She was completed in 1906 and was only a partial success. She spent most of her time on training and experimental duties and was re-acquired after the First World War by her builders as a museum exhibit. Although damaged during the Second World War, she has been restored and can be seen in the Deutsches Museum in Munich. Displacement: 237 tons (surfaced) 282 tons (submerged). Armament: 1 18-in torpedo-tube (bow); 3 torpedoes carried. Speed: 10.8 knots (surfaced) 8.7 knots (submerged)

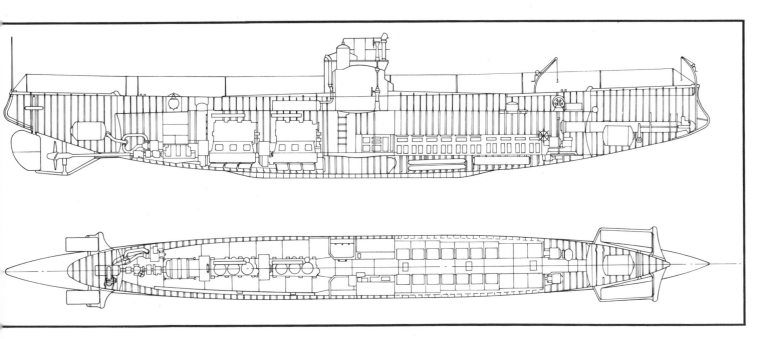

Submarines at War

The first moves to be made by submarines when war broke out in August 1914 were timid in the extreme. Neither side was ready to do more than establish patrol lines, the Germans being obsessed with the need to guard against the expected onslaught by the British, and the British in turn only watching out for movements of surface ships. The British set up a patrol line in the Heligoland Bight immediately, and it was here that the U-Boats were stationed too. Information from the six British boats led to a spirited foray by surface forces later in the month, but due to a variety of circumstances the U-Boats took no part in the action. But the U-Boats had not been idle for, on 6 August, ten were sent on their first offensive patrol; they were to try to find out more about British dispositions, and to go as far north as the Norway–Orkneys line. This was a hazardous trip for submarines at this early stage, and particularly so for the U-Boats, which had never ventured so far afield, even in peacetime.

The U-Boats' pioneer cruise showed what the new weapon could achieve, but it also showed its limitations. *U9* broke down on the second day, but the others reached Fair Isle and even sighted British battleships at gunnery practice. At dawn the next day the British cruiser *Birmingham* suddenly caught sight of *U15*, apparently immobilised with engine trouble, and turned to ram. With hardly any damage to herself the cruiser sliced through the luckless submarine, which went down with all hands. When the rest of the U-Boats returned to Heligoland it was discovered that *U13* was also missing, and she is believed to have been mined on 12 August. The first attack on the British had not merely failed, but cost two U-Boats.

There were compensating factors however; on the one hand the British had cause to be uneasy, as their pre-war estimates of a U-Boat's radius of action had been too low, while on the other hand, the easy sinking of *U15* caused a marked degree of complacency about the risk to surface ships. This was to be rudely dispelled on 22 September, when *U9*, under the first of the U-Boat aces, Kapitän-Leutnant Otto Weddigen, sank three 12,000-ton armoured cruisers within the space of little over an hour. The three ships were, even by the standards of 1914, in an exposed position, and were known to their crews as the 'Live Bait Squadron',

but the joke rang hollow when it was realised that HMS *Aboukir, Cressy* and *Hogue* had taken over 1,100 men with them. On 15 October, Weddigen was again able to strike a numbing blow against the Royal Navy, when he sank the 23-year old cruiser *Hawke* off Aberdeen. Once more the loss of life was heavy, about 500 officers and men, for these older ships had only minimal protection against modern torpedoes, and carried large crews.

The only answer

The British by now had learned the hard way that the only answer to U-Boat attack was to screen all ships with destroyers, and soon units of the Grand Fleet moved at all times with a large force of escorting destroyers. Although the destroyer had no special weapons for dealing with submarines she was fast, highly manoeuvrable and so difficult a target that she could normally ignore the threat to her own safety. Apart from using her quick-firing guns she could ram a submarine in the same way as the *Birmingham* had sunk *U15*. This rapidly became the standard method, and new destroyers were fitted with a strengthened forefoot to their bows to act as a 'can-opener'.

Bundesarchiv

But there was no means as yet of detecting a submarine, and all countermeasures depended on a submarine giving her presence away, ie. waiting for the sight of a periscope or an accidental surfacing. Unfortunately such opportunities were rare, particularly with experienced submarine commanders, and in any case a periscope was hard to spot in rough weather.

The discomfiture of the British was completed when they realised that nothing prevented U-Boats from entering their main fleet's base at Scapa Flow. The result was a major upheaval, with the Grand Fleet moving to a series of temporary refuges while the necessary defences were installed at Scapa Flow, principally net barrages and blockships to seal the approach channels. Thus the submarine

had achieved its first strategic victory over the surface warship, and had the German High Seas Fleet been in a position to take advantage of the U-Boats' achievement the Grand Fleet would have been caught in a difficult situation.

To make things worse, the British lacked

a suitable mine, so even the defensive fields laid by minelayers proved useless. Indicator nets were the next step; these were nets of heavy wire mesh, kept afloat by indicator buoys and attended by armed drifters. Not only did a submarine run the risk of fouling her hydroplanes and pro-

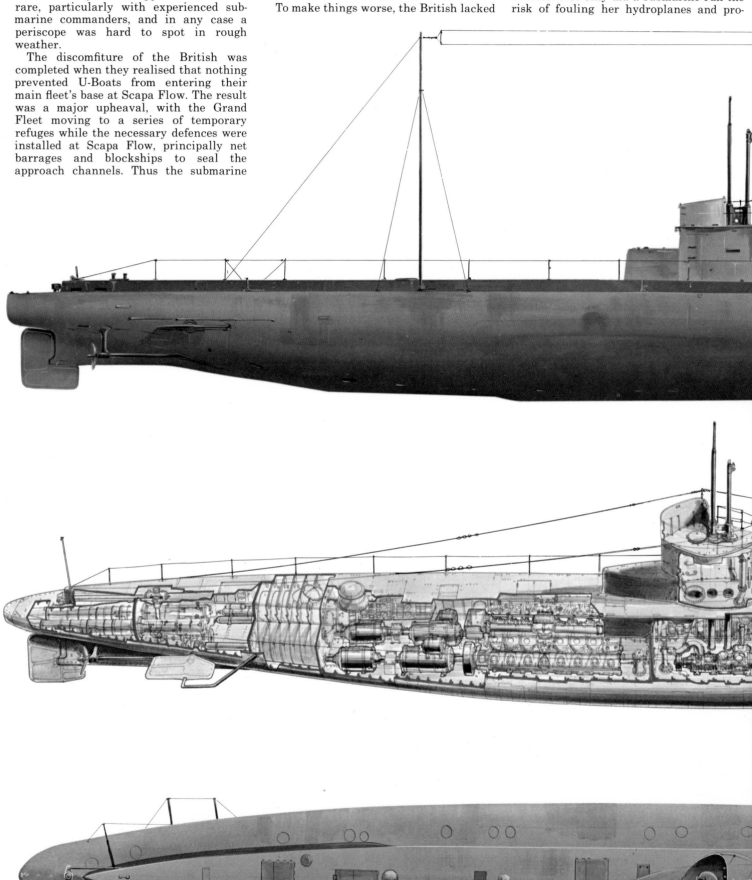

pellers in trying to force a way through the net, but she gave her position away to the drifters above.

So, to give the drifters a weapon to attack a submarine which surfaced alongside, the lance bomb was developed. This was an explosive charge and detonator fixed to the end of an ash pole, and intended to be hurled downwards on to the deck of a submarine. Unlikely as it may sound, a lance bomb was once used, but it inflicted only minor damage to the submarine.

At the outbreak of war all belligerent and neutral countries regarded themselves as bound by International Law and the Hague Convention as far as the conduct of warfare at sea was concerned. With little precedent later than the Napoleonic Wars to guide them, the maritime nations of the world assumed that a submarine (or any warship, for that matter) was not allowed to open fire on an enemy merchant ship 'on its lawful occasions' ie. not carrying offensive weapons and not acting in a hostile manner. On the contrary, the submarine would have to stop the merchantman, examine her papers, identify herself and then sink the victim or sail her home under a prize crew.

This idea was very favourable to the British as the major sea power and the world's largest mercantile shipowners, but it took little account of the peculiar nature of the submarine. Since it is impossible to stop and search a ship without being on the surface, a submarine would be almost completely ineffective as a weapon against commerce; moreover, she carried too small a crew to provide prize crews for her capture, or to accommodate prisoners.

German *U31*
U31 was a typical U-Boat of pre-1914 design, ordered in 1912 but not completed until late 1914. She was lost in the North Sea in January 1915 from unknown causes (probably a mine) She was armed with two torpedo-tubes in the bow and two in the stern, and carried a 10.5-cm deck gun. On the surface her two-shaft diesels gave her an endurance of 4,440 miles at 8 knots, but when submerged this fell to 80 miles at 5 knots. Length: 212 ft 6 in. Beam: 20 ft 9 in. Crew: 35 officers and men

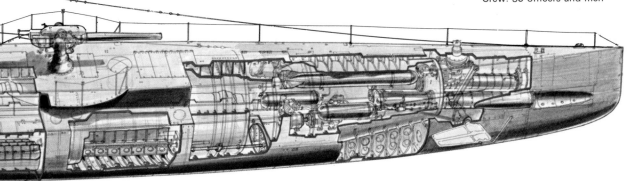

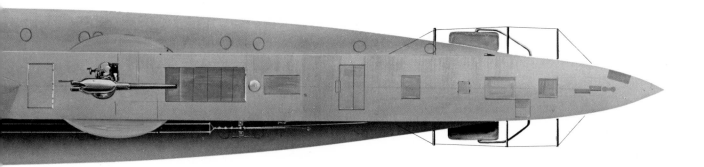

Every student of Mahan's books on naval strategy knew in 1914 that while Great Britain's seaborne commerce was her main strength, it was also a great source of weakness. At first the Germans had tried using their cruisers on the trade-routes to dislocate shipping, but by the beginning of January 1915, eight of the nine German cruisers operating outside the North Sea were either sunk or securely blockaded by Allied forces, and despite the vigour of their operations they had inflicted less than two per cent loss on British shipping.

On 20 October 1914, U17 under K/L Feldkirchner stopped, searched and scuttled the steamer Glitra off Norway – the first time a submarine had tried to abide by the rules, and also one of the last. This insignificant little ship has gone down in history as the first victim of the submarine war on trade, but it was not long before other U-Boats began to attack shipping. As all British warships were now escorted by a screen of destroyers, there were fewer naval targets, and inevitably merchant ships made easier prey.

The problems faced by a submarine commander in identifying the type of target are demonstrated by U24's torpedoing of the SS Amiral Ganteaume without warning off Cap Gris Nez on 26 October 1914: as the ship was loaded with Belgian refugees, the sinking was denounced as an atrocity, but in fact she was probably mistaken for a French troop transport.

No time for niceties
The view from a submarine's periscope is very limited, and was even more so with the crude instruments available in the First World War; there was distortion of size and blurring of the image, so any careful examination of a ship from a submerged submarine (which would involve counting guns, number of people visible and type of uniform worn, etc.) was quite impossible. Furthermore, the vessel's slow speed under water gave the submarine commander little time for a leisurely assessment of possibilities, and the time available for making an attack could be limited to minutes or even seconds. In short, the very nature of the submarine, which made it such a lethal weapon against ships, also made a breach of international maritime law inevitable.

The Glitra sinking certainly inspired the idea of using U-Boats against British shipping, and the German Naval Staff were encouraged by Great Britain's ruth-

less interpretation of the law of contraband. Under the impression that all foodstuffs had been commandeered by the German government, the British retaliated by treating cargoes of food as contraband, even when destined for a neutral port such as Copenhagen, providing that their ultimate destination could be proved to be Germany.

The problem was that both sides had drifted into total war, but everybody was still under the impression that life and business for civilians on both sides would carry on as usual while the dirty work was done by the armed forces. But as the land war in Flanders bogged down, and hopes of reaching Berlin or Paris by Christmas faded, it became clear to the leaders of both sides that the war would be a long one, and that it would also be a grim economic struggle. The Germans declared the waters around the British Isles a War Zone on 4 February 1915 and warned that British and French ships entering it would be sunk without warning, and that it would 'not always be possible' to prevent attacks on neutral shipping. In other words, the U-Boats were to be unleashed in an all-out offensive to cut off supplies to Great Britain and France.

The losses quickly mounted up; 32,000 tons of British shipping had been sunk in January 1915, and 15,900 tons of French and neutral shipping, but by March the figures had risen to 71,400 tons and 9,300 tons respectively. After a drop in April the figures jumped to 84,300 tons and 35,700 tons a month later, and by August they had had climbed inexorably to the peak of 148,400 tons of British shipping and 37,400 tons of French and neutral shipping.

International opinion was soon up in arms, and no country's attitude was more crucial that that of the United States. The demands of the British war economy provided a growing boost to American industry, and manufacturers were only too happy to provide the sinews of war to both sides. As the British blockade prevented supplies from reaching Germany there was some friction between British and American interests, but on the other hand the needs of the British and the French were so enormous that the loss of the potential German market was hardly noticed. Furthermore, American public opinion had been prejudiced against Germany from the outbreak of war, first by her violation of Belgian neutrality and then by stories of brutality during the advance through Belgium and France.

Although there was a certain amount of latent anti-British sentiment to be exploited by German propaganda, this was more than balanced by a sentimental regard for France which went back to the War of Independence, and so State Department irritation at British high-handedness in operating the blockade was frequently eclipsed by far greater anger over the deaths of American citizens in neutral ships sunk without warning. The fiercest outburst came after the torpedoing of the British liner Lusitania by U20 off Southern Ireland on 7 May, for she was running on the regular route from New York to Liverpool and was carrying 159 American passengers. The British were naturally quick to denounce the sinking, but the outcry in the United States was far stronger, and a diplomatic Note from Washington to Berlin demanded that German submarines should refrain from sinking ships carrying passengers.

Looking back on the Lusitania incident we should try to be as dispassionate as possible. Although some lurid claims have been made recently, there is no credible evidence to suggest that the Lusitania was armed, or that she was carrying a large cargo of high explosives. True, she was carrying 5,500 cases of small-arms ammunition and shell-fuses, totalling 37 tons, but this is hardly a lethal cargo, since rifle ammunition and nose-caps are not liable to be set off by a nearby torpedo explosion.

Much has been made of a mysterious second explosion reported by survivors, but this can easily be attributed to an implosion of the boilers, and if anyone doubts that a large ship would sink so quickly from a single hit, the very large boiler-rooms in a liner would fill rapidly and cause the ship to sink fast. Most of the accusations about hidden guns and vast cargoes of TNT prove on analysis to be either counter-claims made by Germany to evade charges of inhumanity, or confusion in the minds of laymen as to the differences between an armed merchant cruiser, an ammunition ship and a liner.

In any case, K/L Schwieger's own report shows that he had been warned to look out for troopships from Canada, but first mistook the liner for a 'number of destroyers in line'; only when the ship came closer did she turn out to be a large four-funnelled ship, and Schwieger immediately fired a torpedo from a bow tube. There is no mention in his report of seeing guns, for it would have been impossible to pick out that sort of detail, and when he reported the second explosion he simply put forward boilers, coal or munitions as a likely cause, without further comment.

The British had gambled that the Germans would not dare to sink a liner carrying American nationals; when they did so, and then insisted on justifying their conduct, the British seized the opportunity to work up American sympathy. Although the sinking of the Lusitania was neither the first occasion on which American citizens were killed, nor the reason for America's entry into the War, it did mark a clear turning point in American public opinion, which finally decided that its sympathies lay more with the Allies.

Left: Inside the control room of a French submarine, showing the cramped conditions in which the crew had to work

The Mediterranean

At first the war in the Mediterranean involved little or no submarine activity, despite the fact that most of the French submarines were stationed at Toulon and Bizerta. The lack of targets was partly responsible, for the overwhelming number of British and French ships in the Mediterranean had no difficulty in blockading Austrian and Turkish ships in their harbours. There were only seven Austrian submarines, all based at Cattaro (now Kotor in Yugoslavia) and they did not achieve anything approaching the Germans' exploits in the North Sea. But after an unsuccessful attack on the French armoured cruiser *Waldeck Rousseau* by the submarine *VI* (all Austrian submarines were originally known by a distinguishing Roman numeral; they did not adopt the U-prefix until late in 1915), the battleship *Jean Bart* was badly damaged by a torpedo from *XII*, and only just reached Malta.

This boat had a quaint history, for she had been ordered by the builders at Fiume for demonstration purposes; she was then taken over in August 1914, and became *XII*. Four months later, in April 1915, the armoured cruiser *Léon Gambetta* was sunk by two torpedoes in a skilful night attack by *V*, under Linienschiff-Leutnant von Trapp. Including Admiral Sénés, 650 officers and men were lost.

Meanwhile, the French submarines did not remain idle, and in December 1914 the *Curie* made a very bold attempt to enter Pola harbour, hoping to torpedo one of the Austrian warships based there. The barrage of nets proved too strong, and when she became hopelessly entangled her captain blew tanks and scuttled her before surrendering to the Austrians. Naturally the Austrians were interested in the *Curie*, which was a modern submarine completed in 1913, and they salvaged her. After repairs she was recommissioned in March 1915 as *XIV* (subsequently *U14*), and

finally returned to French ownership after the Armistice.

In March 1915, much greater submarine activity was sparked off by the Anglo-French expedition to the Dardanelles. Suddenly Germany's new partner, Turkey, was under attack, and it was felt that a small reinforcement of submarines offered the only hope of interfering with the massive Allied naval effort. Accordingly, K/L Hersing was asked to attempt a passage of the Straits of Gibraltar in *U21*, and he left the Ems on 25 April 1915 via Spain and Cattaro. Although he was spotted by a patrolling torpedo-boat off Gibraltar, Hersing made a landfall at Cattaro without incident on 13 May, where he completed some urgent repairs before heading for Gallipoli. In the meantime the Germans had taken steps to reinforce the Austrians by sending ten new coastal U-Boats in sections down to Cattaro by rail. These were six of the 127-ton UB-type coastal submarines, *UB1, UB3, UBs7* and *8* and *UBs 14* and *15*, and four of the 168-ton UC-type small minelaying boats, *UCs 12–15*.

After re-assembly they were commissioned under the German flag, and three of them were sent to Gallipoli in May 1915 in a brave attempt to distract the Allies. One of them, *UB3*, was lost without trace in the Aegean, but the other two passed through the Dardanelles and reached Constantinople safely. This was to be their only success for the moment, and it was left to *U21* to strike the first important blow. On 25 May, Hersing stalked the battleships *Swiftsure* and *Vengeance* without success, and then saw the *Triumph* off Gapa Tepe, firing her 10-in guns at the Turkish positions. The battleship was moving, with her anti-torpedo nets out, and Hersing had to wait for two hours for a good shot, but when it came, one torpedo hit her amidships and this sent the

old battleship over on her beam ends.

Hersing escaped by diving *under* the sinking *Triumph*, an appalling risk which was justified by his escape without detection. Two days later he saw the old battleship *Majestic* off Cape Helles, and moved into the attack. This time, the target was at anchor with nets out, and surrounded by colliers and patrols, but all to no avail. To a man like Hersing it was only a matter of time before a gap opened, and when it did he fired a single torpedo. Seven minutes later the one-time pride of the Channel Fleet keeled over and sank in 150 ft of water.

Although his targets were old and highly vulnerable ships with virtually no chance of surviving a torpedo hit in a vital spot, the Admiral commanding at the Dardanelles felt that he was about to see his entire supporting fleet of warships and transports picked off one by one, and so all bombarding ships larger than destroyers were sent away to Mudros. This alone put new heart into the hard-pressed Turkish infantry, and correspondingly dismayed their enemies. But the greatest enthusiasm was in Constantinople, where *U21* had a Roman triumph on 5 June.

The entry of Italy into the War on the Allied side on 24 May gave the German and Austrian submarines new targets. On 9 June the light cruiser HMS *Dublin* was badly damaged by a torpedo from *IV*, and a day later the newly re-assembled *UB15* caught the Italian submarine *Medusa* on the surface off Venice, and sank her. These UB-craft were tiny and only barely adequate, and were known to their crews as 'tin tadpoles', but the same *UB15* was able to torpedo the armoured cruiser *Amalfi* in the Gulf of Venice. Yet another cruiser was sunk on 18 July, when *IV* sank the *Giuseppe Garibaldi* off Gravosa, near Ragusa, while *V* sank the submarine *Nereide* on 5 August near Pelagosa.

Italian 'F' Class
The Italian Fiat-Laurenti designs were most successful, and were built under licence for several foreign navies. The 21 units of the 'F' Class were built during the First World War, and served until the 1930s. Armament: two 17.7-in torpedo-tubes; one 3-in AA gun. Speed: $12\frac{1}{2}$ knots (surfaced) 8 knots (submerged)

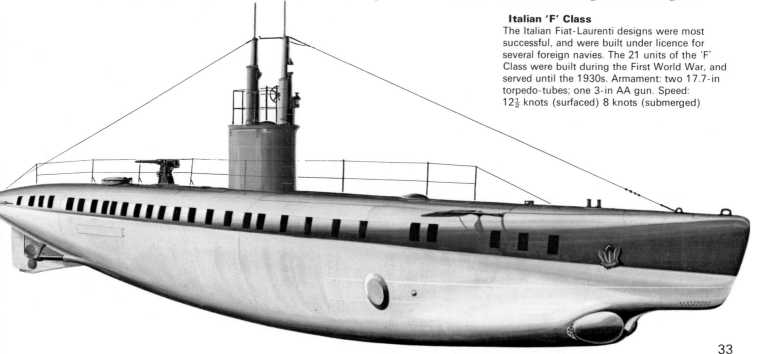

For a time the pretence was kept up that the German submarines were operated by the Austrian Navy, and *UB15* and *UB1* were formally transferred in June 1915 as *X* and *XI*. By October all the Austrian submarines bore U-prefixes with Arabic numerals, just like the German U-Boats, (and in many cases duplicating the German numbers). The five U-Boats at Constantinople, however, were not handed over to the Turks, but formed instead into a half-flotilla for operations in the Sea of Marmora and the Black Sea. Hersing in *U21* was the senior officer, and during the summer of 1915 he was reinforced by *UB14* and *UC13*. He and his captains pursued a vigorous campaign, but *UC13* was lost by stranding in the Black Sea, while his own boat developed defects which forced him to return to Cattaro for repairs lasting four months.

Forcing the Narrows
The British and French had not allocated any modern submarines to the Dardanelles forces at first, as they had envisaged it as nothing more than a shore bombardment and landing of troops. At the end of 1914, however, three of the elderly 'B' class boats from Malta and the French boats *Brumaire* and *Circé* were sent to help maintain the blockade of the Dardanelles. This was principally to guard against a breakout by the German battle cruiser *Goeben* and her consort, the light cruiser *Breslau*, but it soon became clear to the naval staff that it might be possible to take a submarine up the 27 miles of the Narrows between the Gallipoli Peninsula and the mainland of Asia Minor, to attack any German or Turkish warships which could be found.

Only a submarine could get through the five rows of mines which guarded the Narrows; the biggest problem was whether these small, under-powered boats could breast the 4–5-knot current which swept through the mile-wide gap between Chanak (Cannakale) and Kilid Bahir. The competition was fierce among the five boats, but finally the British *B11* was chosen on account of new batteries; her hydroplanes were fitted with special guards to prevent mine-cables from fouling them, and she was sent off on 1 December 1914.

After an exciting passage, the little submarine reached the smoother waters above the Narrows, and found to her delight that an elderly Turkish warship, the *Messudieh*, was lying at anchor. Lt Holbrook closed to 800 yards, fired one 18-in torpedo, and the target rolled over and sank. Hailed in the Allied newspapers

British 'B' Class
The British 'B' Class were the second stage in the development of the original Holland design bought from the Americans in 1901. Their gasoline engines were their weak point, and they were too small for anything more than harbour defence. Yet in December 1914 *B11* managed to get through the Dardanelles minefields and torpedoed the Turkish 'battleship' *Messudieh*

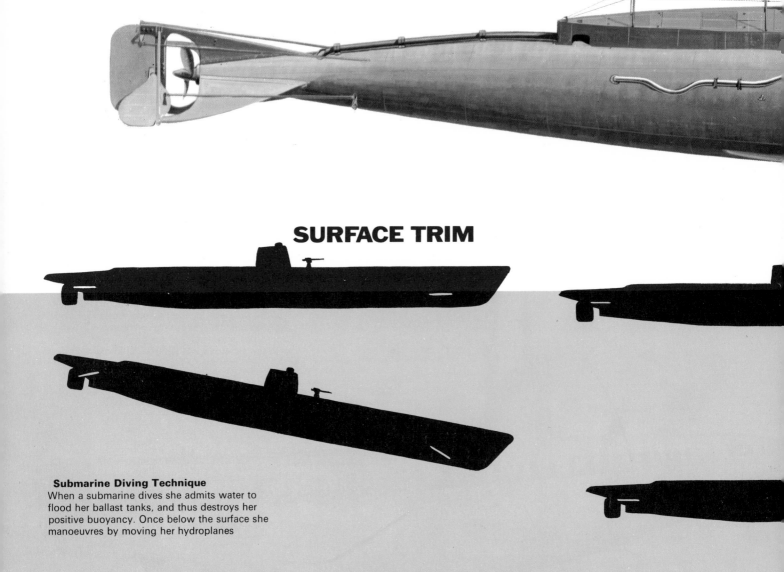

SURFACE TRIM

Submarine Diving Technique
When a submarine dives she admits water to flood her ballast tanks, and thus destroys her positive buoyancy. Once below the surface she manoeuvres by moving her hydroplanes

as a battleship, the *Messudieh* was in reality a very old steam frigate reconstructed for coastal defence, but it was an audacious success to put against the recent achievements of the U-Boats.

More significantly, it showed the Allies how they could strike at the Turks, for if *B11* could penetrate the Narrows, a larger boat with more power and endurance could even reach the Sea of Marmora which lay between the Narrows and Constantinople. An immediate request for larger submarines was made by the officer commanding the British submarines at the Dardanelles, and as soon as the landing operations were sanctioned, orders were given for no fewer than seven of the 'E' Class to go out to the Dardanelles with the other naval reinforcements. The stage was set for one of the classic submarine campaigns of history.

The first attempt to force the Straits met with disaster, when *E15* ran aground off Kephez Point after being caught by the fierce current. As she was under the guns of Fort Dardanos it proved extremely difficult to prevent the Turks from salvaging an example of the very latest type of British submarine. After attempts to torpedo her, using both destroyers and submarines, two battleships tried to destroy her with gunfire; success was finally achieved by sending in a pair of picket boats which were armed with small torpedoes.

But the fiasco was only a minor interruption, and by 26 April 1915 the Australian submarine *AE2* was signalling from the Sea of Marmora; although she did not last long, being sunk by a Turkish torpedo-boat a day later, her sister *E14* had already arrived. Nor were the French submarines

inactive, but unfortunately the *Saphir* ran aground off Nagara Point in similar circumstances to *E15*, and the *Joule* was mined on 1 May, making the toll four out of five. But the Allied armies had sustained such tremendous casualties during their landings on 26 April that *E14*'s report of three ships sunk – and the alarm and confusion spread among the Turks – made it imperative to try to exert more pressure on the Turkish seaborne supply route. On 19 May, *E11* relieved *E14*, and began a career of destruction which earned Lt-Cdr Nasmith the Victoria Cross.

Building up strength
During the following months *E2*, *E7*, *E11*, *E12*, *E20*, *H1* and the French *Turquoise* were among the submarines which successfully forced the mine-barrier and the currents of the Narrows to get to the

AWASH

PERISCOPE DEPTH

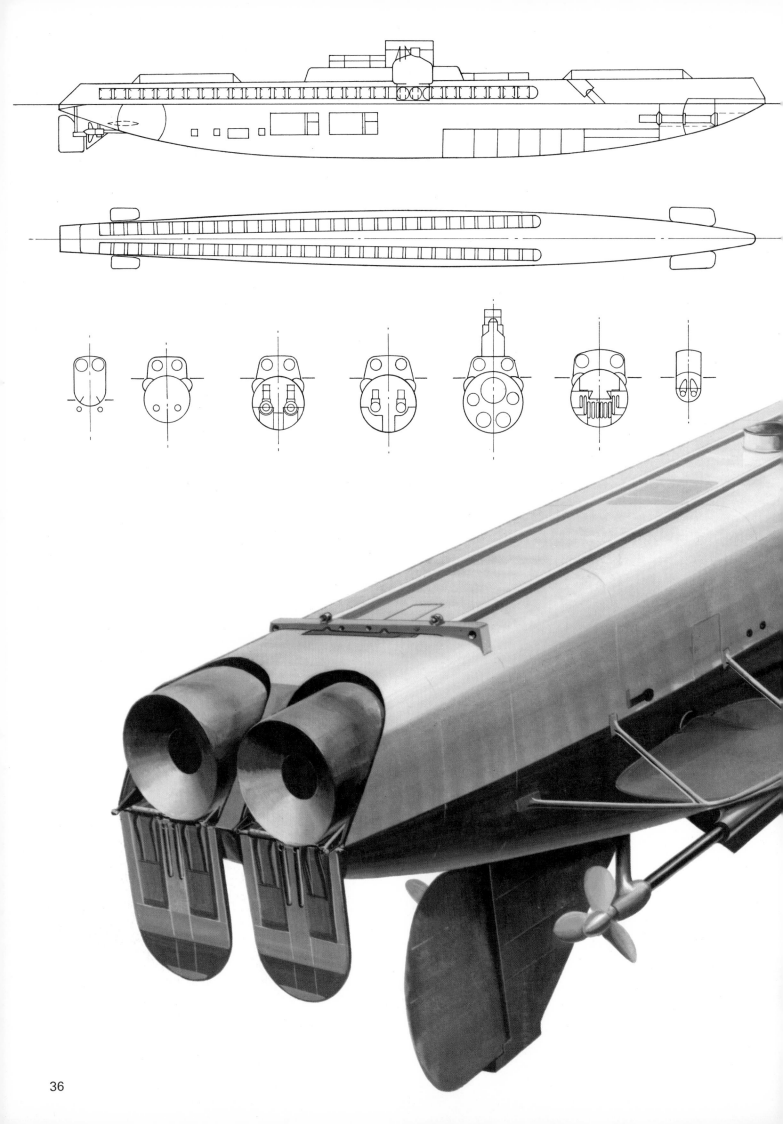

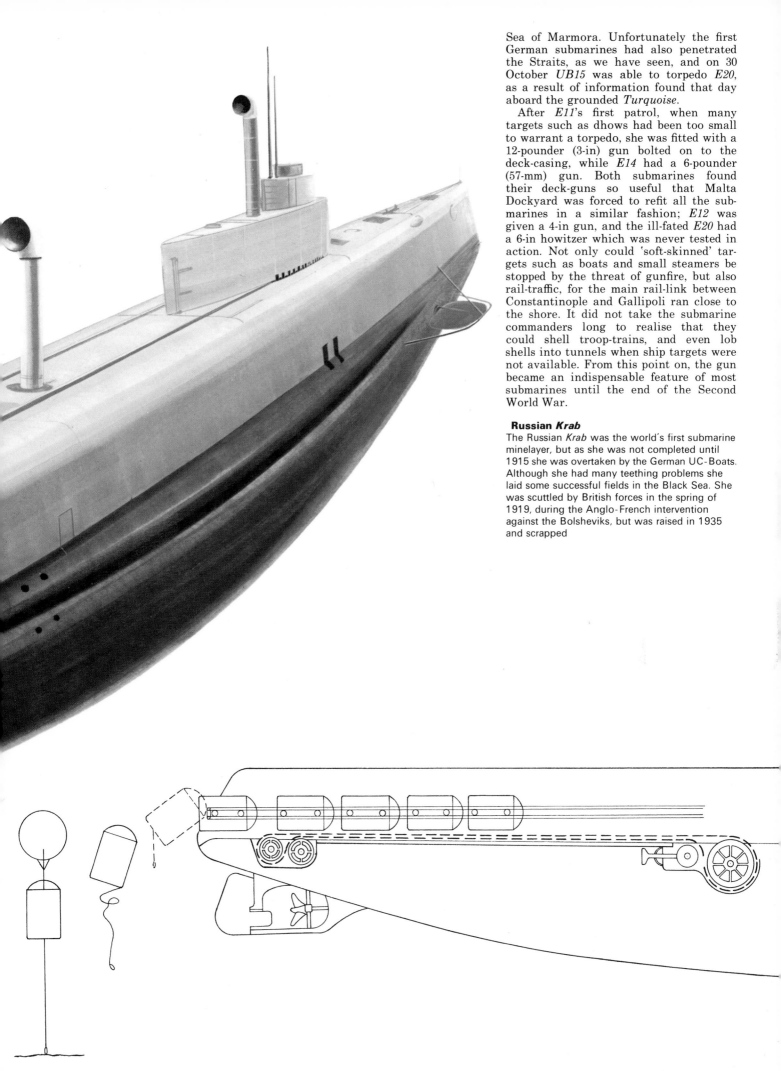

Sea of Marmora. Unfortunately the first German submarines had also penetrated the Straits, as we have seen, and on 30 October *UB15* was able to torpedo *E20*, as a result of information found that day aboard the grounded *Turquoise*.

After *E11*'s first patrol, when many targets such as dhows had been too small to warrant a torpedo, she was fitted with a 12-pounder (3-in) gun bolted on to the deck-casing, while *E14* had a 6-pounder (57-mm) gun. Both submarines found their deck-guns so useful that Malta Dockyard was forced to refit all the submarines in a similar fashion; *E12* was given a 4-in gun, and the ill-fated *E20* had a 6-in howitzer which was never tested in action. Not only could 'soft-skinned' targets such as boats and small steamers be stopped by the threat of gunfire, but also rail-traffic, for the main rail-link between Constantinople and Gallipoli ran close to the shore. It did not take the submarine commanders long to realise that they could shell troop-trains, and even lob shells into tunnels when ship targets were not available. From this point on, the gun became an indispensable feature of most submarines until the end of the Second World War.

Russian *Krab*
The Russian *Krab* was the world's first submarine minelayer, but as she was not completed until 1915 she was overtaken by the German UC-Boats. Although she had many teething problems she laid some successful fields in the Black Sea. She was scuttled by British forces in the spring of 1919, during the Anglo-French intervention against the Bolsheviks, but was raised in 1935 and scrapped

A photograph of a captured German mine, taken during the First World War. When laid by a submarine, the frame and mine sank to the sea bed where a soluble plug released the mine on a length of cable and allowed it to float to the correct height; then it was anchored by the legs. This was an accurate system, but had the drawback that the plug was liable to dissolve too quickly, releasing the mine immediately under the submarine

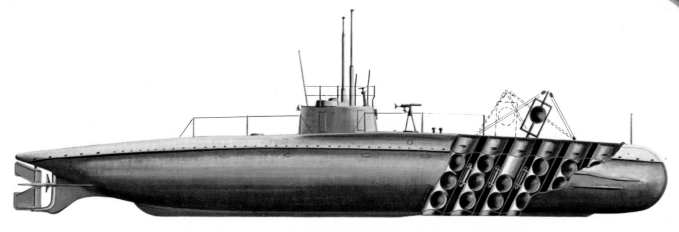

German *UC1* (above)
The first German minelayer, *UC1* appeared in 1915. Apart from a machine-gun on deck she had no armament, but she carried twelve mines in six vertical chutes. The drawing shows how each mine was loaded in a frame; it was laid downwards through a hatch in the keel. This class had very limited endurance

German *UC26*
An inboard view of the German minelayer *UC26*, showing how much of the forward space was taken up with the mine-wells. The *blue* areas indicate torpedo-tube spaces; *red* indicates machinery; *mauve* indicates the control room and conning tower and *yellow* indicates the accommodation spaces

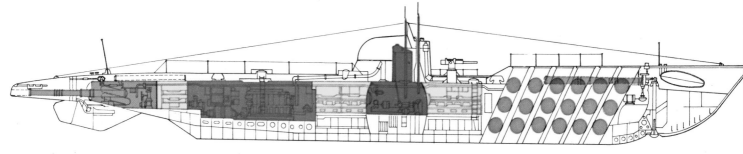

German _UC71_
The minelayer _UC71_ had two external torpedo-tubes to leave more internal space for her mines. All the later minelayers were given a torpedo armament to allow them to sink ships on their homeward trip. This submarine did not commission until 1917, and survived the war only to be sunk by accident while crossing the North Sea to surrender

Although the failure of the Gallipoli Campaign and the final evacuation of the Peninsula in January 1916 meant the withdrawal of Allied submarines from the Sea of Marmora, there was still a lot of work left for them to do. Their skilled commanders were sent home for service in the North Sea, but the boats themselves remained. Six British submarines were sent to join the French boats watching the mine barrage in the Straits of Otranto, laid to prevent the Austro-Hungarian Fleet from breaking out of the Adriatic, and eight were dispersed on anti-U-Boat patrols. Only _E2_ was left to keep a lonely vigil off the Dardanelles, guarding against a breakout by the _Goeben_ and the _Breslau_; unfortunately, when

the German ships did finally appear, on 19 January 1918, the _E2_ was in dock with a fractured shaft. In a last desperate attempt to cripple the battle cruiser, _E14_ was transferred from Corfu and, although she penetrated the Narrows with some difficulty, she failed to find her target, and was sunk by Turkish patrol vessels on 27 January.

The little 'B' Class boats, which had done so much better than expected in 1914/15, were by 1916 regarded as unsafe to dive, and six were converted by the Italians to surface patrol vessels in 1916/17. _B6–B11_ became _S6–S11_, with raised wheelhouses and 12-pounder guns, but on 9 August 1916 _B10_ was sunk by an enemy aircraft while under conversion at Venice.

Submarine Minelaying Techniques
There are two main systems of laying mines from submarines. _Above:_ vertical chutes inside the pressure hull (or in the saddle tanks). _Below:_ a horizontal deck or tubes. Both types needed precise compensating gear to adjust the trim while laying, to prevent the submarine from suddenly 'porpoising'

British 'M' Class
The British replied to the U-Cruisers with the 'M' Class, which mounted 12-in guns removed from battleships. The three 'M' Class were never tested in action, but they evolved a special method of using their guns. Known as the 'dip-chick' method, it involved a sudden rise to the surface, a round fired from the 12-in gun, and then a rapid dive again, all in 30 seconds

German *UB86* and *UB59*
Two examples of the UB type of small U-Boat, which were developed from small coastal submarines first ordered in November 1914. *UB59* (right) and *UB86* were both 500-tonners armed with four bow tubes, one stern tube and a deck gun. This type, the UBIII, grew steadily in size until it equalled the pre-war U-series, and it was chosen as the model for the Type VII U-Boats when Germany began to build U-Boats again under Hitler

US 'H' Class (right)
The American 'H' Class were built to a successful
design which was also used in Canada and Italy.
H4–9 were originally ordered by the Imperial
Russian Navy as *AG17–20* (AG = American
Holland) but after the Revolution in 1917 they
were taken over by the US Navy. Armament: four
18-in torpedo-tubes. Speed: 14 knots (surfaced)
10 knots (submerged)

The Baltic

The other theatre in which British submarines distinguished themselves was the Baltic. As early as October 1914 two British submarines, *E1* and *E9*, set out from Gorleston, bound for Libau (now Liepaja), which was held by the Russians as a forward base. In some ways the passage of the Kattegat and the Baltic was as hazardous as the Dardanelles. The shallowness of the water and the number of German patrol craft, combined with a large number of minefields, made the Baltic a difficult area for submarines, but they did have the advantage of a friendly Russian base from which to operate.

When the first two boats arrived at Libau, however, they found the Russians busily engaged in demolishing the port in expectation of its capture by advancing German troops, and the British were forced to reshape their plans hurriedly. The Russians had set up a new base for the submarines at Lapvik in the Gulf of Finland, and here they were able to rest and effect repairs. The third boat, *E11* under Nasmith, had to turn back because of persistent attacks by patrol craft in the Kattegat, and was transferred to the Dardanelles – where, as we have already seen, there was no shortage of action.

The mere presence of two hostile submarines had a disturbing effect on German dispositions in the Western Baltic, for this was the secluded training area and private preserve of the High Seas Fleet. Outnumbering the Russian Fleet at Kronstadt, and facing a submarine force which lacked the leadership and the modern boats (many of the new Russian boats were without engines, as these had been ordered in Germany) which could have made it more dangerous, the Germans had good reason to think themselves secure in the western half of the Baltic.

The first intimation to the contrary came when *E1*, while on passage to Libau, fired a torpedo at the cruiser SMS *Viktoria Luise* which ran under the target, and when *E11*'s attempted passage was detected it was obvious that more than one submarine was involved. Max Horton, promoted to Commander on 1 January 1915, caused further unrest by taking *E9* out of Lapvik during the depth of the Russian winter, when ships were normally iced in. Entering Kiel Bay, he found the destroyer *S120*, but the torpedo hit the bottom under her and she was only severely shaken. The German Commander-in-Chief was convinced that the British had an entire flotilla, with a secret depot-ship hidden in a bay, and two squadrons of heavy ships were withdrawn to Swinemünde while the depot-ship was located.

Extraordinary exertions

But the main victims of *E1* and *E9* were the ships carrying iron ore from Sweden to Germany, and when the thaw came the two submarines ranged far and wide in pursuit of targets. The Russian *Drakon* was also able to drive off the cruiser SMS *Thetis* on 14 May, and this ship was again attacked unsuccessfully by the *Alligator* a month later. The *Okun* was similarly unable to hit a squadron of cruisers, and escaped from a ramming by a destroyer with slight damage. But reinforcements were on the way for the British Government had been agreeably surprised by the extraordinary exertions of Horton and Laurence in *E9* and *E1*. Four more 'E' Class, *E8*, *E13*, *E18* and *E19* were to go out to join their sisters, while the old 'C' Class boats, *C26*, *C27*, *C32* and *C35*, were to be stripped down, sent by sea to Arkhangelsk, and then transported by rail and canal barge to Lapvik. *E8* arrived first, on 18 August, but the next one, *E13*, ran aground off the Danish

island of Saltholm, and was destroyed by German torpedo boats. The other two arrived without mishap, making a total of five modern submarines at Lapvik, with four smaller 'Cs' available as soon as they could be re-assembled.

The results were soon evident. On 5 October one Russian and two British submarines sortied from Reval, and several merchant ships were sunk. Later that month four steamers and two cruisers were sunk by the British, while the Russian *Kaïman, Krokodil, Makrel, Som* and *Alligator* accounted for two between them. The year 1916 seemed to start well enough, and in May the British were again joined by the Russians, but the Germans' success on land swung the tide of battle slowly in their favour. Then came the so-called 'February Revolution' in March 1917, followed by a steady decline in the effectiveness of the submarine effort as Russian support for the British flotilla became less enthusiastic.

After the October Revolution came the Peace Treaty of Brest-Litovsk, in which the Germans stipulated to the new Communist masters of what was shortly to become the Red Fleet that the British submarines must be surrendered. There was only one way out for the submariners, and on 8 April 1918 a still-friendly Russian icebreaker led the surviving seven submarines out of their final base at Helsingfors (Helsinki) to be scuttled in deep water. The Baltic was no longer 'Horton's Sea'.

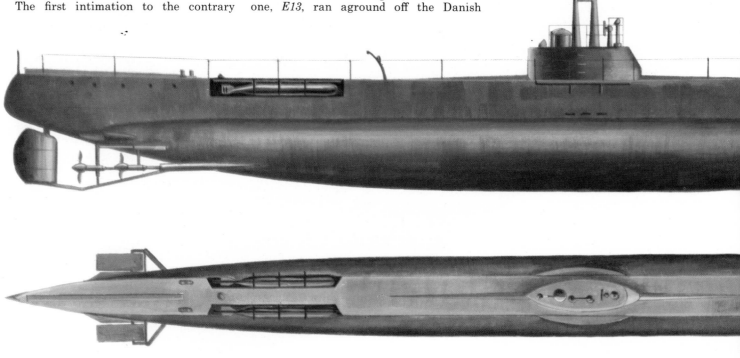

British 'C' Class

The 'C' Class were an enlarged version of the 'B' Class, and despite their gasoline engines they gave good service in the First World War. In 1915 four were dismantled and sent by rail and canal from Arkhangelsk to the Gulf of Finland, to attack German shipping. They were armed with two 18-in torpedoes in the bow

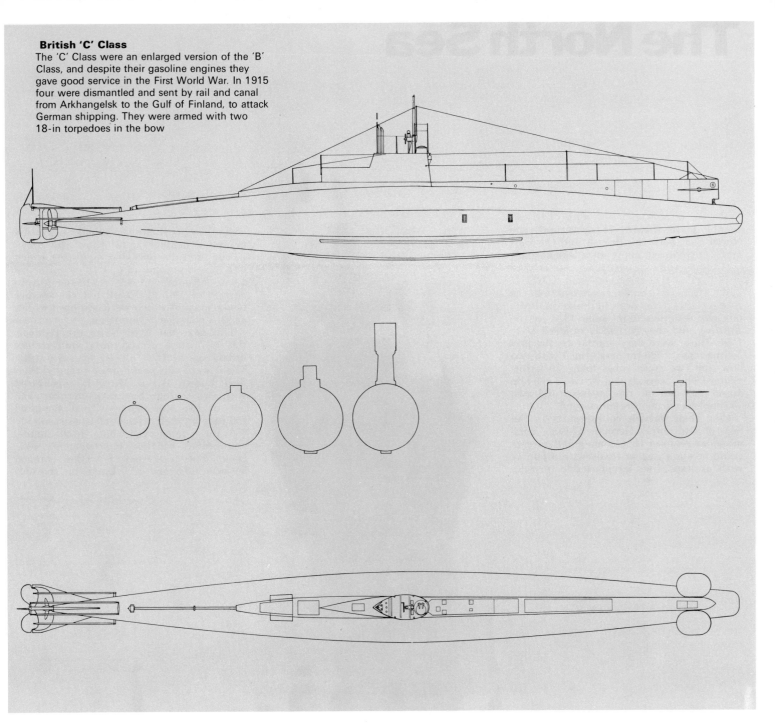

Russian *Akula*

The *Akula* was considered by the Russians to be their most successful design before 1914. She was much bigger than the *Minoga*, and was armed with eight torpedoes in drop-collars. After an active career in the Baltic she was lost in a German minefield near the Gulf of Riga in November 1915

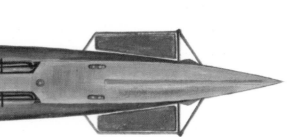

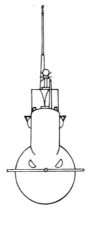

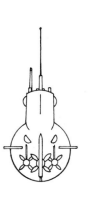

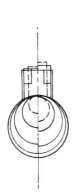

The North Sea

In the main theatre of operations, the North Sea, both the British and the Germans introduced many new submarines, both repetitions of existing classes and novel types. The Germans had *U31–U41* and *U43–U50* under construction in August 1914 (*U42* was building in Italy, but she was seized in June 1915 as the *Balilla*), and they promptly ordered *U51–U56*. These were very similar to the preceding class – 720-tonners armed with two bow and two stern tubes firing 20-in torpedoes. They were driven by two 1,100 bhp diesel engines on the surface, and two 550 ehp electric motors submerged.

Like their British counterparts in the Sea of Marmora, German U-Boat commanders realised that some small targets could be sunk just as easily with a gun as with an expensive, irreplaceable torpedo,

and the ocean-going submarines soon mounted heavier guns than the small 37-mm on a disappearing mounting which had been standard up to *U18*. A variety of 3.4-in (88-mm) and 4.1-in (105-mm) were carried in 1915–18 by all, but the smaller boats, most of which were equipped with a small 4-pounder (50-mm) gun.

The next batch of boats ordered was the *U57* class of six units, followed by orders up to *U70*, placed by early 1915. These were the workhorses of the U-Boat fleet, known as the 'Mittel-U' type, fitted with two to four bow torpedo-tubes, and one or two stern tubes. They displaced 750 tons on the surface and approximately 830 tons submerged, but these figures changed as wartime improvements were made. Speeds varied, but they ranged between 15.5 and 17.5 knots on the surface from twin diesels, and 8 to 9 knots from the twin electric motors while submerged.

In November 1914, when the German High Command realised that there would be no early victory on land, orders were placed for two new types of U-Boat to allow the Navy to prosecute the war more effectively. These were the little 'UB' coastal submarines and the 'UC' mine-layers, which were comparable in size to the early British 'A' and 'B' classes. However, both types were developed until they were bigger and more successful than the earlier Mittel-U types.

The first minelayers, *UC1* to *UC15*, were unique in that they had no torpedo armament, and they carried only 12 mines, stowed in six vertically inclined tubes. Also, they reverted to using the Körting heavy oil engine which had been such an undesirable feature of the early U-Boats. Their low endurance and lack of sea-keeping meant that they could only lay mines in the Channel and off the South East coast of England, but they never-theless added a new and sinister dimen-sion to the submarine war.

For some time the British were only dimly aware of the danger, when mysterious fields were discovered off the East Coast in June 1915, but on 3 July, after a steamer reported colliding with a submerged object, British divers found the wreck of the newly completed *UC2*. The Italians salvaged the wreck of *UC12* in March 1916 after she had blown herself up on her own mines in Taranto harbour, and the British recovered *UC5* almost intact when she ran aground on Shipwash Sand in April. More news came to light

when the French found charts of mine-fields aboard *UB26*, after she had been caught in nets outside Le Havre.

The British reacted in a similar fashion to the Germans and ordered a further 38 of the 'E' Class in November 1914; unlike the Germans they had put a number of experimental submarines in hand in 1913, in order to evaluate foreign ideas. Three of the 'S' Class were built to the Italian Laurenti design, using Fiat diesels, and the four 'Ws' were built to French plans purchased from Schneider-Laubeuf. Vickers had also been allowed to build four 'V' Class to their own designs, while there were two more very unusual types, a large ocean-going boat and one driven by steam. Although the French had given up

the idea of steam-propulsion as long ago as 1908, the Admiralty was looking for a surface speed which was beyond the capacity of existing diesel engines.

Too novel for war

Had the war not started when it did this interesting spawning of types might have had more effect, but as it turned out the 'S' and 'W' Classes proved too novel for wartime use, and all seven were trans-ferred to Italy between October 1915 and August 1916, on the grounds that the Italian Navy might know how to work them. The big ocean-going boat was called *Nautilus*, the first British submarine to have a name instead of a number. Although she was a dismal failure and never became

German 'UB' and 'UC' type specifications

	UB1–17	UB18–46	UB48–136	UC1–15	UC16–79	UC90–120
Length (ft)	92	118.5	181.5	111.5	170	184
Breadth (ft)	10.25	14.25	191.3	10.3	17.1	18.2
Draught (ft)	10	12.15	12	10	12	12.35
Displacement (tons) surface/submerged	128/143	275/304	521/657	170/185	417/509	496/575
Surface hp	1×60	2×282	2×1100	1×90	2×500 or 2×600	2×600 or 2×650
Submerged hp	1×120	2×280	2×760	1×138	2×460	2×600
Oil fuel (tons)	3.5	22	34	2.5	46.6	63.6
Endurance at 5–8 knots (miles)	1,600	6,500	8,500	800	8,700	8,000
Speed (knots) surface/submerged	6.5/5.5	9/5.8	13.5/7.5	6.5/5	11–12/7	11–12/6.5
Torpedo tubes (in)	2×17.7 Bow	2×19.7 Bow	4 Bow; 1 Stern	None	2 Bow; 1 Stern	1 Stern; 2 ext.
Guns	1 MG	1×50mm or 1×88mm	1×105mm	1 MG	1×88mm	1×105mm
Complement	14	23	34	16	28	32

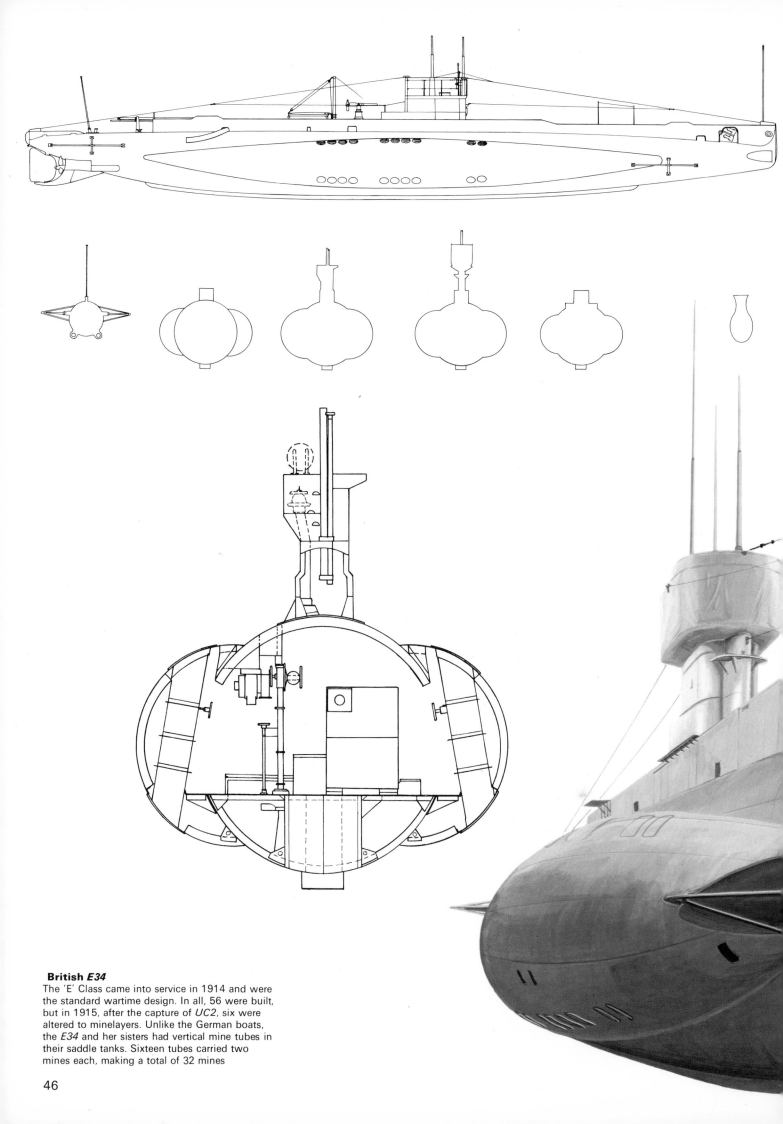

British _E34_

The 'E' Class came into service in 1914 and were
the standard wartime design. In all, 56 were built,
but in 1915, after the capture of _UC2_, six were
altered to minelayers. Unlike the German boats,
the _E34_ and her sisters had vertical mine tubes in
their saddle tanks. Sixteen tubes carried two
mines each, making a total of 32 mines

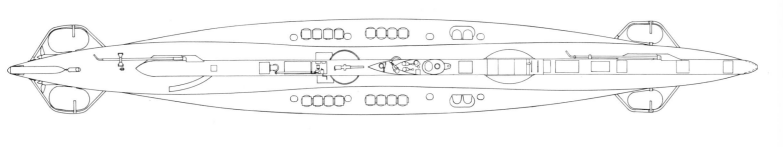

E34

operational, the steam-driven *Swordfish* did carry out trials and proved that steam turbines could be used in submarines. Beyond that point she could not be made to go, and in July 1917 she was recommissioned as a surface patrol vessel, with built-up superstructure and guns like those of the little 'B' Class in the Mediterranean.

Being able to tap the enormous resources of America gave the British a great advantage. As part of a deal arranged with the head of Bethlehem Steel, Charles M Schwab, Vickers' Canadian subsidiary company in Montreal was given a contract to build ten submarines based on the contemporary 'H' Class building for the US Navy and for the Russians as the 'AG' Class, while the Fore River Plant at Quincy, Massachusetts, was to build a further ten. The American-built group, numbered *H11* to *H20*, were to be delivered unarmed to Canadian Vickers, who would

then arm them, but this stretching of the neutrality laws finally goaded the State Department into action, and they were held up until the United States entered the war in 1917.

As it turned out, the British had by then more submarines than they could man, and six of the 'Hs' were ceded to Chile as compensation for warships seized in 1914, while the Canadians were given two. Out of the first group, *H1* and *H4* were sent to the Dardanelles in 1915; *H3* was lost in a minefield off Cattaro in 1916, but *H6* went aground off the coast of Holland and, after being interned, was purchased by the Dutch Navy. A further eight 'Hs' were built in Canada for the Italian Navy, and the Royal Navy liked theirs so much that in 1917 they ordered a further 34 to a modified design – which must constitute a record: one basic design was built in three countries, and the class served in seven navies. Incidentally,

H5's crossing of the Atlantic established a record for the longest voyage by a submarine to date.

The Admiralty panics
One notable feature of the naval war was the way in which the Admiralty was apt to be panicked by rumours. In 1915 a report was received in England to the effect that new German U-Boats would be capable of much higher surface speeds, and to meet this threat it was thought necessary to build 20-knot submarines. A further requirement was for long endurance and a more powerful wireless set, for the 'D' and 'E' Class boats patrolling in the Heligoland Bight could only transmit over a range of 50 miles. The resulting 'J' Class were over 100 feet longer than the 'E' Class, and had the remarkable speed of 19 knots on the surface, making them the fastest submarines in the world.

Unfortunately this led to the dangerous

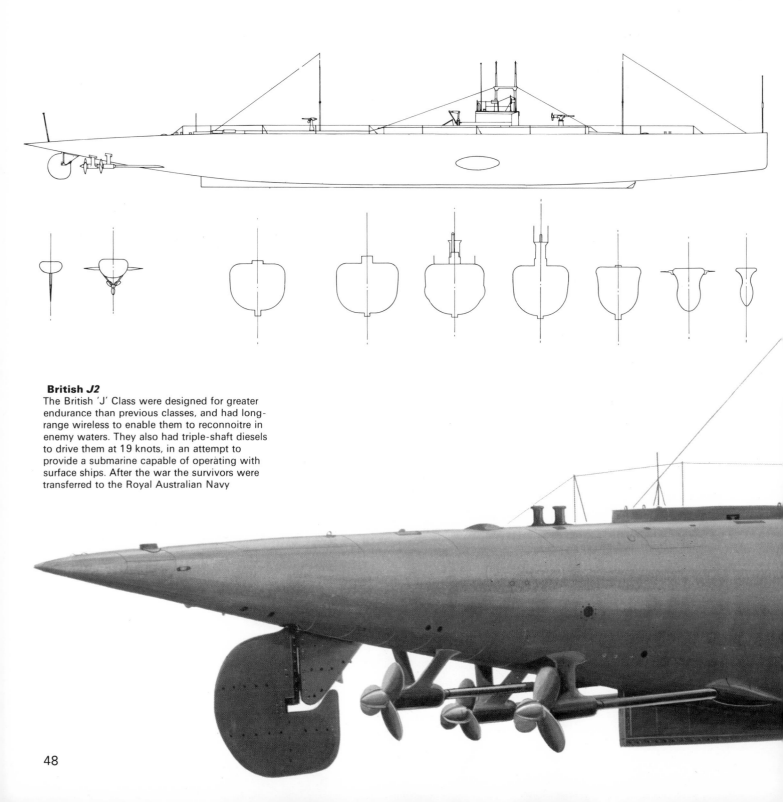

British *J2*
The British 'J' Class were designed for greater endurance than previous classes, and had long-range wireless to enable them to reconnoitre in enemy waters. They also had triple-shaft diesels to drive them at 19 knots, in an attempt to provide a submarine capable of operating with surface ships. After the war the survivors were transferred to the Royal Australian Navy

illusion that it would be a great advantage to have submarines capable of operating with the main battle fleet, the object being to lure the enemy's ships into a submarine trap. Up to this point the submarine's development had been rapid but logical, and under the stress of war enormous improvements in efficiency were being made, but now the designers were faced by an insoluble problem; the diesel could not be up-rated or developed any further, and even in the 'J' Class engine-power had only been achieved by linking three Vickers 1,200 bhp 12-cylinder engines. As a result, when Vickers were planning early in 1915 a so-called 'Fleet Submarine' there was no question of giving her the speed of a battleship (21 knots) with diesel engines, and so their designers fell back on the steam turbine unit which was being installed in the experimental *Swordfish*.

The ill-starred 'K' Class were the most bizarre submarines yet seen, for their 10,000 shaft hp turbines could drive them at 24 knots, with an auxiliary diesel for charging the batteries in addition to the electric motors giving them a total of three propulsion systems. In anticipation of their role in a surface action they were at first armed with twin revolving 18-in torpedo-tubes in the superstructure, as well as four bow and four beam tubes.

"Too many holes"

The 'K' boats merit a history of their own to do them full justice, but it will suffice to say here that their short-comings derived from two different causes: first, they were doing the wrong job, and second, their highly ingenious design was so complex that it was vulnerable to small defects. Submarines have never had any part to play in company with large war-ships; they have always been weapons of stealth and ambush. Furthermore, they are so dangerous that even friendly war-

ships are likely to shoot first and ask questions later, and because of their low profile they are badly equipped for sur-face navigation at speed in close formation. The 'K' Class had two oil-fired boilers, each with a small funnel which had to fold down into a watertight well, and as these boilers required large air-intakes, these also needed watertight seals. In the succinct words of a contemporary sub-mariner, 'too many damned holes', and a minor obstruction like a paint canister or a wire rope was sufficient to jam a vent open just as the submarine was ready to dive.

A chapter of accidents befell the seven-teen boats of the 'K' Class, some of them the sort of mishaps that submarines are prone to suffer, but because of their role with the Fleet they were unduly exposed to the risk of collision. The worst event was the 'Battle of May Island' on the night of 31 January 1918, when two flotillas of 'K'

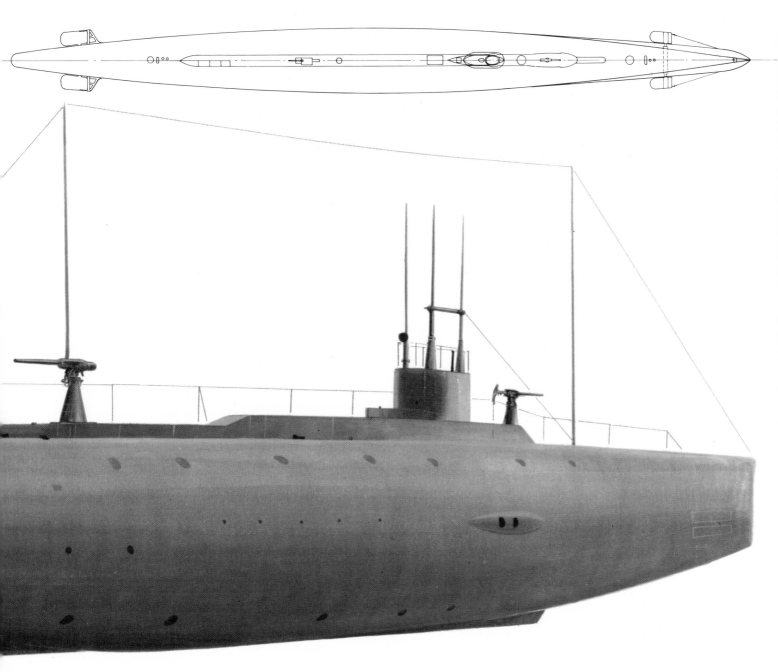

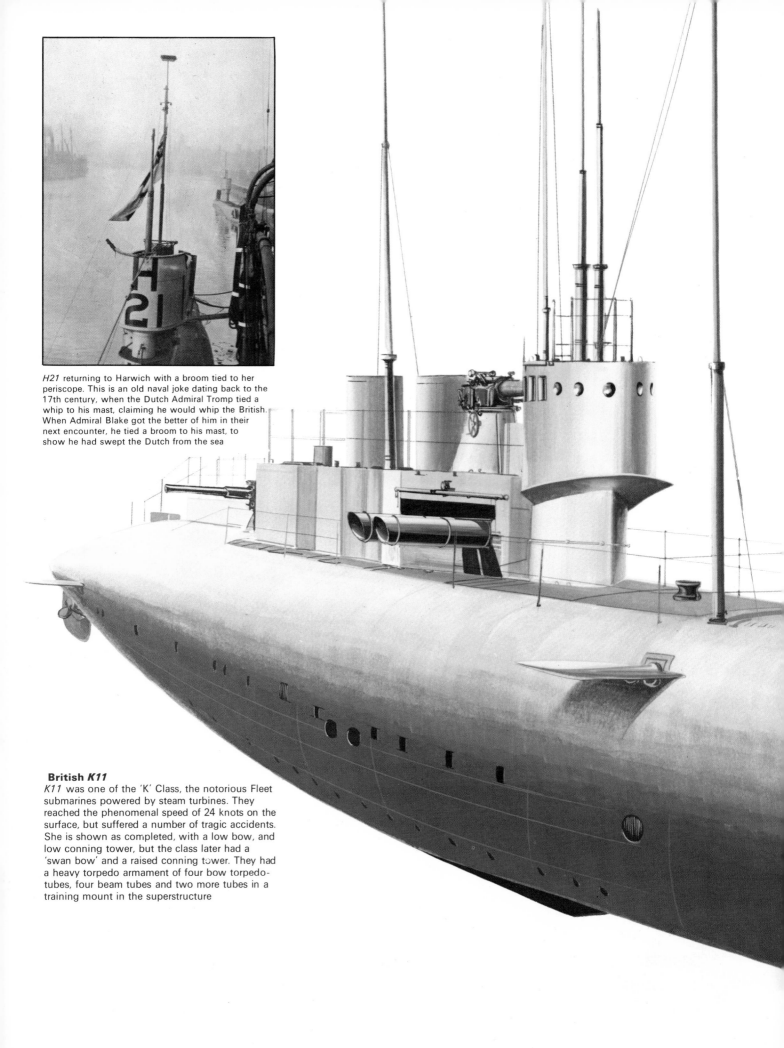

H21 returning to Harwich with a broom tied to her periscope. This is an old naval joke dating back to the 17th century, when the Dutch Admiral Tromp tied a whip to his mast, claiming he would whip the British. When Admiral Blake got the better of him in their next encounter, he tied a broom to his mast, to show he had swept the Dutch from the sea

British *K11*

K11 was one of the 'K' Class, the notorious Fleet submarines powered by steam turbines. They reached the phenomenal speed of 24 knots on the surface, but suffered a number of tragic accidents. She is shown as completed, with a low bow, and low conning tower, but the class later had a 'swan bow' and a raised conning tower. They had a heavy torpedo armament of four bow torpedo-tubes, four beam tubes and two more tubes in a training mount in the superstructure

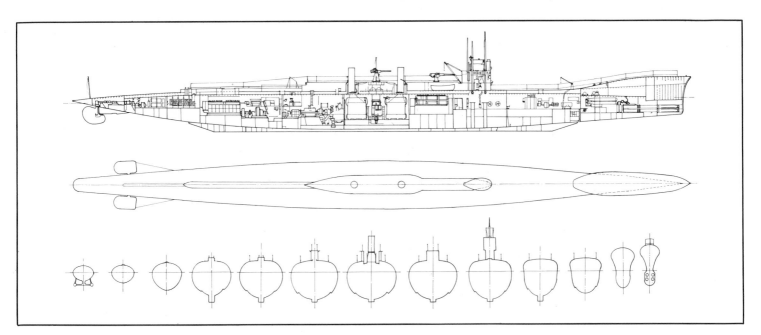

British _Swordfish_ (top)
The _Swordfish_ was the first British submarine to adopt steam propulsion, the only way to provide high surface speed. She was not a success, and was finally converted into a surface patrol vessel in 1917, but she paved the way for the 'K' Class

British 'K' Class
The 'K' Class had to be redesigned to eliminate various faults. The internal view above shows the arrangement of boilers and machinery, and shows how the bow was raised to accommodate a quick-blowing tank to help them surface faster. The funnels folded down into wells which were sealed with hatches

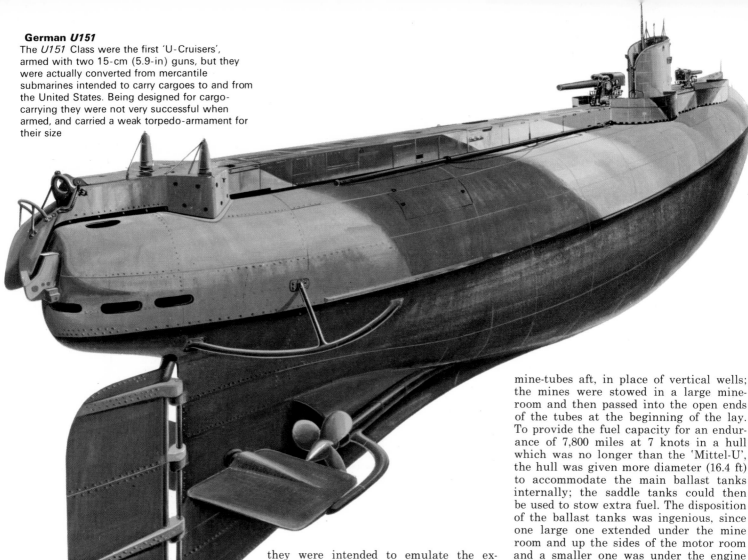

German _U151_
The _U151_ Class were the first 'U-Cruisers', armed with two 15-cm (5.9-in) guns, but they were actually converted from mercantile submarines intended to carry cargoes to and from the United States. Being designed for cargo-carrying they were not very successful when armed, and carried a weak torpedo-armament for their size

boats operating with battle cruisers on a night exercise were involved in multiple collisions. _K4_ was sunk by _K6_, and _K17_ was sunk by a cruiser. To confirm the growing suspicion of a hoodoo on the class, an inquiry revealed that the disaster was caused by a jammed helm in _K22_, which was actually _K13_ renamed after she had drowned most of her crew on her maiden voyage. With their long hulls they proved very difficult to handle, for at 338 ft overall and displacing 2,650 tons when submerged, they were larger than any contemporary submarine including the German 'U-Cruisers'.

Profiting by their capture of a UC-Boat, the British rapidly made provisions for submarine minelaying, and altered six 'E' Class during construction, but instead of putting the chutes inside the pressure hull as in the German boats, they put them in the side ballast tanks, ten chutes in all, with two mines in each. To compensate for the extra weight the two 18-in beam torpedo-tubes were omitted.

The next British development was also inspired by German ideas, for the news of U-Cruisers with 5.9-in guns prompted the Admiralty to order four submarines armed with a single 12-in gun each. These were the famous 'M' Class, of which the fourth was cancelled and only _M1_ saw war service; they mark the ultimate in gun-armed submarines. It is generally thought that

they were intended to emulate the exploits of submarines in the Sea of Marmora, but recent evidence of trials against simulated submarine targets suggests that they were intended for use against U-Boats, although the reasoning behind this remains obscure.

The other notable British development was the anti-submarine submarine, or to give it a more modern name, the hunter-killer type. Twelve of these craft, the 'R' Class, were ordered in December 1917, and they were nearly 30 years ahead of their time in having a streamlined fish-shaped hull, single-shaft machinery and enlarged battery-capacity to give a higher speed underwater than on the surface. Not only were the 'R' Class ahead of their time, they actually worked quite well, and reached 14 knots submerged, which remained a record until the closing stages of the Second World War. Had they been equipped with a better detection device than the hydrophone they could have hastened the development of the modern submarine, but even so an 'R' boat is credited with torpedoing a U-Boat in October 1918 – and if the torpedo had not failed to explode, the class might have earned more respect; instead they were seen as freaks.

German developments
Returning to the Germans, production of the 'Mittel-U', 'UB' and 'UC' types continued throughout the war, but there were a number of other interesting designs as well. In January 1915 orders were placed for ten 'UE' Class ocean-going minelayers, _U71_ to _80_, and they differed in many ways from the UC type. Apart from being bigger, they were fitted with horizontal

mine-tubes aft, in place of vertical wells; the mines were stowed in a large mine-room and then passed into the open ends of the tubes at the beginning of the lay. To provide the fuel capacity for an endurance of 7,800 miles at 7 knots in a hull which was no longer than the 'Mittel-U', the hull was given more diameter (16.4 ft) to accommodate the main ballast tanks internally; the saddle tanks could then be used to stow extra fuel. The disposition of the ballast tanks was ingenious, since one large one extended under the mine room and up the sides of the motor room and a smaller one was under the engine room and on either side of it. There were no internal torpedo-tubes, just two in the superstructure.

A further ten, _U117–126_, were ordered in May 1916, but they differed in many ways. By increasing the size considerably the designers were able to increase range, mine capacity and armament, and thus made very formidable craft out of these 'UE II' boats. Not only was the mine-room extended to enable 42 mines to be stowed, but 24 torpedoes could be carried, 12 externally in watertight cylinders and 12 internally, to be fired from four bow tubes. In addition, the gun armament was heavy, comprising a 5.9-in or two 4.1-in guns, and one can see in the 'UE II' Class the forerunner of successful Second World War designs like the Type IXA.

A development which attracted much more interest and caused great alarm at the time was the 'UK' or 'U-Cruiser' type of large boat with 5.9-in guns. This was a result of experience in 1915/16 very similar to that of British submarines, when it was shown that gunfire would sink a small target more effectively than a torpedo. The first class was the _U135–138_ group ordered in May 1916, and they were followed three months later by _U139–141_; orders for an even larger type, _U142–150_, were never completed.

The importance of the gun-calibre was grossly over-estimated in the minds of both the British and the Germans. In practice a U-Cruiser could do nothing that a smaller U-Boat could not do with a gun of 88-mm or 105-mm calibre, and the time taken to build these large and clumsy submarines would have been better spent

German *U155*

U155 was the former mercantile submarine *Deutschland*, and she carried the heavy armament of two 15-cm and two 8.8-cm guns. To compensate for her weak torpedo armament of only two bow tubes she was later fitted with six internal tubes, shown by dotted lines. In 1916 she made two famous trips to the United States, but was converted to a military submarine after America's entry into the war. The photographs below show *top: U90* at sea; *centre* and *bottom:* postcards printed after the war of the torpedo room and the control room, looking forward

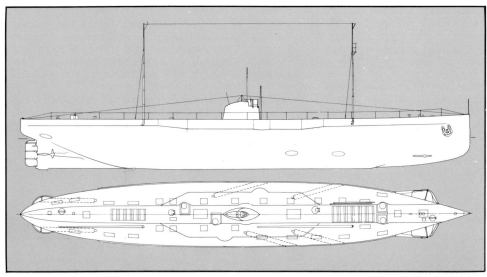

in building more of the standard types. On the British side there was wild talk of re-arming merchant ships with 6-in or 7.5-in guns, with no thought of the limitations of a submarine in a straight artillery duel. It is one thing for a submarine to shell a target from close range and quite another for her to face a ship armed with a 4.7-in or 6-in gun, for the submarine is so low in the water and so devoid of any fire-control equipment that her shooting is bound to be poor. U-Boats very rarely got the better of duels with decoy-vessels (Q-ships), and were either sunk outright or escaped with damage.

The effect of the British blockade was almost complete from the beginning of the war, for those German merchant ships which were not captured or sunk by Allied warships very quickly made for neutral ports and were interned. In 1915 it was decided to build two mercantile submarines which could run the blockade with ease, not so much for the cargoes they could carry but for the tremendous effect it would have on American opinion. Not only would the British be shown to have no defence against the U-Boat, but the Americans would be given a gentle warning about the dangers they would face if they chose to side with the enemies of Germany.

Intimidation fails

At one time it was hoped that the Kaiser would sanction a declaration of unrestricted submarine warfare to coincide with the arrival of the first submarines in American waters. It was thought that this double blow to the hopes of the pro-Allied politicians in the United States would paralyse any effective moves to put pressure on Germany, but one can doubt today whether this would have happened, any more than it did at the time of Pearl Harbor, 25 years later. In the event the Germans overplayed their hand.

The first cargo-carrier, *Deutschland,* left Kiel on 23 June 1916 under Captain König, carrying dyes, mail and precious stones; she made a landfall at Baltimore, Maryland on 9 July and, as she was clearly not armed, the US authorities had to treat her as a merchantman. After loading copper, nickel, silver and zinc, and having created world-wide interest, she sailed for Bremen on 2 August. Her sister *Bremen* was ordered to make a similar voyage to Norfolk, Virginia but this time *U53* was ordered to 'blow a path' through the waiting warships and to make an unannounced visit to Newport, Rhode Island. Although the *Bremen* disappeared without trace somewhere off the Orkneys (she was probably mined), the *U53* under Hans Rose reached Newport on 7 October.

The appearance of a belligerent warship caught the US Navy completely off balance; after an amusing conversation

with an American admiral who was frantically spinning out the talk while waiting for instructions from Washington, Rose took his submarine out of US territorial waters as quietly as he had come. Then, in accordance with his orders, he began to sink shipping within sight of the Nantucket lightship. Despite American annoyance at this effrontery there was little that could be done about it, and *U53* sank five ships in all before returning to Germany, with Rose convinced that he had struck terror into the hearts of the United States Navy and Government.

But fear does not always breed subservience, and the Americans became more worried than ever about Germany's long-term intentions. The mission was already pointless as the *Bremen* had failed to arrive, and the Kaiser could not bring himself to sanction an all-out U-Boat offensive. The surviving mercantile submarine *Deutschland* was ordered to be converted to a U-Cruiser, and five more were ordered in February 1917. These were numbered *U151–157*, of which *U155* was the ex-*Deutschland*, and they were armed with two 5.9-in guns and two 88-mm

guns staggered forward and aft of the conning tower. The large cargo hold abaft the conning tower was converted to a magazine for shells and charges, and the refrigerating plant provided for cooling the hold was removed. One unusual feature was the fact that the surface power was exactly the same as the submerged power.

The only other development of interest was the 'UF' type, a small submarine intended for operations off the Flanders coast. Between December 1917 and July 1918, 92 were ordered but none was completed before the Armistice. They approxi-

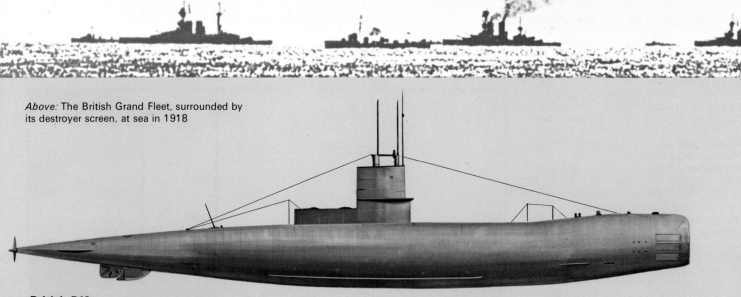

Above: The British Grand Fleet, surrounded by its destroyer screen, at sea in 1918

British *R12*
The British 'R' Class are outstanding as the first attempt to produce an anti-submarine submarine, or 'hunter-killer' as they are known today. They were also a quarter of a century before their time in having a streamlined hull designed for higher speed under water than on the surface. The bulbous bow contained listening gear, and the armament of six 18-in torpedoes was designed for maximum effect against submarines. Speed: 9 knots (surfaced) 14 knots (submerged)

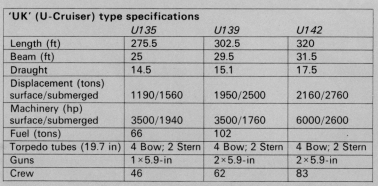

'UK' (U-Cruiser) type specifications			
	U135	*U139*	*U142*
Length (ft)	275.5	302.5	320
Beam (ft)	25	29.5	31.5
Draught	14.5	15.1	17.5
Displacement (tons) surface/submerged	1190/1560	1950/2500	2160/2760
Machinery (hp) surface/submerged	3500/1940	3500/1760	6000/2600
Fuel (tons)	66	102	
Torpedo tubes (19.7 in)	4 Bow; 2 Stern	4 Bow; 2 Stern	4 Bow; 2 Stern
Guns	1 × 5.9-in	2 × 5.9-in	2 × 5.9-in
Crew	46	62	83

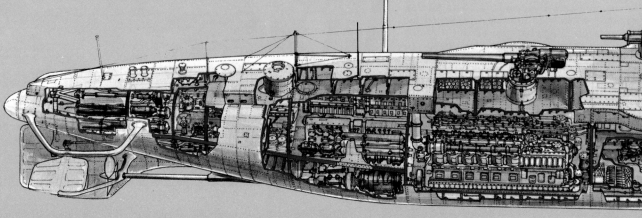

mated to the *UB18* class in size, but had more power and higher speed. Only two other types call for comment, the *UA* which was originally ordered as the Norwegian *A5*, and the cancelled 'UD' Class, which were 4,000-ton underwater cruisers incorporating the same armament as the *U151* class. When the Armistice came in November 1918 the Imperial German Navy had ordered 811 submarines of all types, 768 of them after the outbreak of war. Out of this vast number over 400 were either cancelled or incomplete, and 178 were lost.

This means that over 47 per cent of the German Navy's U-Boat arm was lost, with 515 officers and 4,849 other ranks, or roughly 40 per cent of the total personnel. Against this fearful casualty rate they could boast over 11 million tons of shipping sunk and a further 7.5 million tons damaged. Great Britain alone lost over 2,000 merchant ships and 14,000 merchant seamen from the activities of submarines, and nearly lost the war through starvation.

During the appalling month of April 1917, when merchant ship losses rose to 881,000 tons, and one ship in four destined

for the British Isles was sunk, the food reserves were calculated at only six weeks. Had these losses not been checked, the submarine would have won by itself a war in which enormous armies were still trying to achieve a victory after three years. Had the British Isles been starved out the sequence of events would have been inexorable: a negotiated peace between Great Britain and Germany followed by the collapse of France. Not even the resources of the United States could have reversed the verdict, for her troops and supplies would never have reached Europe.

British *L52*

The British *L52* represents the final evolution of the standard submarine in the Royal Navy. Basically an improved 'E' Class, they had a heavy torpedo- and gun-armament, and were highly successful in service. Three survived until the Second World War. They were armed with six 21-in torpedo-tubes and two 4-in guns

German U-Boat losses				
	'U' Type	'UB' Type	'UC' Type	Total
1914	5	—	—	5
1915	14	2	3	19
1916	7	8	7	22
1917	19	12	32	63
1918	17	42	10	69
Total	62	64	52	178

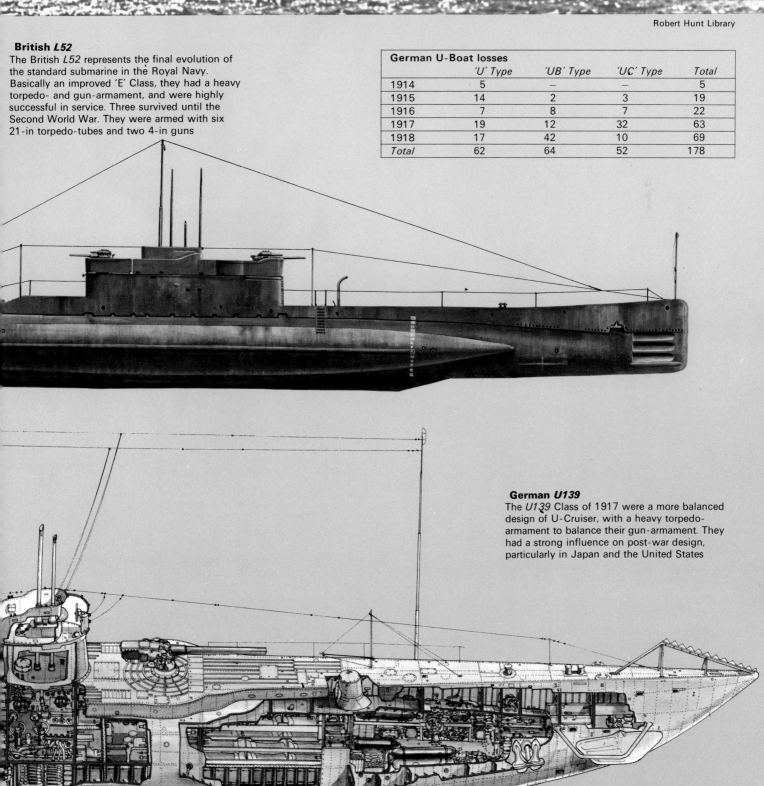

German *U139*

The *U139* Class of 1917 were a more balanced design of U-Cruiser, with a heavy torpedo-armament to balance their gun-armament. They had a strong influence on post-war design, particularly in Japan and the United States

Weapons and Tactics

Left: The explosion of a depth-charge.

As we have already seen, the only weapons against the submarine in 1914 were the ram and the gun. However, both these methods depended on the submarine surfacing or giving away her position, and so opportunities for using them were limited. In all only 14 U-Boats were sunk by ramming, and it tended to damage the attacking ship. In 1918 the old destroyer *Fairy* sank after damage sustained from ramming *UC75*, but at the other end of the scale *U29* was sunk by the battleship HMS *Dreadnought* like a cobra crushed by an elephant.

However, there were two passive methods of defence, minefields and nets, and these were quickly put into effect by both sides. First came indicator nets and then mine nets, which had small charges attached to the netting to explode on contact. Although the British took some time to develop a properly effective mine, when they finally introduced the H2 pattern in 1916 it rapidly became the most effective weapon against U-Boats and sank 25 per cent of the total.

The depth-charge was introduced in 1916 to solve the problem of attacking a submerged submarine; it was basically a 300-lb bomb fitted with a hydrostatic device to detonate it at a pre-set depth. Then came the battle to devise a sensor to detect the submarine before it attacked, and out of this were developed various types of hydrophone. This was simply an underwater listening device which was made directional to trace the noise made by a submarine's electric motors. In July 1916 the motor boat *Salmon* brought off the first successful attack using both depth-charges and hydrophones, when she sank *UC7*. Late in 1918 scientists began to test more advanced methods of sonic location, and from the initials of the Allied Submarine Detection Investigation Committee came the name Asdic, but that story belongs to the post-war period.

The simplest defence for a ship was to follow a zigzag course, for the U-Boat's commander had to estimate the target's course and speed by eye. Any error in estimation of the speed or inclination of the target could result in the torpedo missing, and so ships were also given false bow-waves to give a wrong impression of high speed. This in turn led to 'dazzle-painting', a form of camouflage which utilised extreme colour variations and linear patterns to obscure features such as the waterline, deckline or bridge structures which helped the U-Boat commander to estimate course and angle of inclination. Submarines also used camouflage to make themselves hard to pick out at a distance, and were even reported to have hoisted sails on occasions to imitate fishing vessels.

Although the depth-charge eventually proved to be the best weapon against a submerged U-Boat there were a number of intermediate steps. The first was the explosive sweep, which was developed from minesweeping gear and comprised a charge towed from a destroyer's stern, and kept below the surface by a special float. If the sweep fouled a submerged object this registered on an indicator, and the sweep could then be fired electrically. Another device was the explosive para-

vane, two of which could be towed at high speed by a destroyer, in the hope that a submarine would draw the infernal machine on to herself. But both these gadgets proved very unpopular with ships' captains, who did not relish the idea of towing explosive charges with a penchant for wrapping themselves around propeller shafts.

The depth-charge thrower was only the culminating development in a series of projectors which could hurl an explosive charge some distance from the ship to the area in which the submarine had last been seen. There was the 7.5-in howitzer, which was simply a breech-loading recoilless weapon firing a spherical bomb; it was trained by means of a shoulder-piece, and as it weighed only 35 cwt it could be mounted in small ships like trawlers. The 10-in bomb-thrower was muzzle-loading, and could fire either a normal shell or a spherical stick-bomb weighing 200 lb; its main weakness was the tendency of the stick to rust to the barrel.

An even more fearsome weapon was the 11-in breech-loading howitzer, which fired a 350-lb shell some 3,000 yards; it could only be carried by cruisers, and as it fired a conventional shell it was mainly for use against diving or surfaced submarines.

By far the most spectacular weapon against submarines was the decoy vessel or 'Q-Ship', simply a merchant ship with concealed armament and designed to lure a U-Boat within gun-range and then open fire. The first Q-Ship victims were quite easily trapped, but inevitably some U-Boats escaped and reported the news, and so a deadly game of bluff developed. The impression given had to be one of an innocent steamer whose crew had taken to the boats, and so a 'panic party' had to leave the ship in the lifeboats, leaving the gun-crews still concealed behind cover. If the U-Boat commander was mildly suspicious he might then indulge in some leisurely gunnery practice, and in some cases three 'panic parties' left before the lethal game could be resolved.

As the U-Boat always had the option of simply torpedoing the Q-Ship some of them were filled with timber to increase their chances of staying afloat, in the hope that the U-Boat would then surface to finish her off with her deck-gun. In 1917 a specially constructed Q-Ship was completed, HMS *Hyderabad*; she had one 4-in gun, two 12-pounders, four bomb-throwers, and torpedo-tubes and depth-charges, all on a draft of only 6 ft 9 in so that torpedoes would pass under her. Many of the 'Flower' Class escort sloops were either modified or completed as 'Flower-Qs', resembling small coasters, and twenty of the so-called P-Boats were similarly converted to PC-Boats. The essential difference between these ships and the Q-Ships was that they functioned as normal warships, whereas the decoys were clandestine by nature and adopted false names so as to mislead spies.

The trawler trap

A variation of the decoy trick was tried in 1915, when U-Boats began to attack the British trawler-fleet off the north-east coast of Scotland. In each group of trawlers was one naval trawler (commissioned but unarmed), which was towing an old 'C' Class submarine, to which she was also connected by telephone. The

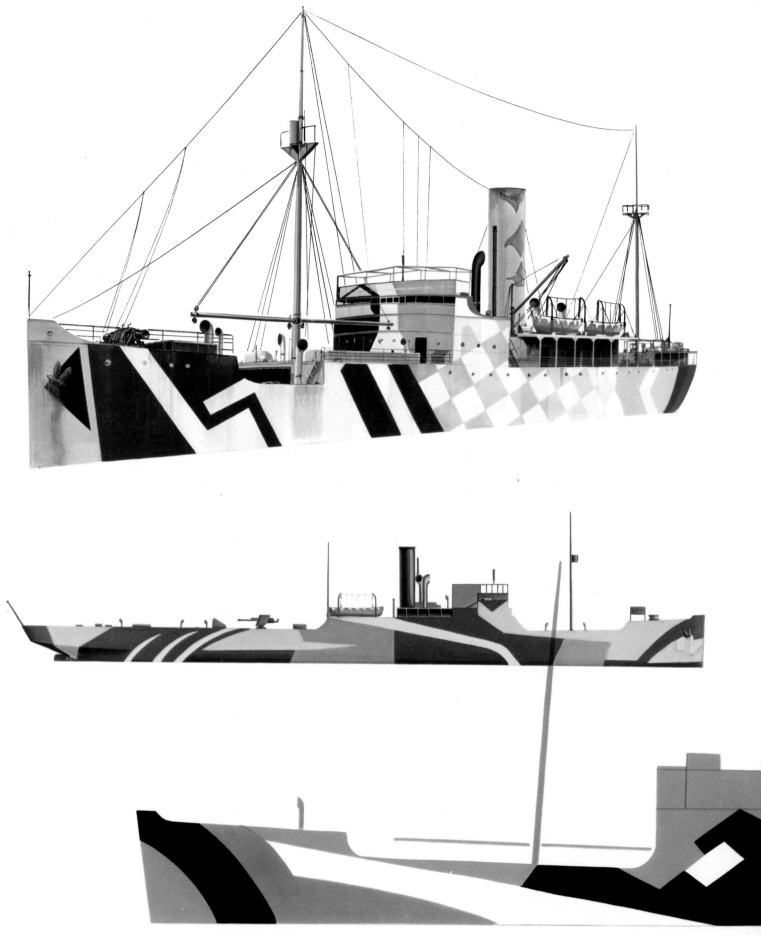

theory was that the trawler would give the essential data to the submarine via the telephone link, and the submarine would then slip the tow and work herself into a position for attacking the U-Boat. The first time it was tried, in June 1915, the cable refused to slip, but despite the fact that the submarine *C24* had 100 fathoms of tow rope and telephone cable dangling

from her bows she managed to torpedo *U40*. Nearly a month later *C27* had another chance; this time the telephone link failed, but the submarine commander was able to work out what was happening on the surface and finally succeeded in torpedoing *U23*.

However, the problem still remained of how to find submarines, and in April 1917

the shipping losses showed clearly that all counter-measures had failed. The fundamental problem was – and still is – that the ocean was far too big for the escorts to cover. The answer was Convoy, or sailing merchant ships in groups defended by warships, the classic counter to harassment of seaborne commerce since the 14th century. But for a variety of reasons,

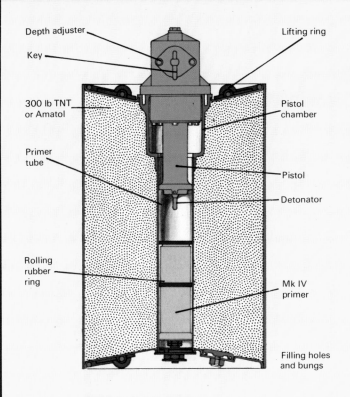

British Depth-charge

The 'D' Type depth-charge Mk III. This simple weapon proved to be the most successful method of sinking U-Boats, but it was not ready until 1916, and only available in quantity in 1917. The hydrostatic device was set to the estimated depth of the U-Boat by hand, and the depth-charge was then rolled off the stern of the escort. Known to the Germans as the 'Wasserbom' or 'Wabo' for short, it could destroy a U-Boat up to 25 ft away, and inflict damage as much as 50 ft away

Labels on diagram:
- Depth adjuster
- Key
- 300 lb TNT or Amatol
- Primer tube
- Rolling rubber ring
- Lifting ring
- Pistol chamber
- Pistol
- Detonator
- Mk IV primer
- Filling holes and bungs

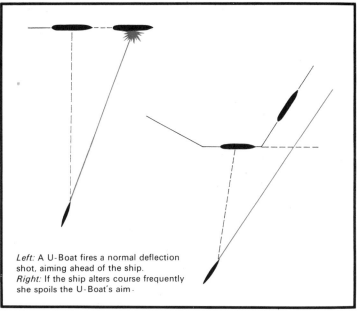

Left: A U-Boat fires a normal deflection shot, aiming ahead of the ship.
Right: If the ship alters course frequently she spoils the U-Boat's aim.

Zig-zag Evasion Technique

Zig-zagging was an important defence for ships against U-Boats. One of the biggest problems was the co-ordination of zig-zagging in a convoy formation; to avoid collisions, it was done to a pre-arranged system

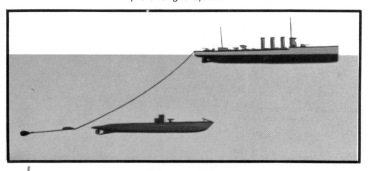

Explosive Sweep

The Explosive Sweep was an early device for towing behind destroyers. It was fitted with an electric indicator which registered an obstruction, and the explosive charge could then be fired from the destroyer

Dazzle-painted Anti-submarine Escorts

These innocent-looking coasters were in fact commissioned warships. The sloops *Gardenia*, shown here in her official dazzle-painted scheme, and *Polyanthus* (opposite, top) were converted during construction from conventional escorts, while *PC69* (opposite, centre) was a converted P-Boat or patrol vessel. They were armed with a variety of 4-in and 3-in guns, depth-charges and bomb-throwers, and differed from the 'Q-Ship' decoys in that they were warships pure and simple. The armament was concealed behind shutters under the deck-houses amidships and at the stern

20th century naval tacticians could not accept that a method which had proved itself during the Napoleonic Wars could have any validity in the age of steam and armour. As late as January 1917 the Naval Staff stated that convoy could not be recommended as a defence against submarines, despite the fact that the Grand Fleet's immunity to submarine attack had been, in essence, due to a form of convoying ever since the outbreak of war.

There was no 'inventor' of convoy in 1917, but much of the credit must go to influential advisers like the Secretary to the Cabinet, Hankey, who pressed it on Lloyd George, the British Prime Minister. The first change was in February 1917, when at French insistence the cross-Channel collier traffic was convoyed; in April 1917 at the worst moment of the U-Boat war the collier losses were 0.19 per cent. With grave misgivings the first ocean convoy sailed at the end of April, and within one month the loss rate dropped from 25 to 0.24 per cent.

The system worked for the simple reason that convoys concentrated the

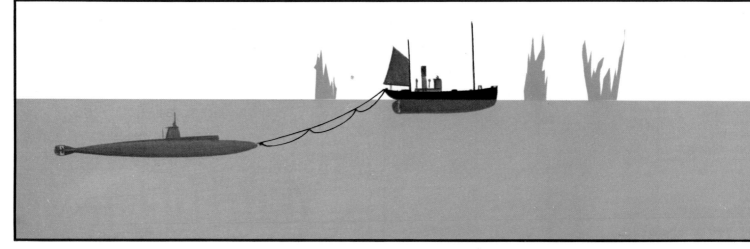

targets and so forced the U-Boats to come to the convoys, where they could be attacked. The memoirs of U-Boat commanders bear this out, for they had hitherto lain in wait at strategic points where merchantmen were bound to pass, whereas after the introduction of convoys the seas were suddenly emptied of shipping. And when shipping did appear it was surrounded by destroyers, sloops and patrol vessels of all sizes.

Once the appalling slaughter of merchant ships was halted, the U-Boats were put on the defensive. A new minelaying offensive was mounted against the U-Boat bases in the Heligoland Bight and on the Flanders coast. With the aid of crypt-analysis British minelayers laid both conventional and magnetic mines in the U-Boats' exit routes, and losses began to rise. Although the enormous Anglo-American Northern Barrage between Norway and the Orkneys was of little use in sinking submarines, the Dover Barrage was finally made submarine-proof in 1918. In the Mediterranean the Allies tried to seal German and Austrian sub-

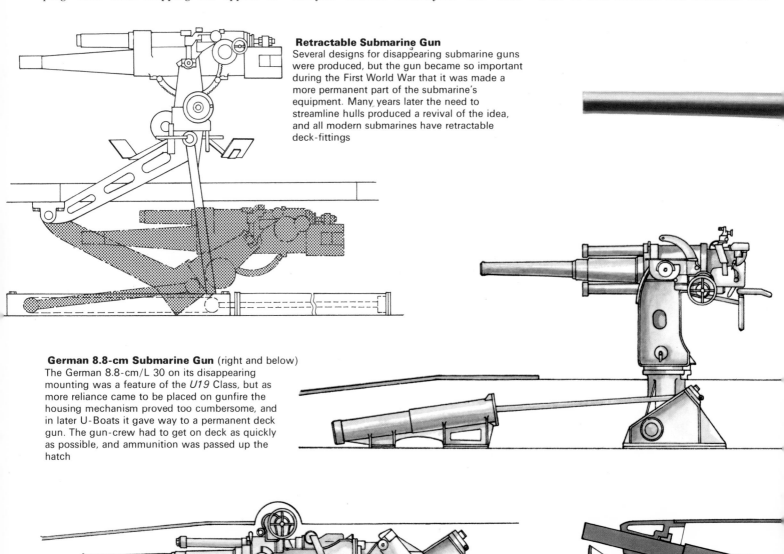

Retractable Submarine Gun
Several designs for disappearing submarine guns were produced, but the gun became so important during the First World War that it was made a more permanent part of the submarine's equipment. Many years later the need to streamline hulls produced a revival of the idea, and all modern submarines have retractable deck-fittings

German 8.8-cm Submarine Gun (right and below)
The German 8.8-cm/L 30 on its disappearing mounting was a feature of the *U19* Class, but as more reliance came to be placed on gunfire the housing mechanism proved too cumbersome, and in later U-Boats it gave way to a permanent deck gun. The gun-crew had to get on deck as quickly as possible, and ammunition was passed up the hatch

Fielding Submarine Gun
A Mr Fielding patented this idea for a bow-mounted gun in a submarine

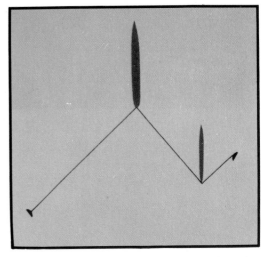

marines in the Adriatic with the Otranto Barrage, but with less success due to the depth of water.

In the final analysis it was the convoys that forced the U-Boats to take greater risks, both in entering mined waters and in broadcasting the endless stream of messages that gave the Allies the intelligence that they needed. Convoyed ships totalled 84,000, of which the U-Boats sank only 257, or 0.4 per cent; during the same period 2,616 ships were lost while sailing independently.

The other weapon to be developed during the First World War as a potent anti-submarine measure was the aircraft. Technically the first submarine to be sunk by air attack was the British *B10*, in dock at Venice in August 1916, but the first true attack on a submarine at sea was made by two Austrian seaplanes against the French *Foucault* off Cattaro on 15 September 1916. The submarine was taken by surprise and was forced to the surface after being damaged. The British introduced 'Blimps', or non-rigid airships, for anti-submarine patrols, and they

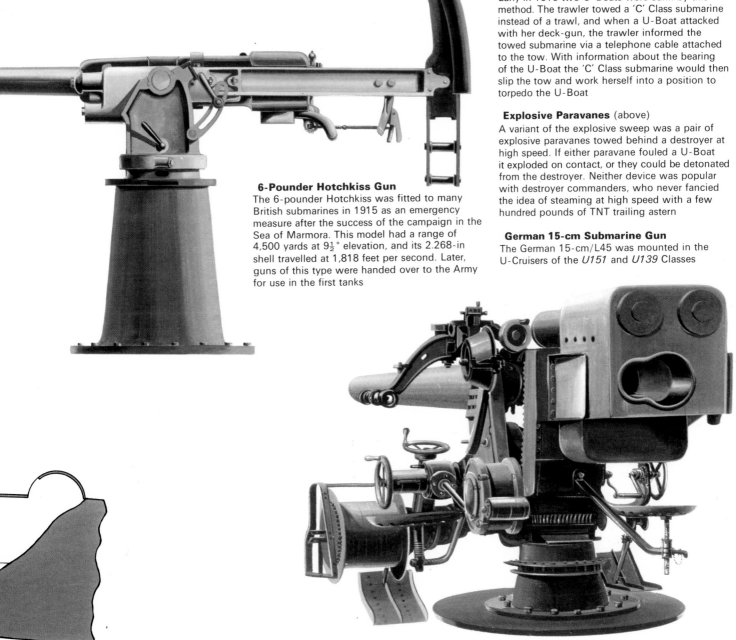

6-Pounder Hotchkiss Gun
The 6-pounder Hotchkiss was fitted to many British submarines in 1915 as an emergency measure after the success of the campaign in the Sea of Marmora. This model had a range of 4,500 yards at $9\frac{1}{2}°$ elevation, and its 2.268-in shell travelled at 1,818 feet per second. Later, guns of this type were handed over to the Army for use in the first tanks

'Trawler-submarine trap' (above left)
Early in 1915 two U-Boats were sunk by this method. The trawler towed a 'C' Class submarine instead of a trawl, and when a U-Boat attacked with her deck-gun, the trawler informed the towed submarine via a telephone cable attached to the tow. With information about the bearing of the U-Boat the 'C' Class submarine would then slip the tow and work herself into a position to torpedo the U-Boat

Explosive Paravanes (above)
A variant of the explosive sweep was a pair of explosive paravanes towed behind a destroyer at high speed. If either paravane fouled a U-Boat it exploded on contact, or they could be detonated from the destroyer. Neither device was popular with destroyer commanders, who never fancied the idea of steaming at high speed with a few hundred pounds of TNT trailing astern

German 15-cm Submarine Gun
The German 15-cm/L45 was mounted in the U-Cruisers of the *U151* and *U139* Classes

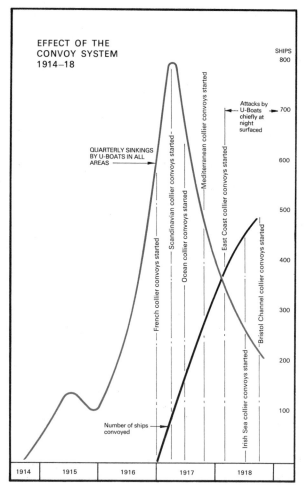

EFFECT OF THE
CONVOY SYSTEM
1914–18

SHIPS
800
700
600
500
400
300
200
100

QUARTERLY SINKINGS
BY U-BOATS IN ALL
AREAS

Attacks by
U-Boats
chiefly at
night
surfaced

French collier convoys started
Scandinavian collier convoys started
Ocean collier convoys started
Mediterranean collier convoys started
East Coast collier convoys started
Bristol Channel collier convoys started
Irish Sea collier convoys started

Number of ships
convoyed

1914   1915   1916   1917   1918

These graphs illustrate the effects of the convoy system on
the U-Boats' anti-trade war. The number of merchant ships
sunk by submarines fell dramatically (*above*) in direct
relation to the number of ships convoyed, and in spite of
the number of U-Boats at sea (*below*)

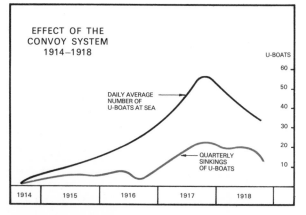

EFFECT OF THE
CONVOY SYSTEM
1914–1918

U-BOATS
60
50
40
30
20
10

DAILY AVERAGE
NUMBER OF
U-BOATS AT SEA

QUARTERLY
SINKINGS
OF U-BOATS

1914   1915   1916   1917   1918

7.5-in Bomb Thrower

This was only one of a series of interim weapons
produced before the depth-charge thrower was
introduced. It propelled its 100-lb stick-bomb to
a range of 2,100 yards at its maximum elevation
of 45°, but its usefulness was limited because
the bomb had no hydrostatic fuse to allow it to
explode at a fixed depth. It was meant primarily
for disabling a submarine on the surface or just
after she had submerged

Loading Torpedoes

Striking down a torpedo in a U-Boat. This remains
essentially the same today in all submarines
because of their narrow beam. The torpedo is
lowered by a boom or derrick rigged temporarily
on deck, through a loading hatch onto guide-
rails, and then down into the torpedo room

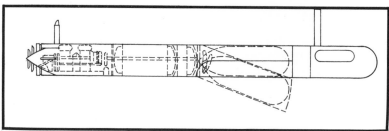

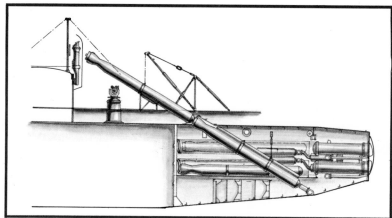

Myers Torpedo Mine

Among several ideas patented during the First
World War was the 'torpedo mine' designed by a
Mr Myers. It was a torpedo which dropped a mine
at the end of its run

proved particularly valuable when convoys were introduced. The Davis Gun was
specially introduced to provide a recoilless
weapon for aircraft and airships to use
against submarines, and of course bombs
and machine-guns were available. It has
been claimed that in all only two ships
were sunk in convoys that were accom-
panied by aircraft.

What defence had the U-Boat against
all these counter-measures? She faced
armed merchant ships, Q-Ships and
ordinary warships, as well as a growing
horde of armed yachts and similar
auxiliary patrol craft. The early war days
showed that a sharp-eyed lookout was
essential to give warning of the approach
of a warship, but as long as the submarine
was still functioning she could dive in
time. Nets were countered by fitting net-

cutters on the bows, either a saw-backed
frame as in U-Boats or a hardened edge
to the bow as favoured in British
submarines.

Periscope design also improved, from
the early crude single instrument to the
provision of separate search and attack
periscopes. The search periscope had a
wide-angle lens to allow the maximum
field of vision, whereas the attack type
had a narrow field; by the end of the war
special air-search periscopes had been
produced, with a high-angle head to allow
a search for aircraft. Aircraft could also be
met with gunfire, but the state of anti-
aircraft gunnery was in an even cruder
state than aerial bombing, and the outcome of aircraft/submarine duels was
largely a matter of luck at this stage.

The biggest problem was the lack of

endurance while running submerged, and
there was a steady growth in battery
capacity as wartime construction progressed. Although the provision of deck-
guns became standard as a means of
conserving torpedoes, the Germans were
forced to rely on the torpedo after the
introduction of convoy in 1917, for there
was little reward in engaging a large number of merchant ships and escorts on the
surface.

As submarines had increased in size it
became possible to provide extra torpedoes as reloads, and this reached its
peak in the UEII Class, with an extra 12
torpedoes stowed outside the pressure
hull. As early as 1915 the British *E14* went
on patrol in the Sea of Marmora with
spare torpedoes lashed on the casing, but
this was an extreme measure that was not

German Air/Sea Search Periscope (right)
The growing danger from aircraft is reflected in this German Goerz air/sea search periscope, which could tilt from the horizontal to 80° elevation. The growing complexity of submarine operations led to the provision of separate periscopes, a wide-angle one for search purposes, and a narrow-angle one for attack

Depth-charge Thrower (below right)
The English firm of Thornycroft designed a small mortar for throwing depth-charges about 75 yards clear of the ship. With one on each side of the stern and a rack for dropping depth-charges, it was then possible to drop a 'pattern' with more chance of destroying the U-Boat

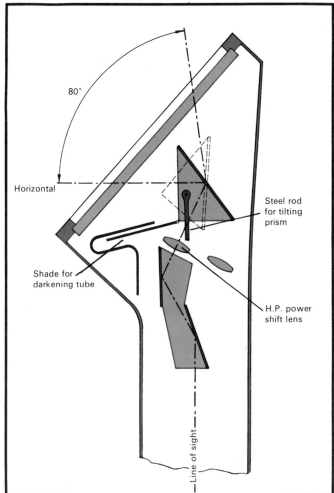

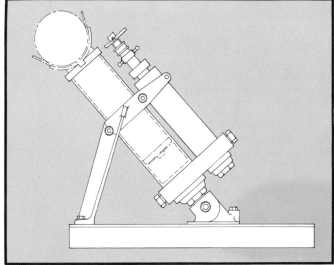

encouraged. On one occasion a British submarine commander swam out to an unexploded torpedo to screw down the safety device before reloading it into the tube.

The war showed that submarines could function in worse conditions than had ever been dreamed of in peacetime. Conning towers were modified to allow greater protection to personnel, but the submarines proved to be more robust than many surface ships. Spray interference and lack of visibility were the limiting factors because of a submarine's low silhouette, but as submariners knew, really rough weather could be dodged simply by submerging, as the effect of waves does not go very deep.

The worst problems of habitability were the cramped quarters and the ever-present condensation. One of the most grisly

reports on conditions was sent in from a British submarine in the Sea of Marmora, when the crew were stricken by dysentery, but that could be matched by stories of U-Boats operating in the North Atlantic in winter. Many of the problems could only be solved by increasing the size of submarines, and there was a clear link between the size of a boat and her efficiency on a long patrol. This was one of the main post-war improvements.

The submarine came of age during the First World War in more ways than one. First came the realisation at top level that she was a dangerous threat to all surface ships, and then as the war went on came the perfection of the weapon itself. This particularly involved the personnel, as submariners learned how to use their boats to the best of their ability, but it

was matched by increased reliability of the equipment. Machinery improved dramatically, and so did torpedoes, and by 1918 the submarine had gone through a revolution of design as rapid as the one undergone by the military aircraft in the same period.

When we look at those quaint examples and wonder how men could dare to put to sea in them we must remember that in 1918 a submariner might wonder how anyone had the courage to take a Holland or a Lake boat to sea. The answer must surely be that submariners have always had a special brand of nerve to enable them to master their strange element. That is the sad paradox of the submarine, that it called for the highest type of bravery and yet waged the most ruthless form of warfare.

The Rearmament Race

When the exhausted world powers turned to negotiation in 1918, as an alternative to the four years of destruction which had been endured, it was with a wholesome respect for the submarine. Whether the war would have ended sooner without the submarine is arguable, but there can be no doubt that it would not have been so ruinously expensive. The British Empire, having started the war as the world's largest ship-owner and operator, lost over 9 million tons, as against 4 million tons lost by all other countries put together. This represented about 90 per cent of the steamships under British registration in 1914, and the loss of national wealth went far beyond the actual cost of the cargoes.

The submarine had proven its worth as a fighting weapon during the First World War, as the fearful slaughter of ships showed only too well. When the Armistice was signed on 11 November 1918 between Germany and the Allies, one of the key clauses stipulated that the U-Boats must be surrendered at a designated port. All boats fit for sea had to retain their armament, but those unfit for sea were to be disarmed and immobilised.

On the morning of 20 November a melancholy procession began, with batches of U-Boats going to the British east coast port of Harwich until the early months of 1919; others surrendered at Sevastopol or in neutral ports, and even more were put out of action in German ports. A total of 176 boats were surrendered, and immediately the victors seized the chance to study the sinister weapon which had cost them so much in blood and treasure. The U-Boats were parcelled out as follows:

Great Britain
105 boats, of which at least U126, U161 and one of the UC90 class wore the White Ensign for a time

France
46 boats of which 10 were incorporated into the French Navy and renamed:

U79/Victor Reveille	U162/Pierre Marrast
U105/Jean Autrice	U166/Jean Roulier
U108/Léon Mignot	UB98/Trinité Schillemans
U119/Réné Audry	UB99/Carissan
U139/Halbronn	UB155/Jean Corré

Japan
7 boats renamed:

U125 – O1	UC90 – O3
U46 – O2	UC99 – O5
U55 – O3	UB125 – O6
	UB143 – O7

Italy: 10 **USA**: 6 **Belgium**: 2 originally allocated to Great Britain

With the exception of the ten French boats listed, all these submarines were scrapped and disposed of by 1922/23 by agreement between the nations concerned (the French arrangement having been a special case) to compensate for wartime losses. But the lessons had been learned and would be incorporated in future construction.

Despite the fact that wartime experience had not justified the 'U-cruiser' type, with its large, clumsy hull and superfluous heavy guns, every navy plumped for cruiser-submarines. The two nations whose navies were expanding rapidly were Japan and the United States, and both took possession of the larger types of U-Boat as their share of surrendered tonnage. The United States took over U140, a 311-ft vessel armed with two 5·9-in guns, and incorporated many of her features into the so-called V-series, the *Barracuda* Class, and the *Narwhal* Class, both with high endurance and heavy torpedo-armament, and in the case of the two *Narwhals*, having two 6-in guns. The sixth

in the V-series was the giant *Argonaut* which was also based on *U140*, but incorporated the minelaying system of the UEII type *U117*, which was also among the US Navy's booty.

The first Japanese cruiser-submarine was the *I52* laid down in 1922, and she was modelled on the *O1* (ex-*U125*), another UEII type. A year later an even larger type, the 'Junsen Type 1' or Cruiser Submarine Type 1 was begun; the four vessels *I1–4* displaced 2,135 tons on the surface and 2,791 tons submerged, had an armament of two 5·5-in guns and carried 20 torpedoes. In 1926 *I1* showed her capabilities by cruising for 25,000 miles and diving to 260 ft, the deepest dive recorded by a Japanese submarine up to that date. No mines were carried, as the minelaying features of the UEII type were incorporated in a further class, the *I21–24*, which approximated more closely to the original design in size.

The British also rushed headlong into experiments with cruiser-submarines, and

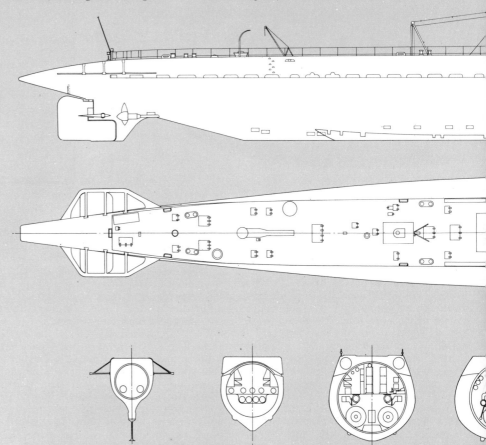

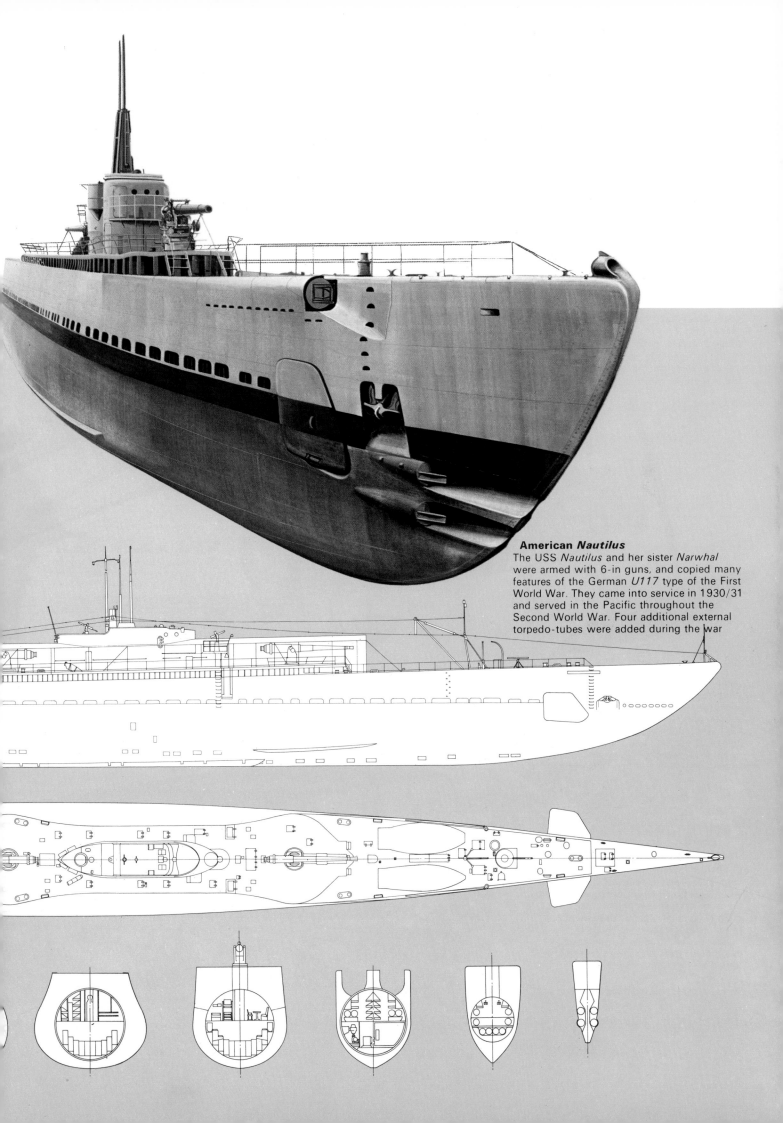

American _Nautilus_

The USS _Nautilus_ and her sister _Narwhal_ were armed with 6-in guns, and copied many features of the German _U117_ type of the First World War. They came into service in 1930/31 and served in the Pacific throughout the Second World War. Four additional external torpedo-tubes were added during the war

in 1923 they launched the giant *X1* under conditions of exaggerated secrecy. She was based on the uncompleted *U173* class of giant U-cruisers, and even used similar M.A.N. twin diesels for surface running. German diesel engines had enjoyed a high reputation for reliability, but in this case they proved to be the reason for many of *X1*'s problems; although extremely safe and capable of diving very deep, with a radius of 12,400 miles on the surface, she was plagued by mechanical troubles and was finally scrapped after only five years' active service. Thereafter British interest in giant submarines lapsed, and only the French stayed in the game, with their *Surcouf*.

Nothing if not logical, the French took the terms of the Washington Treaty at face value, and as the Treaty stated that submarines might carry guns no bigger than 8 in, that was the calibre chosen. This unique submarine carried not only a seaplane but a twin 8-in turret and twelve torpedo tubes, with ten reloads. An interesting innovation was the provision of a quadruple mounting for firing small (15·7-in) torpedoes against merchant ships; al-

though fast, these torpedoes had a range of only 1,500 yards.

Although the Italian Navy developed large submarines from their UEII type, *U120*, they avoided the extreme examples produced elsewhere. While the number of torpedo-tubes was increased, the gun-calibre was kept down to 3·9 in or 4·7 in, thus avoiding the chief pitfall of the big submarine.

British experience in the recent conflict had taught them one thing, the need for a heavy bow salvo of torpedoes to give greater accuracy at long ranges. This arose because, unlike U-Boats, British submarines had normally attacked well-defended warships. The knowledge that anti-submarine tactics had improved beyond all measure, and would continue to do so, led British submariners to accept the need to fire from a greater distance, and so from the *L52* class of 1917,

British submarines had a standard armament of six 21-in bow torpedo tubes. By comparison, Japanese and American submarines still had only four bow tubes at the expense of two stern tubes, and German U-Boats had largely been armed with two bow and two stern tubes, although in the later boats an extra pair was fitted.

Aircraft from submarines

The other important development in the years after the Armistice was the operation of aircraft from submarines. War experience had shown the importance of reconnaissance to the submarine, especially for locating targets when operating in distant waters. In January 1915 *U12* had operated

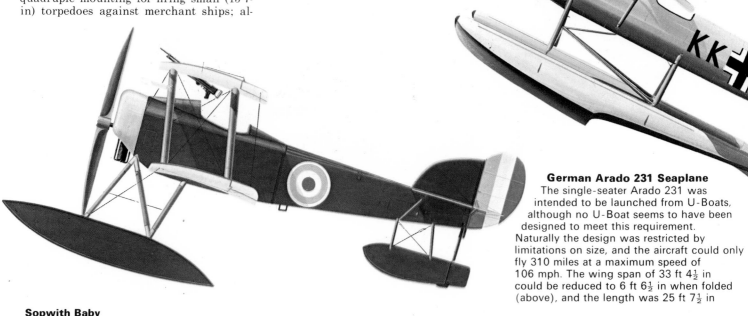

German Arado 231 Seaplane
The single-seater Arado 231 was intended to be launched from U-Boats, although no U-Boat seems to have been designed to meet this requirement. Naturally the design was restricted by limitations on size, and the aircraft could only fly 310 miles at a maximum speed of 106 mph. The wing span of 33 ft 4½ in could be reduced to 6 ft 6½ in when folded (above), and the length was 25 ft 7½ in

Sopwith Baby
With its 25 ft 8 in wingspan and maximum speed of 100 mph, the Sopwith Baby was successfully flown off a British submarine in 1916. Performance and range were too limited to produce any positive results, however, as was the case with similar experiments with German U-Boats

In 1916 the Norwegian Navy bought Farman floatplanes for trials, and when they broke down or ran out of fuel submarines were able to recover them by surfacing gently underneath. In this photograph a recovered seaplane is being lifted off the casing of submarine *A4*. Note the spare float lashed to the submarine's casing

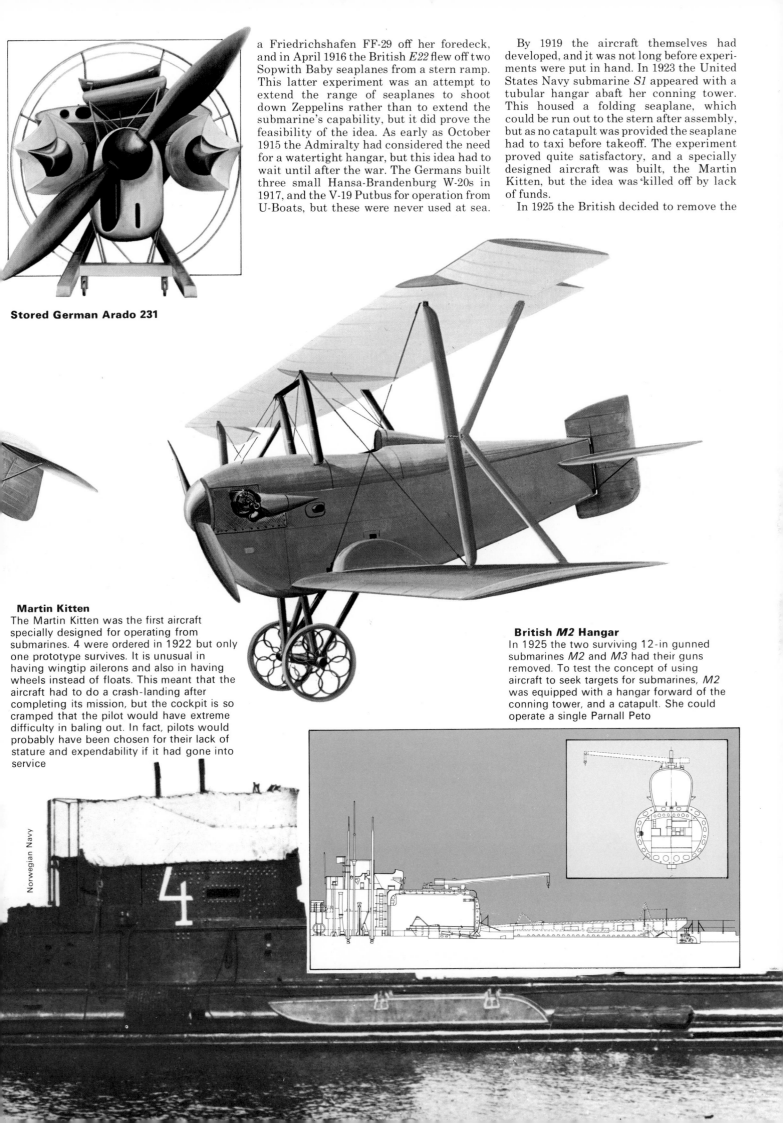

a Friedrichshafen FF-29 off her foredeck, and in April 1916 the British *E22* flew off two Sopwith Baby seaplanes from a stern ramp. This latter experiment was an attempt to extend the range of seaplanes to shoot down Zeppelins rather than to extend the submarine's capability, but it did prove the feasibility of the idea. As early as October 1915 the Admiralty had considered the need for a watertight hangar, but this idea had to wait until after the war. The Germans built three small Hansa-Brandenburg W-20s in 1917, and the V-19 Putbus for operation from U-Boats, but these were never used at sea.

By 1919 the aircraft themselves had developed, and it was not long before experiments were put in hand. In 1923 the United States Navy submarine *S1* appeared with a tubular hangar abaft her conning tower. This housed a folding seaplane, which could be run out to the stern after assembly, but as no catapult was provided the seaplane had to taxi before takeoff. The experiment proved quite satisfactory, and a specially designed aircraft was built, the Martin Kitten, but the idea was 'killed off by lack of funds.

In 1925 the British decided to remove the

Stored German Arado 231

Martin Kitten
The Martin Kitten was the first aircraft specially designed for operating from submarines. 4 were ordered in 1922 but only one prototype survives. It is unusual in having wingtip ailerons and also in having wheels instead of floats. This meant that the aircraft had to do a crash-landing after completing its mission, but the cockpit is so cramped that the pilot would have extreme difficulty in baling out. In fact, pilots would probably have been chosen for their lack of stature and expendability if it had gone into service

British *M2* Hangar
In 1925 the two surviving 12-in gunned submarines *M2* and *M3* had their guns removed. To test the concept of using aircraft to seek targets for submarines, *M2* was equipped with a hangar forward of the conning tower, and a catapult. She could operate a single Parnall Peto

Norwegian Navy

12-in guns from their two surviving 'M' Class submarines, and *M2* was converted to carry a seaplane. A large hangar was built forward of the conning tower, with a large crane on its roof; a light inclined catapult was built on the forward casing, and a specially designed Parnall Peto seaplane was carried. The biggest problem of handling an aircraft on board a submarine was the lack of space, and this dictated very small machines, which in turn lacked the capacity for fuel which would have made them more useful.

Then, in 1932, the Japanese launched their prototype *I5*. They stowed the fuselage and floats in one hangar and the wings in another, sited to port and starboard under the conning tower. The time taken to assemble the seaplane was so long that the submarine would almost certainly have been sunk in the middle of the operation. The *I6* had the same problem, but she did at least have a catapult like the *M2*. Thereafter a seaplane and catapult became a feature of the larger types of Japanese submarines, and special tactics were devised to exploit the combination.

The sister of *M2* was converted to a minelayer at the same time, as a development of the *U71* type. *M3* had a free-flooding casing (i.e. outside the pressure hull) containing twin mine-tracks, which ran from well forward past the conning tower. She was a great success, although ungainly in appearance, and she was followed by a class of six more. The main innovation in the *M3* was the provision of powered chain conveyor gear, which allowed the use of a normal mine and sinker, rather than the special type of mine which had to be used in all First World War minelayers.

The Washington Disarmament Conference of 1921/22 and the Treaty which resulted were the outcome of the rivalry which had grown up between the United States and Japan during the First World War. Although the Treaty is best known for its limitations on large surface warships, it also dealt with submarines. The British delegation was not unnaturally content to see the submarine banned, but this was a futile quest so soon after the great submarine campaign of 1915–18. The Italians and French were particularly anxious to

retain a large fleet of submarines as a cheap alternative to new battleships and aircraft carriers, and the Japanese made little secret of their intentions to build up a big fleet to threaten American superiority in the Pacific. Lord St Vincent's words of 1801 had come true, and neither of the two largest navies really wanted to see any progress made with the weapon most likely to destroy their own superiority.

The best that could be done was to limit the gun-calibre to 8 in, as in heavy cruisers, but the French were particularly obdurate in rejecting limitations on numbers of submarines and in blocking attempts to outlaw unrestricted warfare. The world's

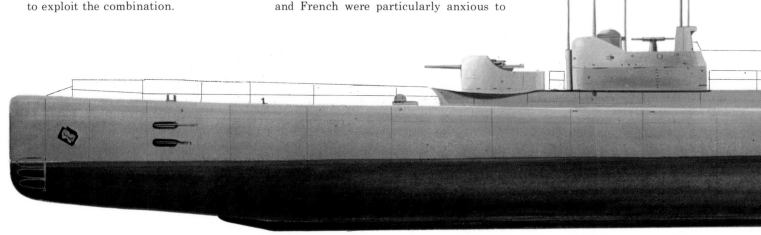

British *X1* (above)
X1 was the largest British submarine ever built until the advent of nuclear propulsion, and was in many ways superior to other cruiser-submarines. Her radius of action was 12,400 miles on the surface, and she could remain submerged for over two days, thanks to her large battery capacity. In addition, her two twin gun-mountings were carried high above the waterline to free them from spray interference, but despite all these advantages her unreliable machinery prevented her from being a success

French *Surcouf* (below)
Not only the largest submarine in the world, the *Surcouf* was also the only one to have the maximum calibre of guns allowed under the Washington Disarmament Treaty. Her 8-in guns were carried in a twin power-operated turret, and could each fire three 260-lb shells per minute to a range of 30,000 yards. In addition, she carried a seaplane in a cylindrical hangar abaft the conning tower. She operated under the Free French flag in the Second World War, but was accidentally rammed by an American freighter in 1942

Cruiser-submarine comparative specifications					
Type	Tonnage (surf/sub)	Length/ Beam (ft)	Speed (kts) (surf/sub)	Guns	Torpedoes
U117 (Germ.)	1164/1512	276·5/24·5	14·7/7	1×5·9 in	4×20 in (20 reloads)
U139 (Germ.)	1930/2483	311/29·75	15·8/7·6	2×5·9 in	6×20 in
U151 (Germ.)	1512/1875	213·25/29·25	12·4/5·2	2×5·9 in; 2×3·4 in	2×20 in
U173 (Germ.)	2115/2790	320/29·75	17·5/8·5	2×5·9 in; 2×3·4 in	6×20 in
Barracuda (US)	2000/2620	341/27·25	18/11	1×5 in	6×21 in
Argonaut (US)	2710/4080	381/34	15/8	2×6 in	4×21 in
Narwhal (US)	2730/4050	371/33·25	17/8	2×6 in	6×21 in
X1 (UK)	2425/3585	363·5/29·75	19·5/9	4×5·2 in	6×21 in (6 reloads)
Surcouf (Fr.)	2880/4304	361/29·5	18·5/10	2×8 in	8×21·7 in (10 reloads) 4×15·7 in
I52 (Jap.)	1500/2500	330·75/25	22/10	1×4·7 in; 1×3 in	8×21 in (9 reloads)
I1 (Jap.)	2135/2791	320/30·25	18/8	2×5·5 in	6×21 in (14 reloads)
Ettore Fieramosca (Ital.)	1556/2128	275·6/27·25	19/14	1×4·7 in	8×21 in (6 reloads)

major navies, denied the opportunity of building unlimited numbers of surface warships as much by economics as by international agreement, plunged into an orgy of submarine building.

The smaller navies were also conscious of the value of submarines, and the Netherlands and the Scandinavian countries had developed their own designs with some success. The Royal Swedish Navy had been building submarines since 1908, but the first fully indigenous design, the *Sjölejonet* Class, was not ordered until 1934. They displaced 580 tons on the surface, were 210 ft in length, and had a submerged speed of 9 knots. The disposition of torpedo tubes was unusual – three 53-cm (21-in) bow tubes, two rotating deck tubes similar to those on French boats, and a single stern tube; two single 40-mm deck guns were carried in retractable mountings, an idea derived from Dutch submarines. Three were completed in 1938/9, and a further six were ordered when the international situation worsened.

Denmark lacked the resources of Sweden, but she too produced original designs like the 'H' Class, whereas Norway was more

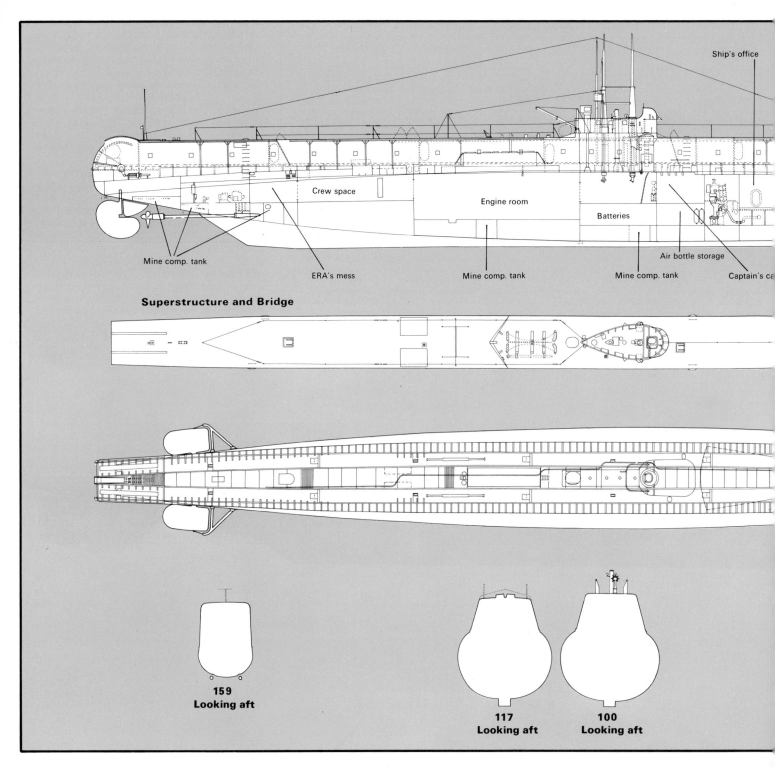

Crew space

Engine room

Batteries

Mine comp. tank

ERA's mess

Mine comp. tank

Mine comp. tank

Air bottle storage

Captain's ca

Ship's office

Superstructure and Bridge

159
Looking aft

117
Looking aft

100
Looking aft

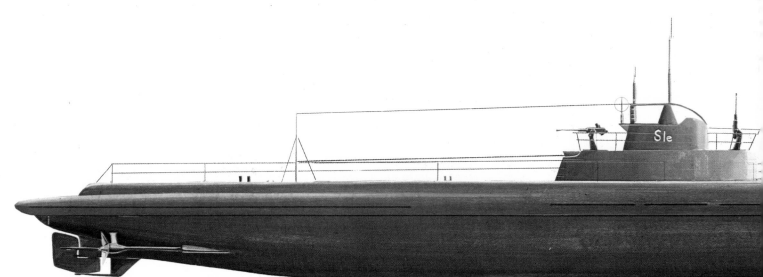

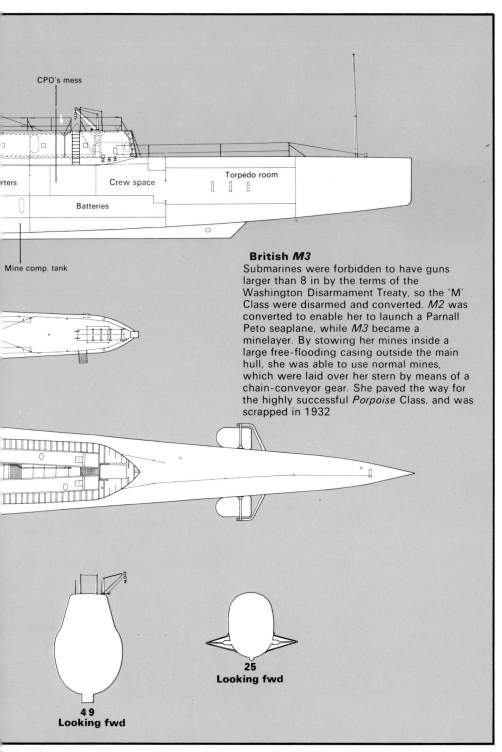

CPO's mess

...rters   Crew space   Torpedo room

Batteries

Mine comp. tank

British M3

Submarines were forbidden to have guns larger than 8 in by the terms of the Washington Disarmament Treaty, so the 'M' Class were disarmed and converted. *M2* was converted to enable her to launch a Parnall Peto seaplane, while *M3* became a minelayer. By stowing her mines inside a large free-flooding casing outside the main hull, she was able to use normal mines, which were laid over her stern by means of a chain-conveyor gear. She paved the way for the highly successful *Porpoise* Class, and was scrapped in 1932

25
Looking fwd

49
Looking fwd

Swedish *Sjölejonet*

...e *Sjölejonet* Class were ordered in 1934, ...d were the first fully Swedish design of ...bmarine. They had an unusual arrangement ...torpedo-tubes, with three in the bow ...wo over, one under), and one internal ...be and an external pair of revolving tubes aft. They also mounted two short-barrelled 40-mm Bofors guns on disappearing mountings, as a defence against aircraft. *Displacement:* 650 tons (surfaced) 760 tons (submerged) *Speed*: 16 knots (surfaced) 9 knots (submerged)

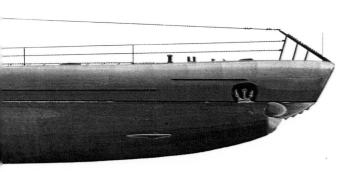

Submarine Building 1921–1936						
Programme	Britain	USA	France	Italy	Japan	Russia
1921	1				3	
1922			9		4	
1923	3	1	10		9	
1924			2	4		
1925		2	9	8		
1926	6		11	3		
1927	6		9	6	1	3
1928	6*		7	4		
1929	6*	1	11	7		25†
1930	3		11	12		4
1931	3	2		5	9	6
1932	3			4		12
1933	3	4				5
1934	3	6	2	10	4	20
1935	3	6		20		25†
1936	8	6	2	11		26

*3 cancelled from each programme. †These programmes were subsequently spread over later years.

content to rely on foreign designs. The 'B' Class were completed in the early 1920s to an American Electric Boat Company design of 1914 vintage, but *B1* nevertheless served in the Second World War. Poland had a small force of five boats, comprising the Dutch-built *Sep* and *Orzel* and a trio of French-built 980-tonners, the *Rys, Wilk* and *Zbik*, of which the *Orzel* and *Wilk* managed to escape to Britain in September 1939 in a desperate dash for freedom.

The Dutch had originally built two types of submarine, those with 'K' numbers for the East Indies, and those with 'O' numbers for home waters, but in 1937 the two series were combined under 'O' for 'Onterzeeboot'. The *O21* class of five boats were laid down in 1937/38 for general service at home and in the Far East. They were conventional in all ways but one: they were the first to incorporate an 'air mast' for charging batteries while running at periscope depth, a vital step in extending the submerged endurance of submarines.

Alas, like other prophets the Dutch were without honour in their own country, and with their Allies for that matter; when *O21–24* arrived in England in May 1940 the first thing the Royal Navy did was remove the air masts, and only in 1943 did the Germans realise the worth of the gadget they had found in a Dutch shipyard. Looking around in desperation for an antidote to the danger of recharging batteries on the surface at night, when aircraft and escorts were using radar, they re-examined the air mast and perfected it as the 'schnorchel'.

After their spectacular experiment with the *Surcouf* the French Navy reverted to more conventional submarines. In March 1920 the Chairman of the Naval Estimates Committee in Parliament had suggested quite seriously that a fleet of 250 to 300 submarines would answer all needs hitherto met by cruisers and battleships. Fortunately this extreme argument was met by a reasoned rebuttal, for it was clear to naval officers that, despite its potency, the submarine had only recently suffered a catastrophic defeat. Furthermore it was correctly argued that on a ton-for-ton basis the complexity of a submarine made it just as expensive as a surface ship to build and maintain, and also reduced its effective life. Although submarines were to be built in large numbers, they were nonetheless part of a balanced fleet. Two types were built after 1922, 1st Class boats of some 1,000 tons, and 2nd Class boats of 600 tons, the larger being intended for overseas patrol duties and the smaller ones for defensive patrol duties in home waters.

An interesting feature of French submarines of this period was their external torpedo-tubes, fitted in training mounts in the casing and capable of being trained over a wide arc. The purpose of this fitting was to assist the submarine in sinking merchant ships, and the idea was extended by the provision of 15·7-in (400-mm) light short-range torpedoes for use against 'soft-skinned' targets. Unfortunately this torpedo proved a total failure, and even the 24V 21·7-in (550-mm) proved unreliable on gyro-angling runs, although good on a straight run.

Two notable French classes of submarine were built between the wars. The six *Saphir* Class minelayers were of moderate dimensions, and had their mines in vertical wells in the saddle tanks. Although this was officially known as the Normand-Fenaux system it was actually a later version of the British system introduced in the 'E' Class in 1915. The *Rubis* operated with great success under the Free French flag during the Second World War, and notched up a high score of victims. Thirty-one large ocean-going boats of the so-called '1500-tonne' type were laid down in batches each year under the 1924–30 programmes, and proved successful; two travelled over 14,000 miles from Toulon to Saigon in 1935 without mishap.

The most famous of the class was the *Casabianca*, which was the only vessel to escape the holocaust which ensued when the Germans tried to capture Toulon by treachery in 1942. She joined the Allies in North Africa and sank three enemy ships during the invasion of Corsica a year later. The next class of large submarines had only just been started when their hulls were scuttled to prevent them from falling into German hands in June 1940, and a similar fate befell their 2nd Class contemporaries.

Russia rebuilds

The Russian Navy, or the Red Fleet as it became after the Revolution, took some years to recuperate from the aftermath of the Civil War and the anti-Bolshevik intervention by Great Britain and the rest of the erstwhile allies of the First World War. Many of the submarines which survived the vicissitudes of 1917–19 were unserviceable, and unfortunately the majority of the new construction had been scuttled. Only ten boats remained in the Baltic by 1922, one in the Arctic and five in the Black Sea. It was to be another nine years before the first new submarines joined the Fleet, which explains why the British submarine *L55* was salvaged and incorporated into the Red Fleet; she had been sunk in 1919 during the Intervention, but was raised in 1928 and recommissioned in 1931.

The first of the new programme was the *Dekabrist* or 'D' Class of six units, which came into service in 1931/32. Based on an Italian design, they displaced 989 tons on the surface, and were armed with a 4-in deck gun, a smaller 45-mm gun and eight 21-in torpedo tubes. The *Leninets* or 'L' Class which followed were of similar size and characteristics, but based on *L55*, and took longer to build; it took from 1933 to 1942 to commission 24 units, and one was never completed. At the same time a smaller

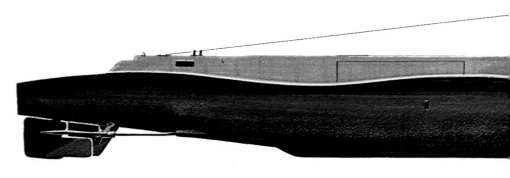

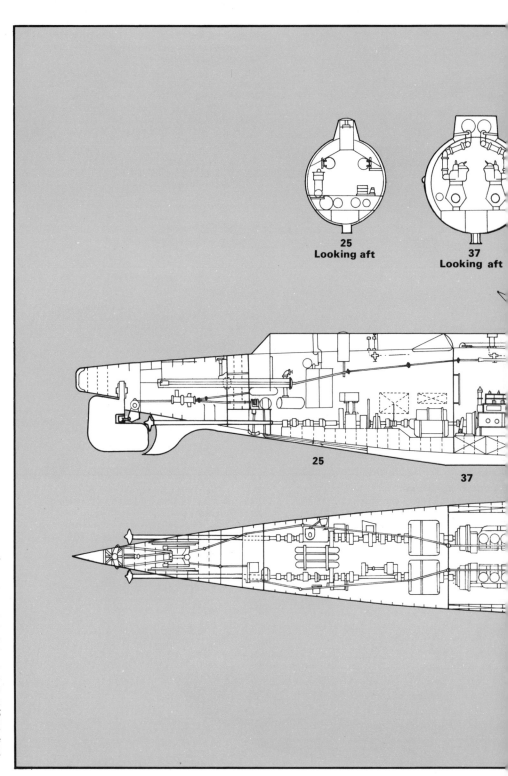

25
Looking aft

37
Looking aft

25

37

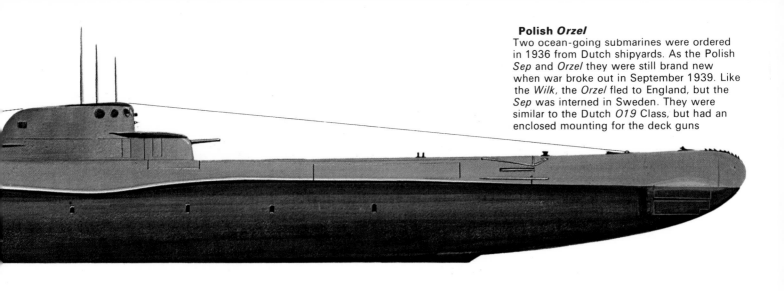

Polish *Orzel*
Two ocean-going submarines were ordered
in 1936 from Dutch shipyards. As the Polish
Sep and *Orzel* they were still brand new
when war broke out in September 1939. Like
the *Wilk*, the *Orzel* fled to England, but the
Sep was interned in Sweden. They were
similar to the Dutch *O19* Class, but had an
enclosed mounting for the deck guns

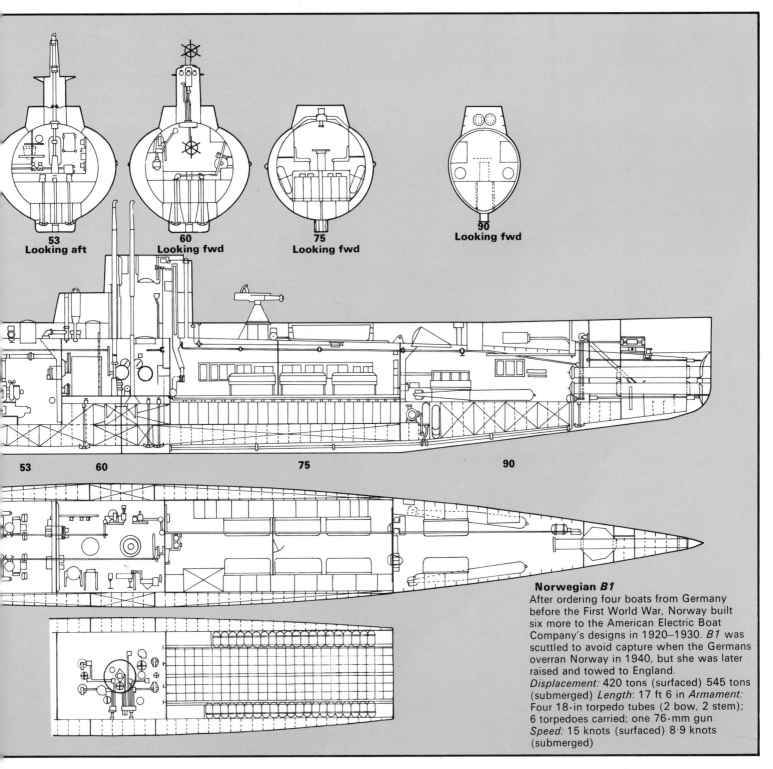

**53
Looking aft**

**60
Looking fwd**

**75
Looking fwd**

**90
Looking fwd**

53   60   75   90

Norwegian *B1*
After ordering four boats from Germany
before the First World War, Norway built
six more to the American Electric Boat
Company's designs in 1920–1930. *B1* was
scuttled to avoid capture when the Germans
overran Norway in 1940, but she was later
raised and towed to England.
Displacement: 420 tons (surfaced) 545 tons
(submerged) *Length:* 17 ft 6 in *Armament:*
Four 18-in torpedo tubes (2 bow, 2 stem);
6 torpedoes carried; one 76-mm gun
Speed: 15 knots (surfaced) 8·9 knots
(submerged)

type was designed, known as the *Shchuka* (Pike) or 'Shch' Class; 90 were commissioned in 1933–42, and three were scrapped incomplete. They displaced 580 tons on the surface, and had six 21-in torpedo-tubes and a 45-mm deck gun. A further intermediate type, the *Stalinets* Class (33 units) and a general patrol type known as the *Pravda* Class (3 units) came into service from 1936 onwards.

The *Pravdas* did not prove very success-

ful, but the *Stalinets* Class were very satisfactory in service, because they were able, by a roundabout route, to make use of German expertise. This came about because the Russian dictator, Marshal Stalin, was anxious to help Germany to evade the restrictions of the Versailles Treaty, which prevented Germany from building U-Boats. German design firms were set up outside Germany, in Spain, Holland and Russia to keep the nucleus of a design team together, and although the orders which resulted went to shipbuilders in the countries concerned, the know-how was German. As a price for their help the Russians obtained plans of the Type IA which was built in Spain for Turkey as the *Gür*, and this design became the basis of the *Stalinets* or 'S' Class.

All these submarines were generally simi-

lar in dimensions to the submarines being built outside the USSR, but there were two more types which represented the upper and lower extremes. The 'Malyutka' (small) Class displaced only 161 tons in surface trim, and had two 21-in torpedo-tubes; they bore some resemblance to the little 'tin tadpoles' of the German UBI Class in 1915. Between 1933 and 1937 over 50 were added to the Russian strength, and two improved types were commissioned between 1938 and 1944. The 'M' types were built in sections, the original Malyutka VI and VIbis series having four sections, the Malyutka XII series six sections, and the final Malyutka XV series seven sections, all small enough to allow shipment by rail and canal for assembly wherever needed.

The other Russian submarine type was the 'Kreiser' or 'Katyusha' type, a big cruiser submarine of 1,390 tons on the surface, armed with two 3·9-in (100-mm) guns, two 45-mm and ten 21-in torpedo-tubes.

French *Rubis*
The French Navy ordered ten minelaying submarines between 1925 and 1939. The *Rubis* was operating under British control at the fall of France in 1940, and under the Free French flag she carried out over twenty successful minelaying trips between 1940 and 1945. Her sister *Perle* survived to be sunk in error by an Allied aircraft in 1944, but the rest were either scuttled incomplete or captured in a wrecked condition in 1942 by the Germans

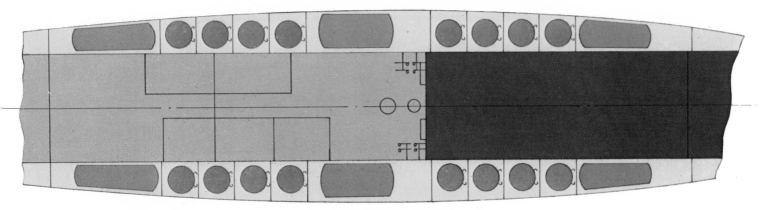

The surface speed was 18 knots to allow them to operate with surface units, and 13 numbered units were commissioned between 1940 and 1942. As the numbers ran as high as *K51* it must be assumed that a large number were not completed during the War. They could dive in 50 seconds, a good time for a large boat.

When Hitler gave the order to attack Russia in 1941, this was the approximate strength of the Red Fleet:

Baltic
7 'K' Class (*K24, K51–56*) – some building
3 'P' Class (*P1–3*)
13 'S' Class (*S1–13*)
4 'L' Class (*L1–3, L21*)
1 'D' Class (*D2*)
1 *L55*
5 'B' Class (*B2, B4–6, B8*)
22 'Shch' Class (*Shch 301–11, 317–320, 322–324, 405–408*)
22 'Malyutka' Class

Far East
4 'S' Class (*S52–53, S57–58*)
12 'L' Class (*L7–14, L16–19*)
41 'Shch' Class (*Shch 101–141*)
30 'Malyutka' Class

Normand-Fenaux Minelaying System
The *Saphir* Class used a system derived from the British method first used in the 'E' Class in 1915. Eight wells on each side, in the saddle tanks, held two mines stowed vertically. The mines were armed and set mechanically from within the pressure hull, and the loss of weight was automatically compensated for. The supply of French Sauter-Harlé mines soon gave out, but by a stroke of good luck Vickers were producing a mine of almost identical pattern for Rumania in 1939, and this was easily adapted

the ex-Estonian *Kalev* and *Lembit* were commissioned as Red Fleet units. They were British-built, and rather similar to the British 'P' Class. In 1944 the British Government transferred four submarines under Lend-Lease for use in the Arctic; these were the *V1* (ex-HMS *Sunfish*) and *V2–4* (ex-*Unbroken*, *Unison* and *Ursula*). In one respect the Russian submarine service was unique in that it assigned numbers according to the Fleet in which the submarines were serving. The two large numbered classes, the 'Shch' and 'Malyutka' types seem to have changed numbers when transferred from, say, the Baltic to the Arctic. Thus Shch *101–141* served in the

endurance, and a reload was provided for each tube in order to extend the operating time. One unfortunate feature was introduced as a result of economy: because the dimensions were restricted, some of the fuel tanks had to be carried in the upper half of the saddle tanks. As it was virtually impossible in a riveted hull to have an oil-tight seam these external tanks tended to give away the submarine's position by leaving a tell-tale oil slick on the surface.

The 'P' and 'R' Classes were generally similar to the 'O' Class but slightly larger. In 1929 a new design for a 'fleet' submarine was produced, the 'River' type with the unusually high surface speed of 22 knots. To accommodate a pair of 10-cylinder diesels the stern torpedo-tubes had to be omitted, and although the design proved successful in service it was soon realised that the concept was wrong. The speed of surface warships had risen since 1915, when the fleet submarine requirement had been put forward, and the only use for 22 knots' speed was in a campaign against commerce in the Pacific or the Indian Ocean.

As the result of the success of the *M3*, six submarine minelayers were built between 1930 and 1938, the famous *Porpoise* Class.

Arctic
6 'K' Class (*K21–23, K1–3*)
12 'S' Class (*S14–16, S19, S51, S54–56, S101–104*)
3 'L' Class (*L15, L20, L22*)
2 'D' Class (*D1, D3*)
8 'Shch' Class (*Shch 401–404, 421–424*)
17 'Malyutka' Class

Black Sea
8 'S' Class (*S31–38*)
6 'L' Class (*L4–6, L23–25*)
3 'D' Class (*D4–6*)
5 'A' Class (*A1–5*)
16 'Shch' Class (*Shch 201–216*)
28 'Malyutka' Class

In addition to these submarines, of which some were still under construction, the Russians took over four boats as a result of their 'liberation' of the independent Baltic republics in 1940, but of these only

Russian 'Shch' Class
This class took its name from the initial letters of the prototype *Shchuka* ('Pike'), and was a medium-sized patrol type begun in 1932. By 1941 nearly a hundred had been built, and they continued in production until 1942. From what can be pieced together it seems that some thirty were sunk during the Second World War

Far East, but Shch *201–216* served in the Black Sea, and when a permanent transfer was made the number seems to have changed as well.

After their attempts to ban the submarine at the Washington Conference, the British settled down to serious submarine construction in 1923. The *L52* Class of 1917 was chosen as the model, and the 'O' Class which resulted was longer and beamier but carried the same heavy bow salvo of six 21-in tubes and two stern tubes. A drop in surface speed of two knots to 15½ knots was more than compensated for by a much increased

These 270-ft boats displaced 1,520 tons on the surface and had a capacity of 50 standard Mk XVI mines in a full-length deck outside the pressure hull. The need for specialised submarine minelayers lapsed when the Royal Navy produced a mine which could be laid from a 21-in torpedo-tube, but the minelayers proved even more successful when used as supply submarines to run precious cargoes to Malta in 1941/42. Their capacious mine-decks were filled with such assorted items as machine-gun ammunition, glycol coolant for Spitfires, and food.

Under the 1929 Estimates a new type of medium submarine patrol submarine was introduced, the 640-ton 'S' Class. They were a breakaway from the large 'O', 'P' and 'R' type, and were meant for work in European and Mediterranean waters which were too confined for large submarines. The result was a great success, and the 'S' Class eventually ran to some 60 units, the largest single class built

Comparison of Russian Type 1A and 'S' Class designs

	1A	Gür	Stalinets
Tonnage (surf/sub)	862/983	750/960	780/1050
Length (ft)	237·5	237·5	256
Beam (ft)	20·25	20·3	21
Draught (ft)	14	13·5	13
Machinery	2800 bhp 1000 chp	2800 bhp 1000 chp	4200 bhp 2200 chp
Speed (surf/ sub) (knots)	17¾/8¼	20/9	20/8½
Torpedo-tubes	6×21-in 4b 2s	6×21-in 4b 2s	6×21-in 4b 2s
Guns	1×4·1-in 1×20-mm	1×4-in	1×3-in 1×45-mm

French *Casabianca*
Thirty-one '1500-tonne' 1st Class submarines were built between 1924 and 1939 for overseas work. Most were scuttled, either at Brest in 1940 or at Toulon in 1942, but the *Casabianca* was able to make her escape from Toulon to join the Allies in North Africa. Later she distinguished herself in the liberation of Corsica by sinking a sub-chaser and damaging another.
Displacement: 1,570 tons (surfaced) 2,084 tons (submerged) *Length:* 302 ft 9 in *Beam:* 27 ft *Armament:* Nine 21·7-in torpedo-tubes (4 forward, 3 and 2 aft); two 15·7-in torpedo-tubes (external aft); one 3·9-in gun; two 13·2-mm AA guns
Speed: 19 knots (surfaced) 10 knots (submerged)

for the Royal Navy. By positioning all fuel tanks inside the pressure hull they cured the worst fault of their predecessors, and had a good diving time. They were too small for overseas work, however, and had to be complemented by the equally famous 'T' Class, which were 70 ft longer, and displaced just over 1,000 tons. Whereas the 'S' Class had six bow tubes only, the 'Ts' had eight bow tubes, including two in a bulbous bow casing, and an extra pair of tubes in the casing amidships, giving them the phenomenal bow salvo of *ten* tubes.

Nothing has been said so far of German developments, for of course Germany was not allowed to have U-Boats under the Treaty of Versailles. As we have seen, the German Navy made sure that it kept abreast of submarine developments by financing design work in other countries. Thus when Hitler and his National Socialist government repudiated the Versailles Treaty and began rebuilding the armed forces in 1934, there was a great deal of expertise available.

particularly in having a much increased number of reload torpedoes.

Among the many experimental ideas was one for a submarine carrying two small motor torpedo-boats on deck in cylindrical hangars. Like the operation of aircraft this was an idea which looked better on the drawing board than it did to an anxious U-Boat commander worrying about the length of time taken to get things in and out of hangars, and it was quietly dropped. Likewise the 2,500-ton minelayers of the Type XA and a trio of aircraft-carrying 3,000-ton U-cruisers were abandoned, no doubt with a sigh of relief from the submariners.

The standard sea-going U-Boat which evolved from this series of prototypes was the Type VII. The first group, known as VIIAs, were developed from a German design built in Finland but in turn the Finnish

The Type VIIC U-Boat had a waterline length of 220 ft, a beam of just over 20 ft, and displaced about 770 tons on the surface. She was of fairly conventional design, with saddle tanks, four bow tubes and two stern tubes; her diesels drove her at 17 knots on the surface and the electric motors could produce 7½ knots for a limited time under water.

Although not an ideal type for the Second World War as it turned out, the Type VII series was simple to build and very handy. Its principal drawback was its endurance, 6,500 miles at 12 knots, which proved insufficient for extended operations, while its lack of internal space imposed extra burdens on personnel. British submariners would have been surprised to learn that their German counterparts regarded Royal Navy submarine accommodation as palatial. Despite these inherent problems the U-Boat Arm waged a most determined and ferocious campaign from the Arctic to the Indian Ocean in conditions ranging from merely spartan to utterly vile.

Five basic types were considered; sea-going types of 500–750 tons, ocean-going boats of 1,000 tons, U-cruisers of 1,500 tons, and coastal submarines and minelayers of 250–500 tons. The sea-going type was based on the Turkish *Gür* which had been built in Spain to a pre-1934 German design, but the first coastal type was based on the UBII Type of the First World War. The ocean-going boats of Type IXA were based on the *U117* or UEII Type of the First World War,

Russian 'K' Class
This class was also known as the *Katyusha* Class, and they were large ocean-going submarines with a heavy armament.
Displacement: 1,390 tons (surfaced)
Armament: Ten or twelve 21-in torpedo-tubes; two 3·9-in guns; two 45-mm AA guns

boat owed a lot to the old UBIII Type of the First World War. *U27* was the first to be launched in 1936, and by the outbreak of the Second World War the improved Type VIIB was in service. The Type VIIC which followed had many improvements over the original A type, such as more powerful diesel engines and greater fuel capacity, and became the standard wartime type. By 1941 the first had been launched, and as the 600-odd which were built came very close to winning the war for Hitler and Nazi Germany, a closer look is indicated.

At this point it is opportune to revert to progress in anti-submarine warfare, for this had kept pace with the frightening increase in the submarine's efficiency between 1919 and 1939. First, the British Admiralty had learned the lessons of 1917, and convoy was to be their standard defence for merchant ships. Meanwhile, in 1918 a secret committee of scientists had been set up to investigate methods of detecting submarines, and their researches had resulted in the brilliant discovery that a sonic beam could be bounced off a submarine's hull and be measured to give a bearing and range. Known from the initials of its parental committee, the Anti-Submarine Devices Investigation Committee, ASDIC, worked on the simple principle

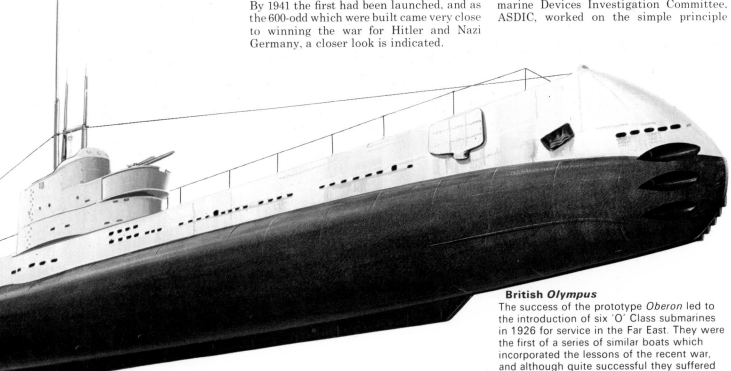

British *Olympus*
The success of the prototype *Oberon* led to the introduction of six 'O' Class submarines in 1926 for service in the Far East. They were the first of a series of similar boats which incorporated the lessons of the recent war, and although quite successful they suffered from having external fuel tanks which leaked oil. This, combined with their size, led to four of the six being lost in the Mediterranean in 1940–42

of passing an electric current through a quartz plate. Although the Germans suspected its existence, they did not uncover the secret until details were captured in France in 1940.

By 1939 the Admiralty had ensured that some 200 escort vessels were fitted with Asdic, and all anti-submarine tactics had been developed to make use of its remarkable properties. It led, however, to a dangerous under-estimation of the threat from submarines, and there were people in the Admiralty who talked of the submarine being a weapon of the past. Not only were there too few escort vessels for the amount of shipping to be protected, but the Asdic had its blind spots; it could not be used against a surfaced submarine, and at that stage in its development it could not hold the target when the searching ship passed overhead. Thus an attack with depth-charges always had to be carried out 'blind'.

The aircraft had shown itself to be a dangerous enemy to submarines during the First World War, and the increased range of aircraft in 1939 made them far more dangerous. It was not foreseen that the ordinary aircraft bomb would be ineffective against submarines, and the lack of sufficient numbers would also prevent aircraft

British *Sealion*

In 1929 the first orders were placed for medium-sized patrol submarines, as the Royal Navy became aware of the need for smaller boats to work in Northern European waters. The problem of leaking fuel tanks was solved by putting them inside the pressure hull, and as speed and submerged endurance were not sacrificed the 'S' Class was most successful. An improved version was put into mass production during the Second World War, making this class the largest single group of submarines built for the Royal Navy: more than sixty units were built over a period of fifteen years.
Displacement: 735 tons (full load, surfaced)
Armament: Six 21-in torpedo-tubes (forward); one 3-in gun *Speed:* 13½ knots (surfaced) 10 knots (submerged)

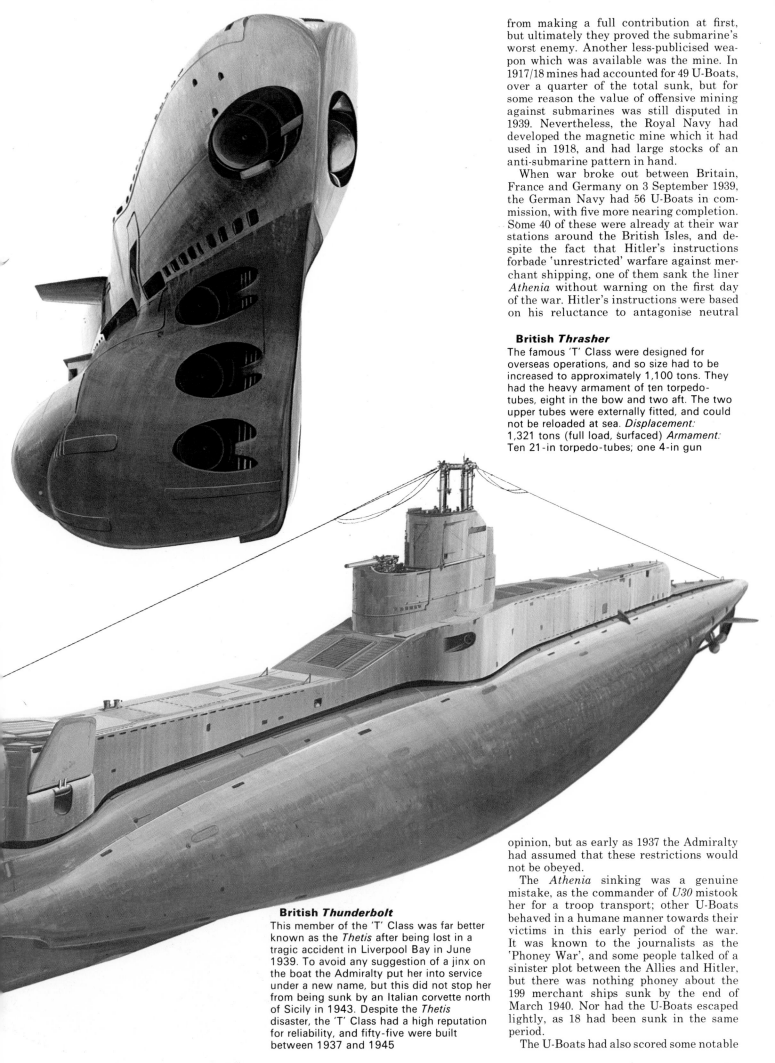

from making a full contribution at first, but ultimately they proved the submarine's worst enemy. Another less-publicised weapon which was available was the mine. In 1917/18 mines had accounted for 49 U-Boats, over a quarter of the total sunk, but for some reason the value of offensive mining against submarines was still disputed in 1939. Nevertheless, the Royal Navy had developed the magnetic mine which it had used in 1918, and had large stocks of an anti-submarine pattern in hand.

When war broke out between Britain, France and Germany on 3 September 1939, the German Navy had 56 U-Boats in commission, with five more nearing completion. Some 40 of these were already at their war stations around the British Isles, and despite the fact that Hitler's instructions forbade 'unrestricted' warfare against merchant shipping, one of them sank the liner *Athenia* without warning on the first day of the war. Hitler's instructions were based on his reluctance to antagonise neutral

British *Thrasher*
The famous 'T' Class were designed for overseas operations, and so size had to be increased to approximately 1,100 tons. They had the heavy armament of ten torpedo-tubes, eight in the bow and two aft. The two upper tubes were externally fitted, and could not be reloaded at sea. *Displacement:* 1,321 tons (full load, surfaced) *Armament:* Ten 21-in torpedo-tubes; one 4-in gun

British *Thunderbolt*
This member of the 'T' Class was far better known as the *Thetis* after being lost in a tragic accident in Liverpool Bay in June 1939. To avoid any suggestion of a jinx on the boat the Admiralty put her into service under a new name, but this did not stop her from being sunk by an Italian corvette north of Sicily in 1943. Despite the *Thetis* disaster, the 'T' Class had a high reputation for reliability, and fifty-five were built between 1937 and 1945

opinion, but as early as 1937 the Admiralty had assumed that these restrictions would not be obeyed.

The *Athenia* sinking was a genuine mistake, as the commander of *U30* mistook her for a troop transport; other U-Boats behaved in a humane manner towards their victims in this early period of the war. It was known to the journalists as the 'Phoney War', and some people talked of a sinister plot between the Allies and Hitler, but there was nothing phoney about the 199 merchant ships sunk by the end of March 1940. Nor had the U-Boats escaped lightly, as 18 had been sunk in the same period.

The U-Boats had also scored some notable

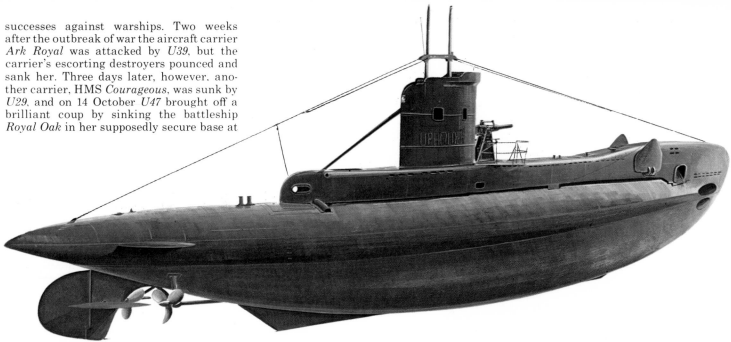

successes against warships. Two weeks after the outbreak of war the aircraft carrier *Ark Royal* was attacked by *U39*, but the carrier's escorting destroyers pounced and sank her. Three days later, however, another carrier, HMS *Courageous*, was sunk by *U29*, and on 14 October *U47* brought off a brilliant coup by sinking the battleship *Royal Oak* in her supposedly secure base at

Scapa Flow. Kapitän-Leutnant Prien took his U-Boat in through the tortuous channels past the rusting blockships which had lain there since 1914, and finally found the battleship at anchor. After one salvo of torpedoes missed, Prien reloaded and fired a spread of three which detonated under the *Royal Oak*'s keel; she capsized and sank with 833 of her crew.

The *Royal Oak* was an elderly second-line unit whose loss could hardly rank with that of the carrier *Courageous* in military value, but *U47*'s exploit had far more impact. The realisation that Scapa Flow could be penetrated by a submarine forced the British to remove their entire Home Fleet to a series of temporary anchorages, just as the Grand Fleet had gone a-wandering in 1914 after a submarine scare. At a crucial moment the whole British strategy for penning the German Navy's surface warships in the North Sea had been drastically changed, all by one submariner and his crew's determination and courage.

Only 38 British submarines were available in September 1939, and although the British blockade of the North Sea denied them any big opportunities for attacking German shipping, they had an important role to play. They were immediately deployed to extend air patrol lines, in order to give warning of enemy naval movements, and to harass U-Boats and surface warships in their home waters. What was not realised for some time, however, was that a policy of sending submarines to lie off enemy bases would expose the submarines to a high loss rate. This is because a base acts like a convoy – in fact a convoy with a reduced perimeter – and thus the advantage swings to the enemy's anti-submarine forces.

In April and May 1940 there was a sudden lull in U-Boat activity, and only 20 ships were sunk; this was because Admiral Dönitz had recalled most of his boats to regroup for the invasion of Norway. The British also had plans for Norway, as they wanted to lay minefields to interrupt the iron-ore traffic from Narvik to Germany. After the end of the campaign only submarine minelayers could be used, and to strengthen the effort the Admiralty persuaded the French Government to lend them the *Rubis*. This famous submarine laid her

British *Upholder* (left)
The first three 'U' Class were ordered in 1936 to serve as unarmed targets for anti-submarine vessels, but they were completed with torpedo-tubes to allow them to carry out normal submarine training as well. In 1940 it was realised that their small size suited them for the North Sea and Mediterranean, and so they were put into quantity production. HMS *Upholder* was commanded by Lt Cdr Wanklyn VC, and she sank over 90,000 tons of German and Italian shipping in the Mediterranean before she was herself sunk in April 1942.
Displacement: 648 tons (full load, surfaced)
Armament: Four 21-in torpedo-tubes; one 3-in AA gun *Speed:* 11¾ knots (surfaced) 9 knots (submerged)

German Type VII (*U236*)
The Type VII U-Boat was the standard design for the U-Boat in the Second World War. It was developed from the Finnish *Vetehinen* design before the expiry of the Versailles Treaty, and many improvements were effected as a result of war experience. *U236* was one of the Type VIIC, the third version, and she came into service in January 1943. She was scuttled in 1945 after suffering damage by air attack.
Displacement: 769 tons (surfaced)
Armament: Five 21-in torpedo-tubes; 14 torpedoes carried; plus a variety of light AA guns *Speed:* 17 knots (surfaced) 7½ knots (submerged)

first mines off Christiansand on 10 May 1940, the first episode in a career which lasted until 1944 and accounted for 15 merchant ships and seven warships sunk, and a merchant ship and a U-Boat damaged.

The increased German naval activity in the Norwegian campaign gave Allied submarines much greater opportunities for attacking. The Polish *Orzel* sank a large troopship, the *Spearfish* damaged the pocket battleship *Lützow* severely, and the *Sunfish* sank four ships, among others. Later the *Clyde* inflicted heavy damage on the battle cruiser *Gneisenau*. These casualties, when combined with the depredations caused by surface action, were sufficient to reduce the Kriegsmarine's strength below the level needed to support the invasion of England planned after Dunkirk. Once more the submarine had intervened decisively in the conduct of war at sea, and had exerted an influence beyond all proportion to her size and cost.

In one respect the British had been extremely lucky throughout this first phase of submarine warfare; whereas their own torpedoes were reliable the Germans' magnetic pistols had proved to be uncertain.

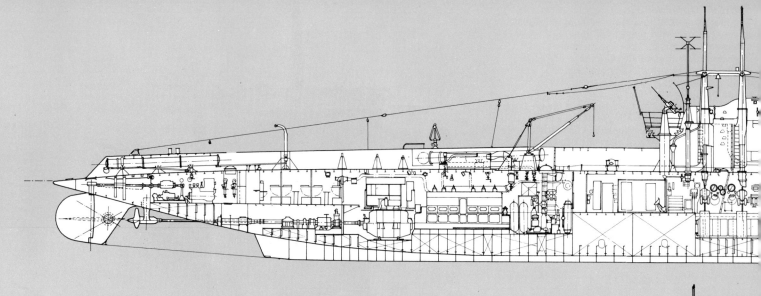

151   147   110

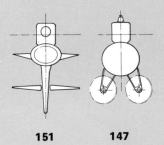   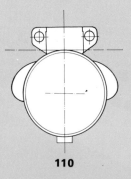   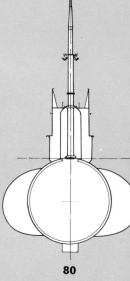

151   147   110   80

British *Telemachus*
Like the German Type VII the British 'T' Class
went through many wartime modifications.
This example shows how many changes had
been made in the original design: a changed
bow shape, external tubes now facing aft,
and a platform on the conning tower for a
20-mm AA gun. She was completed in 1943
and scrapped in 1961

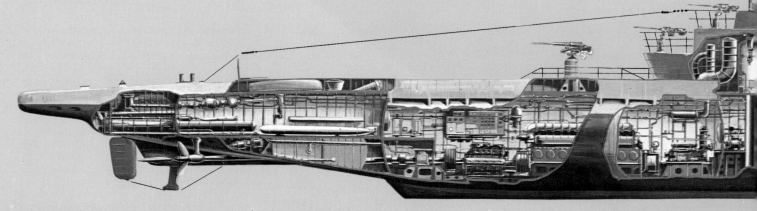

German Type IXB

These ocean-going boats were developed
from the UEII Type of the First World War,
and had more endurance than the Type VII
series. They proved less suitable for the
Western Approaches and were used in
distant waters, but their average of tonnage
sunk was as high as any other group of
U-Boats. Their main drawback was that they
took too long to build, and only 14 were
built. *Displacement:* 1,051 tons (surfaced)
Armament: Six 21-in torpedo-tubes; 22
torpedoes carried; one 105-mm gun; one
37-mm gun; one 20-mm gun *Speed:*
$18\frac{1}{4}$ knots (surfaced) $7\frac{1}{4}$ knots (submerged)

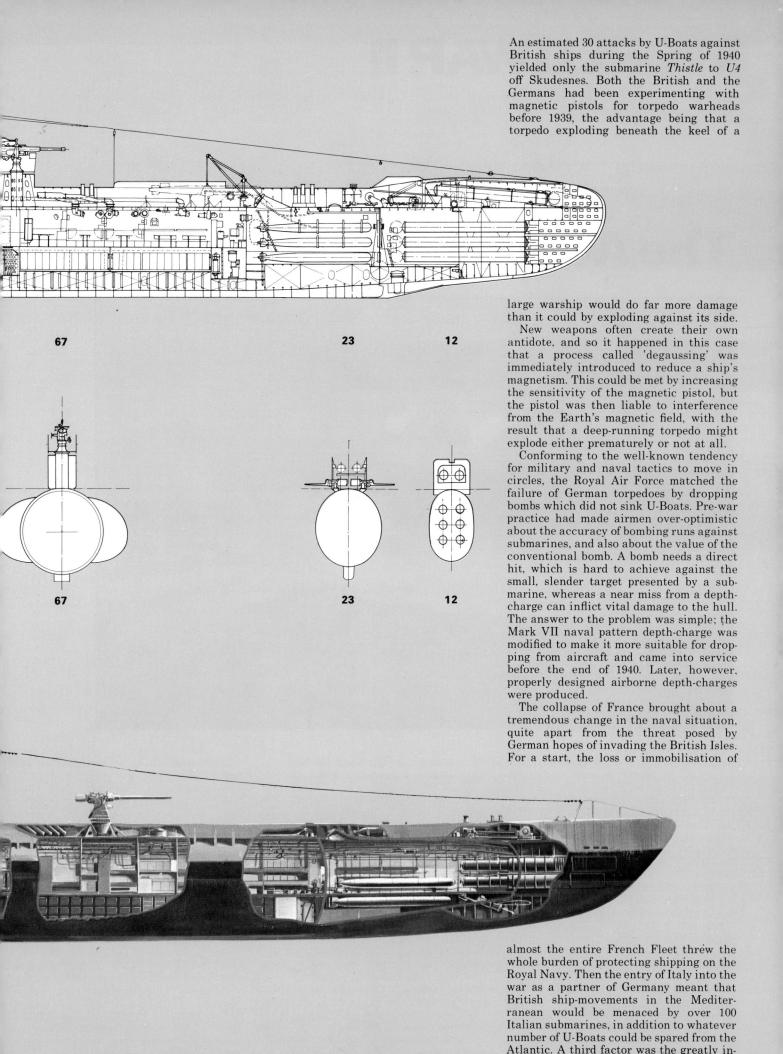

An estimated 30 attacks by U-Boats against British ships during the Spring of 1940 yielded only the submarine *Thistle* to *U4* off Skudesnes. Both the British and the Germans had been experimenting with magnetic pistols for torpedo warheads before 1939, the advantage being that a torpedo exploding beneath the keel of a

67   23   12

67   23   12

large warship would do far more damage than it could by exploding against its side.

New weapons often create their own antidote, and so it happened in this case that a process called 'degaussing' was immediately introduced to reduce a ship's magnetism. This could be met by increasing the sensitivity of the magnetic pistol, but the pistol was then liable to interference from the Earth's magnetic field, with the result that a deep-running torpedo might explode either prematurely or not at all.

Conforming to the well-known tendency for military and naval tactics to move in circles, the Royal Air Force matched the failure of German torpedoes by dropping bombs which did not sink U-Boats. Pre-war practice had made airmen over-optimistic about the accuracy of bombing runs against submarines, and also about the value of the conventional bomb. A bomb needs a direct hit, which is hard to achieve against the small, slender target presented by a submarine, whereas a near miss from a depth-charge can inflict vital damage to the hull. The answer to the problem was simple; the Mark VII naval pattern depth-charge was modified to make it more suitable for dropping from aircraft and came into service before the end of 1940. Later, however, properly designed airborne depth-charges were produced.

The collapse of France brought about a tremendous change in the naval situation, quite apart from the threat posed by German hopes of invading the British Isles. For a start, the loss or immobilisation of

almost the entire French Fleet threw the whole burden of protecting shipping on the Royal Navy. Then the entry of Italy into the war as a partner of Germany meant that British ship-movements in the Mediterranean would be menaced by over 100 Italian submarines, in addition to whatever number of U-Boats could be spared from the Atlantic. A third factor was the greatly increased number of U-Boat bases available.

The Atlantic

Imperial War Museum

By the end of 1940 many U-Boats had been moved to the French Atlantic ports, with 12 flotillas based on Brest, La Rochelle, La Pallice, St Nazaire, Lorient and Bordeaux. Being so much nearer to the Western Approaches and the North Atlantic gave them greater operating time, and so made them far more effective than before. For the same reason, when the Italian Navy offered some of its submarines to the Germans for use in the Atlantic it was decided to base them on Bordeaux rather than make them travel all the way from the Mediterranean.

The first Italian submarines to make a passage of the Straits of Gibraltar were the *Giuseppe Finzi* and *Pietro Calvi* in June 1940. After further attempts had shown how difficult it could be, owing to the currents in the Straits, the Italian Naval Staff decided to embark on the expense of setting up a permanent base at Bordeaux, and this was begun in August 1940. It came to be known as BETASOM, from *Beta* (= 'B' for Bordeaux), and *Som* (= Sommergibili), and by January 1941 the base was able to cater

Above: A Mosquito bomber armed with rockets attacks a diving submarine

for 27 submarines. This massive effort would have been very helpful to the Germans, but for the fact that the design of the Italian submarines proved so poor. They had prodigiously large conning towers, some of which were equipped with a galley and a lavatory for the comfort of watchkeepers, but had only modest surface speed.

BETASOM did its best to remedy the defects, and many desirable features of the German U-Boats were incorporated when possible. The main patrol area was off the Azores, and in the 2½ years in which Italian submarines operated they sank almost 1 million tons of Allied shipping, or an average of some 31,000 tons sunk by the 32 boats involved. When the Italians tried to make a separate peace in 1943, two of the surviving boats at Bordeaux were seized by the Germans and taken into the Kriegsmarine as *UIT21* and *22* (UIT stood for U-Italian).

As soon as the German base facilities were ready Admiral Dönitz switched to the attack once more. In August 1940 Hitler declared a total blockade of the British Isles, thus freeing the U-Boats from the restrictions that had been in force since the beginning of the war. Success did not come easily, for the growing skill of British escorts made coastal waters too dangerous for the U-Boats, and so they had to move out westwards. Here they found the going easier, and between June and November 1940 losses of shipping rose to nearly 1,600,000 tons. Fortunately the United States replaced its 'Cash and Carry' legislation with an agreement to 'lend' war equipment, particularly 50 old but useful destroyers, in exchange for a 99-year lease on various bases throughout the British Empire.

The 'bases for equipment' exchange had little immediate effect on the U-Boat war as the destroyers took some time to be refitted as anti-submarine vessels, but it put heart into the British when they most needed it. It also depressed the Germans, who felt that America was once more trying to rob Germany of her rightful victory, and many senior Nazis urged Hitler to declare war on the United States before she could re-arm and rescue the British. But the Germans had their own problems, particularly in maintaining an adequate number of U-Boats at sea. Surprisingly little equipment from the navies of Europe had fallen into German hands, despite the swift collapse of resistance in May and June; dockyards were wrecked and although some captured submarine hulls were salvageable it would take months before they could be put back into service. The building programme had been stepped up, but like other branches of the armed services, the U-Boat Arm had been equipped for a short war, and pre-war planning for expansion had been unrealistic.

Only four U-Boats were launched between the outbreak of war and the end of 1939, and a further 60 followed in 1940. But in the same period British air and surface forces had sunk 32, and accidents had increased the total to 34. This was a much heavier loss rate than the U-Boats had sustained in the early years of the First World War, and proved that the British convoy escorts were skilled opponents. The withdrawal of destroyers from escort duties to meet the threat of German invasion after Dunkirk had denuded the convoys to a dangerous extent, and although the U-Boats scored more kills than ever before, there were only about thirty at sea at any moment, too few to exploit their enemy's weakness. This was the period of the great U-Boat aces, like Prien and Kretschmer, and some of them sank the staggering total of 200,000 tons of shipping apiece, an achievement which earned them the award of the Knight's Cross with Oak Leaves.

Birth of the 'wolf-packs'

The aces soon found that a night attack on the surface made a U-Boat almost invulnerable. The British escorts' Asdic could not detect a surfaced submarine, and it took an exceptionally sharp lookout to spot the conning tower of a U-Boat. Kretschmer went a step further, and took his U-Boat inside the columns of the convoy, the last place an escort commander would think of looking, and from this 'sanctuary' he could sink ships with impunity while his torpedoes lasted. The answer to this tactic was surface-warning Radar, but in 1940 no escorts were fitted with it, so merchant ships were fitted with illuminant rockets known as Snowflakes; when these were launched at the orders of the escort commander any U-Boat near the convoy would find itself suddenly exposed to view.

It was at this time that Admiral Dönitz began to intervene more directly in the conduct of U-Boat operations. Realising that the exploits of the aces could not be emulated by the newer submarine commanders and crews, he was anxious to use the large numbers of new boats in 'wolf packs'. The essence of the wolf pack tactics was the swamping of a convoy and its escorts by a co-ordinated attack from a group of U-Boats. To achieve this a U-Boat which made contact with a convoy was given strict orders not to attack but to signal its course and position to U-Boat Headquarters, which would then make contact with other U-Boats in the area and direct them to the original U-Boat's position. When the pack was assembled it was launched against the luckless convoy in a series of night attacks, night after night if necessary.

The chief danger from wolf pack tactics was that a U-Boat was both fast and hard to detect on the surface. Running at 17 knots on her diesels, a U-Boat could outpace the trawlers, corvettes and sloops which made up the bulk of convoy escorts in 1940 and 1941. Destroyers were faster, but too few, and in any case the lack of a radar set in all but a few ships made it difficult for any escort to sight a U-Boat. The new tactics were introduced between October 1940 and March 1941, and they proved deadly.

Another factor contributing to their success was the aerial reconnaissance provided by Focke-Wulf Condor aircraft operating from French airfields. These four-engined aircraft were able to locate convoys and shadow them for the benefit of the U-Boats, and until air-cover could be provided for convoys there was virtually no defence against them.

As stated before, the small size of the Type VII U-Boats prevented them from ranging too far in pursuit of targets, and to offset this a 'U-tanker' was introduced. The Type XIV was known to the Germans and the British as the 'Milch Cow', and each one could carry 432 tons of spare fuel and four torpedoes for transfer on the surface. Only ten were completed in 1941/42, and as Allied anti-submarine forces were told to give them top priority all were sunk. A further ten were cancelled because the growing threat from aircraft made refuelling on the surface too dangerous. For the

Italian *Brin*

The 1,000-ton *Brin* Class of four boats were completed in 1938, but a year later another two were added to replace an earlier pair transferred to General Franco during the Spanish Civil War. *Armament:* Eight 21-in torpedo-tubes (forward); one 3·9-in gun; four 13·2-mm machine-guns *Speed:* 17·4 knots (surfaced) 8·7 knots (submerged)

same reason a series of much larger supply boats, the Types XV and XVI were also cancelled.

The British adopted several counter-measures to meet the new threat. In May 1941 the first Type 271 surface search radar set went to sea in a corvette, and as it could detect a conning tower at 2½ miles or more it put paid to surface attacks at night. Another device was High-Frequency Direction-Finding, known for short as Huff-Duff or H/F–D/F. Its principle was well known, but the British had been able to produce a set of great sensitivity which was small enough to be installed in an escort, and this meant that the vital signals sent by a shadowing U-Boat could be traced to within a quarter of a mile. The result was that the U-Boat could at least be forced to dive, and thus silenced; an immediate alteration of the convoy's course then gave the U-Boats the lengthy task of relocating the convoy and re-assembling the wolf pack.

March 1941 was a bad month for the U-Boats. Five U-Boats were sunk in the North Atlantic, including the three aces Prien (*U47*), Kretschmer (*U99*) and Schepke (*U100*). A month later *U110* fell into British hands for long enough to allow boarders to recover her code-books. The result of this exploit was good enough for the Admiralty to keep its secret until well after the end of the Second World War. Even today it is not known exactly how much knowledge of German cyphers was gained, but it can be assumed that some of the successes against U-Boats in 1941 were attributable to the capture of *U110*.

There was no quick answer to the Focke-Wulf Condor, but an interim remedy was to fit some merchant ships with a catapult for launching a single Hurricane fighter aircraft. Although there was no way of recovering the fighter, it was a fair exchange for the degree of immunity conferred on the convoy if the shadower was shot down. Ideally each convoy needed its own aircraft carrier, but in 1941 this was quite beyond the Royal Navy, even if there had been sufficient aircraft to equip the carriers.

The other area in which improvements were made was weaponry. The difficulty in holding a submarine contact with Asdic as the contact came closer to the searching ship has already been mentioned; the answer was to provide a weapon which could project bombs or depth-charges ahead of the ship, while she still held the U-Boat in the Asdic beam. Development of such weapons took time, and in the meantime it was only possible to increase the number of depth-

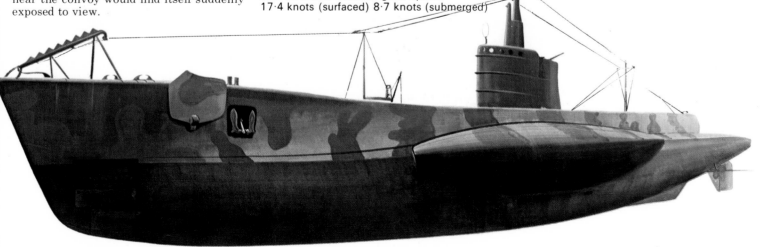

charges which could be dropped. Before the war two depth-charge throwers and a short rack of charges was considered enough, but by 1941 most escort destroyers had surrendered a gun on the quarter-deck for a heavy outfit of four throwers and two extended racks of depth-charges. Better reloading gear was provided so that an escort could keep up a continuous attack, and the pattern of dropping charges was revised to give the maximum chance of destruction.

The standard Mark VII depth-charge had already been modified for use in aircraft, but it was also made heavier to make it sink faster. This was an attempt to reduce that gap between the time the Asdic beam lost contact with the U-Boat, and the explosion of the first charge; obviously the shorter the time interval the more precise was the attack. Another more deadly weapon was the Mark X depth-charge, a 15-ft long canister packed with Minol, one of the new explosives developed during the war. This 1-ton monster could only be fired from a torpedo-tube, and when it exploded at great depth its concussive effect produced damage over a greater radius. It had its drawbacks however: being the equivalent of a full pattern of ten ordinary depth-charges it could blow the ship's stern off if set too shallow or if the ship was moving too slowly.

In 1941 the first 'Hedgehog' appeared. This was a spigot mortar for firing 24 small bombs well ahead of the ship in an elliptical pattern. Each bomb had a 32-lb charge of Torpex (another new explosive) and a hit from one could sink a U-Boat. It allowed the firing ship to hold the target in the Asdic beam, but unlike the ordinary depth-charge a near miss did no harm at all to the U-Boat. In 1943 the British produced a fearsome weapon called 'Squid', which fired three full-sized depth-charges ahead of the ship, and thus combined the advantages of both the earlier weapons.

To be on the receiving end of these weapons was a harrowing experience. For a start there was the audible 'pinging' of the Asdic, and then if a searching escort gained contact would come the repeated concussion of patterns of depth-charges, each one containing 300 lb of high explosive. Light bulbs were shattered and small leaks could be started in the pressure hull. These were particularly dangerous as the mixture of seawater with the sulphuric acid in the batteries generated chlorine gas, which attacks the mucous membranes of the breathing passages.

A prolonged attack could keep the U-Boat down until her air-supply was exhausted even if she had not suffered structural damage. Evasive action was difficult because the noise of the electric motors could be detected by the enemy. If a submarine was trapped by a number of escorts and kept down until her air-supply ran out the choice of options was not inviting: to stay down and die of asphyxiation or blow tanks and try to fight it out on the surface.

Other ideas were germinating. At the end of 1941 the British converted a small merchant ship, the ex-German banana boat *Empire Audacity* into the first 'escort carrier', HMS *Audacity*. She carried only six Martlet fighter aircraft, which had to be parked aft on her small wooden flight deck as there had been no time to provide a lift or hangar. The purpose of this conversion was to provide a defence against the Focke-Wulf Condors which were causing a great deal of trouble to the convoys running from the British Isles to Gibraltar, but it proved that small utility aircraft carriers were a possibility. *Audacity* served for only a month before she was torpedoed off Portugal during a fierce convoy battle, but her aircraft had made so much difference that more conversions were ordered.

The entry of the United States into the war in the same month changed the whole situation, for she alone could provide the numbers of aircraft and the building resources to convert more escort carriers. As a result of strenuous British entreaties six mercantile hulls were converted in April and May 1942, and five of them were immediately transferred to the Royal Navy. However, the Americans were badly equipped for anti-submarine warfare, despite their decisive intervention in 1917, and the first result of their entry into the war was merely an inflation of the losses of merchant shipping. The U-Boats moved over to the Caribbean and the East Coast of the United States, where they found so many juicy targets that they christened the early months of 1942 the 'Happy Times'. It took only 21 U-Boats to sink 500 ships in six months.

The Americans' unpreparedness cannot be blamed on surprise, for the US Navy had been escorting ships bound for the British Isles to a 'Mid-Ocean Meeting Point', called MOMP for short, since September 1941. One destroyer had been sunk and another severely damaged by U-Boat torpedoes during this quasi-war, and the British had freely handed over information about their anti-submarine measures. Furthermore, the Admiralty had ordered 50 American-designed escorts early in 1941.

How was it, then, that the US Navy appeared to have no way of protecting shipping in its own coastal waters? The answer is that senior officers still doubted the wisdom of convoys, even after all experience had shown how vulnerable unescorted ships were to submarine attack. The Americans, having a large number of elderly destroyers, and no specialised escorts like the British sloops and corvettes, pinned their hopes on 'hunting groups', or high-speed patrols by destroyers to seek out the U-Boats before they could attack. It was seriously held by some officers that convoy was too defensive a measure to appeal to the aggressive American spirit – it might suit the more dogged, patient British but it was too old-fashioned an idea to be used by dynamic Americans.

Of course this argument had been the one used by the British from 1914 to 1917 to justify their own 'aggressive' tactics, and it ignored the inescapable fact that it was impossible to cover the ocean with patrol vessels. The submarine by virtue of its invisibility need only hide until the patrolling group had passed, and this is just what happened. During the 'Happy Times' U-Boat commanders reported that they could almost set their watches by the American patrols, which signalled their approach by plumes of smoke and impressive bow waves as a squadron of destroyers tore past at 30 knots. Once past, the length of their patrol line ensured that they would not be back for some time, and the U-Boat could rely on a free hand in running down solitary merchantmen once more. Furthermore security was bad, the American coastline was ablaze with lights, and the merchantmen chattered to one another in plain language, giving their positions regularly. Under these circumstances it is hardly surprising that 505 ships (nearly a third of the total for the whole year) were sunk in American waters before June 1942, when the US Navy finally organised all shipping into convoys.

Galling though these losses were, the

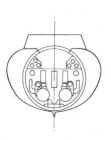
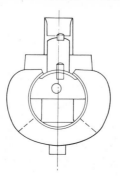

German 'Milch Cow' Type XIV
To extend the range of the Type VII U-Boats, the German Navy built ten submarine tankers in 1941. With a fatter and shorter hull than the Type IX boats, and less power, they could carry sufficient fuel to keep four or five U-Boats at sea for twice as long as usual, and they also carried four spare torpedoes in external stowage. They were made top priority targets for Allied ships and all ten were sunk. *Displacement:* 1,688 tons (surfaced) *Armament:* Two 37-mm AA guns; one 20-mm AA gun; no torpedo-tubes

British and Americans were able to coordinate their counter-measures very well. The programme of 50 British destroyer escorts (BDEs) was hurriedly expanded to 250, and further designs were put into mass-production, so that eventually over 1,000 hulls were on order by 1943. As an emergency measure, Lend-Lease was put into reverse to allow 25 'Flower' Class corvettes to be transferred to the USN, and the new British escort design, the 'River' Class frigate was put into production in American yards. But convoy proved to be the essential measure once again, and when introduced brought the shipping losses back under control.

Not that the position of the Allies was anything but alarming. In 1941 Great Britain had lost a total of 4,328,558 tons of shipping, representing 1,299 ships in all; U-Boats had sunk over 2 million tons (432 ships) while surface raiders, aircraft and mines accounted for the rest. But in 1942 the U-Boats alone sank over 6 million tons, while the total losses from all causes amounted to 7,790,697 tons (1,664 ships). It was April 1917 all over again, except that this time all possible counter-measures had been put into effect and yet the U-Boats were winning. In January 1942 the Germans had 91 U-Boats operational, and although 87 were lost during the year, new construction meant that 212 were operational by December.

The scent of victory

Dönitz and his submarines could smell the scent of victory in the air, and he exhorted them to greater efforts. It was essential for the U-Boats to prevent the Americans from bringing their enormous resources to bear on Europe, and Dönitz calculated that it would take a monthly loss rate of 800,000 tons of Allied shipping to starve out the British and prevent the Americans from implementing their strategic plans to liberate the Mediterranean and the Continent of Europe.

The average monthly losses of shipping in 1942 were running at 650,000 tons, which was far beyond the rate of replacement, so the first priority for the United States was to build more merchant ships. With boundless ingenuity and energy American shipyards devised methods of mass-producing ships, and soon 'Liberty' and 'Victory' standard hulls began to appear in numbers. The British were beginning to see the results of their large warship-building programmes of 1940/41, and in 1942 the first 'River' Class frigates appeared, 1,400-ton twin-screw ships with enough endurance to cross the Atlantic and more speed than a surfaced U-Boat. With more radar sets and H/F-D/F sets available for escort vessels the existing convoy escorts were also better equipped to fight off wolf pack attacks, and this was reflected in the large number of sinkings in 1942.

The U-Boats were helped at this time by the so-called 'black gaps' in mid-Atlantic, five areas which were out of range of shore-based aircraft. In these areas U-Boats could stalk convoys without the fear of being forced to dive by an aircraft, and they sank many ships with little loss to themselves. The introduction of more escort carriers in the late summer of 1942 and the provision of a handful of VLR (Very Long Range) Liberator bombers helped to close the air gap, but the numbers of both would remain small until 1943.

A useful interim measure was the MAC-ship or Merchant Aircraft Carrier, which

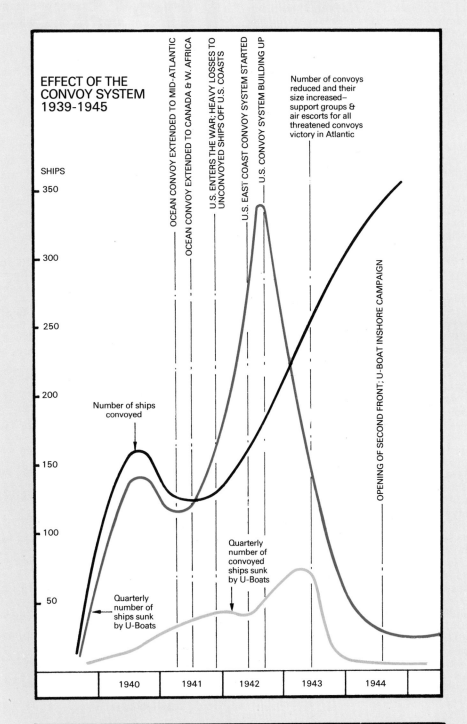

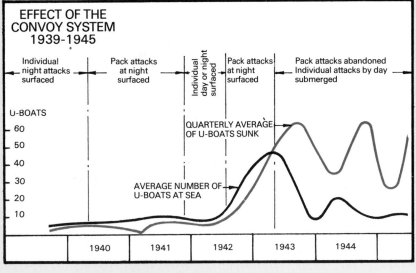

was an oil-tanker or grain-carrier equipped with a plywood flight deck to allow her to operate four aircraft. The virtue of this compromise was that it did not prevent the ship from continuing to carry her valuable cargoes, whereas an escort carrier was completely gutted and converted to a warship. On the other hand an escort carrier operated from 15 to 24 aircraft, and had the necessary communications equipment for controlling aircraft over a convoy.

The U-Boats continued their grim war of extermination, for their goal of 800,000 tons of enemy shipping sunk per month seemed within reach. Indeed Admiral Dönitz believed that they had reached the magic figure, but as in the First World War, U-Boat commanders tended to over-estimate the tonnage of their victims. As we have seen, the losses did not exceed 650,000 tons, which meant that the collapse of the Allies was further away than Dönitz thought. New torpedoes and devices were coming forward, and it was hoped that these would tip the scale. The most important were the homing torpedo and a radar impulse detector, the torpedo to increase the rate of hits and the detector to reduce the chances of being surprised by ship or aircraft on the surface.

The first homing torpedo was issued in January 1943, and was known as the T4 or 'Falke', but after only thirty had been used it was replaced by the better-known T5 'Zaunkönig'. This was the weapon known to the British as the 'Gnat' (for German Naval Acoustic Torpedo), and it travelled at the relatively low speed of 25 knots to reduce interference from its own noise.

Two factors combined to frustrate the Allies' efforts to beat the U-Boat offensive in 1942. The first was the Americans' virtual withdrawal of their escort forces from the Atlantic in June 1942, because these were needed for the Pacific against the Japanese. The second factor was the need to earmark escorts for the large convoys which would be needed for the invasion of North Africa, 'Operation Torch'. Although they were still responsible for coastal escort work, the American ships retained in the Atlantic now formed 2 per cent of the escort forces available, with the British and Canadians sharing the burden in a 50:48 ratio. This dilution of effort was unavoidable, but it gave the U-Boats a chance to inflict even heavier losses than they might have done, when the escorts were at full stretch.

To counterbalance this problem the large number of escort vessels coming into service did allow the British to organise the first experimental support group in September 1942. This was a group of escorts which operated independently in search of U-Boats, but kept itself at readiness to go to the aid of a hard-pressed convoy. It should not be confused with the old-style hunting groups, because it was based on the convoy system rather than being a replacement for it. The basic idea was to leave the convoy's escort to look after the close-range defence, while the support group could pursue and harry U-Boats to destruction. All too frequently a convoy escort had to leave a promising contact because she had to return to the convoy, and the support group idea promised to increase the number of sinkings. This is exactly what happened, particularly because support groups were able to operate in the areas where U-Boats were concentrated.

The Crisis

At the start of 1943 both sides were in a strong position. The U-Boats were well led and their achievements in 1942 meant that officers and men were experienced. Against them were ranged a growing force of aircraft and ships equally determined and skilled. Behind both antagonists were the designers and scientists, whose influence would prove decisive.

The first round went to the U-Boats in March. Acting on intelligence gathered after German cryptanalysts broke into the British convoy cypher, Admiral Dönitz arranged a heavy concentration of U-Boats against two eastbound convoys. This led to a successful interception, by a total of 39 U-Boats, of the slow convoy SC-122, totalling 52 ships, and the faster HX-229, with only 25 ships. Finding the fast convoy first, the U-Boats were able to sink eight ships in a space of less than eight hours. The slow convoy fared rather better when another group of U-Boats attacked, but one U-Boat, *U338*, was able to sink four merchant ships with five torpedoes. During the next three days the convoys were joined to give their escorts a chance to fight back, but even this did not prevent the U-Boats from sinking another nine ships. In all 140,000 tons of shipping had been sunk, for the loss of only three U-Boats.

This great convoy battle marks the high point of the U-Boat offensive. Dönitz almost achieved his dream of making the convoy system unworkable, for the immediate reaction at the Admiralty was to consider the reintroduction of independent sailings until fresh counter-measures could be devised. At no time did Hitler come closer to victory, for if his U-Boats had cut communications

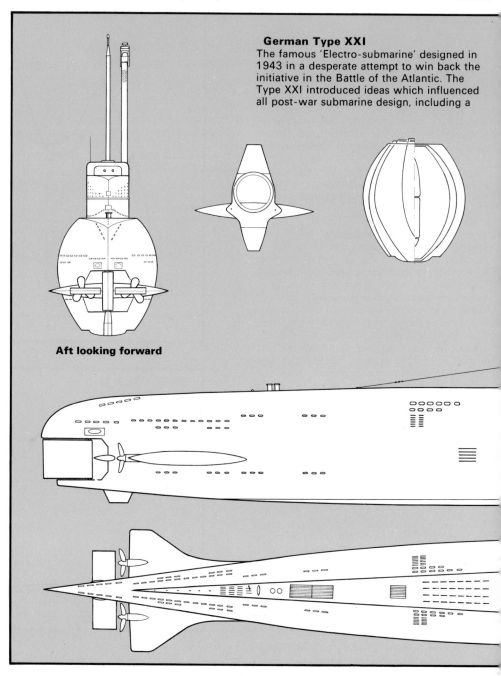

German Type XXI
The famous 'Electro-submarine' designed in 1943 in a desperate attempt to win back the initiative in the Battle of the Atlantic. The Type XXI introduced ideas which influenced all post-war submarine design, including a

Aft looking forward

between Britain and North America, not only would the British have been starved into impotence, but he would have been free to turn his whole might against Russia. Fortunately March 1943 was the turning point, and the U-Boats were shortly to receive their most devastating setback.

The first gleam of hope for the Allies was the intervention of escort carriers and support groups, which had been held back to cover 'Operation Torch'. With that landing successfully achieved, all the vital ships and aircraft which had been taken away from the Atlantic were now thrown back into the battle. Then President Roosevelt intervened to make 61 VLR Liberators available to the RAF, a welcome reversal of policy. But the scientists made the biggest contribution, for they had perfected a short-wave radar set for use in aircraft, the ASV (Air to Surface Vessel) set. ASV transmissions could not be picked up by the U-Boats' existing radar receivers, and losses to aircraft attack rose alarmingly. In May another great convoy battle was fought, but this time aircraft and two support groups intervened, with the result that eight out of twelve U-Boats were lost. It was in a frantic effort to find an answer to this unexpected

reversal of fortune that the U-Boat Command committed two fundamental blunders.

Basing his calculations on the premise that the Metox receiver would give ample warning of any radar-assisted attack, Dönitz decided that submarines could meet aircraft on equal terms provided that each U-Boat had its anti-aircraft armament increased. Conning tower platforms were extended, and a variety of weapons was added forward and aft. The common weapon was the 2-cm Flak 'vierling', a deadly four-barrelled automatic weapon, but single 2-cm and 37-mm weapons were also added, and twin 2-cm. As the main opponents were Sunderland flying boats and Liberator bombers, neither of them very fast or manoeuvrable aircraft, such an array of guns made a surfaced U-Boat an ugly customer, particularly when air crew were not expecting her to stay on the surface to fight it out.

This was the first of the blunders made by Dönitz and his advisers, for skilled air crew did not take long to devise tactics which neutralised the so-called 'aircraft trap'. They simply flew around the U-Boat out of range, while calling up the nearest warship to come and sink her; if at any time the

U-Boat started to dive, the aircraft then rapidly switched to the attack. This led to the 'Battle of Seconds', the U-Boat crews' term for the vital 30–40 seconds needed to clear decks before diving, and many inexperienced U-Boat personnel died simply because they could not get below fast enough.

The second error made by the Germans was a more technical one. Faced with disturbing reports from U-Boat commanders about attacks from aircraft at night when the Metox receiver had given no indication of a radar search, the German scientists refused to consider the possibility of centimetric wave-bands on the grounds that they had already tried this idea without success. A similar reluctance to accept the existence of H/F-D/F in 1942 had caused casualties, but in the spring of 1943 such a mistake was deadly.

The problem was not helped when a captured British bomb-aimer casually revealed that aircraft could track the emissions from a Metox set. When the Germans found that the Metox set did produce emissions which could be tracked, they jumped to the wrong conclusion, and blamed the Metox for all their problems.

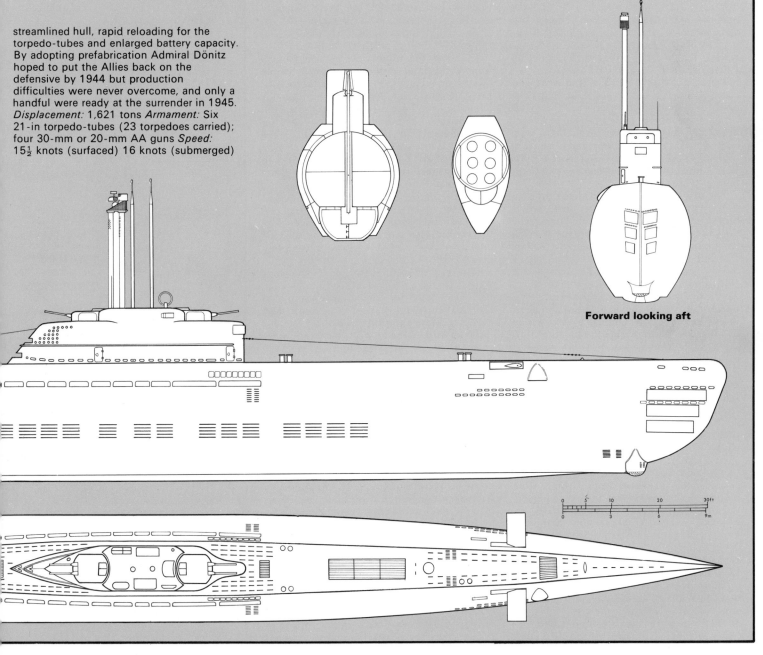

streamlined hull, rapid reloading for the torpedo-tubes and enlarged battery capacity. By adopting prefabrication Admiral Dönitz hoped to put the Allies back on the defensive by 1944 but production difficulties were never overcome, and only a handful were ready at the surrender in 1945. *Displacement:* 1,621 tons *Armament:* Six 21-in torpedo-tubes (23 torpedoes carried); four 30-mm or 20-mm AA guns *Speed:* 15½ knots (surfaced) 16 knots (submerged)

Forward looking aft

However, a new receiver which cured the fault did nothing to halt the sinkings, and only when it was too late to affect the outcome did the Germans discover that however many signals were emitted by the Metox, the centimetric wave-band of the ASV set gave far more accurate bearings, and it was this which was causing the losses.

The collapse of the U-Boat campaign was dramatic. In May a pair of convoys like SC-122 and HX-229 reached Britain without loss, having sunk six U-Boats on the way. In the same month escorts achieved a record, with more U-Boats than merchant ships sunk, and the figures show how savagely the escorts were mauling the U-Boats in revenge:

Month	Shipping sunk	U-Boats sunk
April	245,000 tons	15
May	165,000 tons	40
June	18,000 tons	17
July	123,000 tons	37

Dönitz had no choice but to withdraw his U-Boats from the battle and concede a temporary defeat, while his technicians and scientists worked on the new weapons which were under development.

The new acoustic torpedoes have been mentioned, but there was also the 'Schnorchel', that half-forgotten Dutch device for running diesels at periscope depth. It was hurriedly introduced into service, and was made a standard fitting for new construction as a move to reduce the crippling losses from aircraft. There were passive devices as well, such as the 'Pillenwerfer' or Submarine Bubble Target (SBT), which was a chemical compound released from a torpedo-tube; it acted like a giant Alka-Seltzer to produce bubbles which gave a false Asdic echo, but rarely fooled an experienced operator. Periscopes and even hulls were coated with rubber compounds which it was hoped would absorb Asdic and radar pulses, but again these measures were only partially effective.

The ace up the Germans' sleeve was the new Walther propulsion system, which promised to revolutionise submarine warfare. This was basically a closed cycle steam turbine, which burned an oxidant with oil fuel to dispense with atmospheric oxygen. The Walther system used a concentrated form of hydrogen peroxide known as Perhydrol which decomposed and was burnt with the oil fuel to produce a mixture of gas and steam which drove the turbine. It offered far more power than electric propulsion, and promised underwater speeds in excess of 25 knots.

The first Walther turbine had been tested in an experimental submarine as far back as 1940, but the first production U-Boat to receive it was *U791*. She was not commissioned, but experience with her was incorporated into the Type XVIIA U-Boats, which were coastal submarines powered by two Walther turbines coupled to a single shaft, and capable of about 25 knots. Under considerable pressure from U-Boat Command, the designers produced drawings for improved types, the XVIIB and XVIIG, but to speed construction only one of the turbines was installed. Despite this a speed of 20 knots was attained, more than double that of the conventional Type VII and Type IX U-Boats in service.

There were many drawbacks, however, and the Walther submarine must rank with some of Hitler's more bizarre tank projects as an interesting idea which absorbed far too much material and time at the expense of less ambitious projects which were suffering setbacks.

The chief difficulty was in the manufacture and storage of the fuel, known as 'Ingolin'. This was highly unstable, and any impurity in the storage tanks led to decomposition and spontaneous combustion; only clinical sterility would do, and eventually synthetic rubber was discovered to be the least dangerous material for lining the tanks. Ingolin was also very expensive to make, costing about eight times as much as oil, and was consumed at a prodigious rate, so that a Type XVIIA boat could only travel 80 miles at top speed – which put the clock back to about 1900 as far as operational radius was concerned.

These problems were realised by Dönitz and at a conference with Hitler in July 1943 he mentioned the existence of a new interim design known as the 'Electro' submarine, which was to bridge the gap between the ordinary schnorchel-equipped U-Boats and the first Type XVII boats. This was the famous Type XXI, actually a conventionally-propelled submarine, but redesigned to make use of every possible advance to offset the recent Allied successes. The improvements can be summarised as basically a streamlined hull to reduce underwater drag, and enlarged battery-capacity to give higher underwater speed. Had the Type XXI been available in greater numbers in 1944 U-Boats might have made a comeback and inflicted casualties at the 1942 level.

To boost the underwater speed from 9 knots to 15½ knots it was necessary to treble the battery capacity, but they were also fitted with silent auxiliary motors for 'creeping' at 5 knots. To allow attacks from safer distances the torpedo salvo was increased to six tubes, and 17 reloads were carried. Wartime experience showed that a torpedo-tube took at least 10 minutes to reload by hand, so the Type XXIs were given mechanical loading to reduce the strain on the crew and to give them the chance to follow up an attack quickly. Although the conventional conning tower had given way to a streamlined 'fin', the menace of aircraft called for two pairs of AA guns in remotely controlled positions on top of the fin.

Dönitz promised Hitler that the first Type XXI U-Boat would be ready in November 1944, but Hitler immediately demanded that the Konstruktion-Amt should do better, even if it meant three-shift working. Reichsminister Albert Speer was given the job of organising the mass-production of Type XXIs, and he hoped to produce 20 per month. But in that strange mixture of efficiency and muddle which characterised the war effort of the Third Reich, the obsolescent Type VIIC was allowed to continue in production, while the Type XXI was entrusted to 'diluted' labour, i.e. a small proportion of skilled workmen padded out with old men, women and even children.

The territorial ambitions of the Germans now proved their undoing. The Army's need for manpower and the aircraft industry's over-riding demands for strategic materials meant that even if the U-Boat programme had been completed it was unlikely that the boats could have been manned. Dönitz told Hitler that in the second half of 1943 production would be running at 27 U-Boats per month, and it was hoped to increase this to 30 per month by 1945. But the existing programme was using 6,000 tons of steel each month, 4,500 tons for U-Boat hulls and 1,500 tons for torpedoes. He also pointed out that if production rose to 40 U-Boats per month extra personnel would have to be found. The Kriegsmarine's allowance was 102,984 men, and the estimated manpower requirement was already 334,838 men short.

The Army had taken the largest amount of manpower since April 1942, when Hitler had been preparing for his ill-conceived

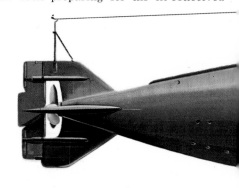

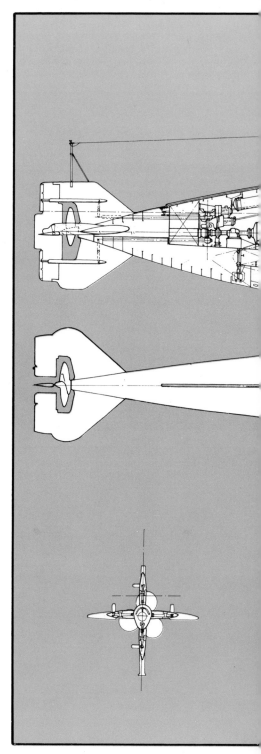

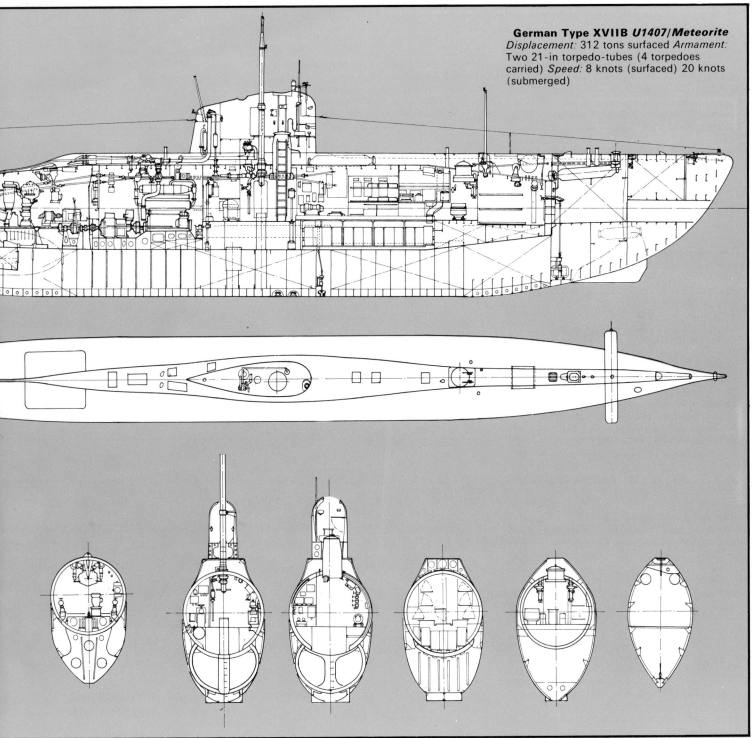

German Type XVIIB *U1407/Meteorite*
Displacement: 312 tons surfaced *Armament:*
Two 21-in torpedo-tubes (4 torpedoes
carried) *Speed:* 8 knots (surfaced) 20 knots
(submerged)

invasion of Russia. At the 1943 rate of U-Boat production (25–30 boats per month) this left the Navy short of 200,000 men. The officer candidates who had entered in the autumn of 1939 had all become commanders by the summer of 1943, and it would be necessary to transfer some officers from the Army and Air Force to make up numbers. This was finally done, and many of the 'expatriate' submariners proved successful, but it is easy to see why the sledgehammer blows of the Allies in the spring of 1943 were able to bring about the collapse of morale in the U-Boat Arm. All had given of their best, and continued to do so, but there was no way of wringing greater effort out of them.

Although the U-Boats continued to be dangerous, throughout the rest of 1943 and 1944 they lacked the ferocious determination that had characterised their earlier efforts. The schnorchel was partly to blame, for its value was negative rather than positive; while using it a U-Boat was relatively safe, but she did not have that freedom of movement which she had once enjoyed on the surface. Even her dangerous acoustic torpedoes were rendered harmless by noise-makers towed astern of escorts, known as 'Foxers', and the schnorchel could be detected by radar in smooth conditions. The invasion of Normandy in 1944 meant the end of the Biscay and Brittany bases, and the loss of Italy closed the Mediterranean to U-Boats. The only area in which U-Boats still enjoyed any measure of success was in Northern Norway and the Arctic, against Allied convoys to Russia.

The emphasis switched to midget submarines and special assault craft known generically as 'K-craft', to hold up invasion fleets. Many different types were built, but they scored very few successes, even against the vast D-Day Invasion fleet of 5,000 ships. The best-known were the 'Molch' (Salamander), 'Hecht' (Pike), 'Seehund' (Seal), 'Biber' (Beaver), 'Marder' (Marten) and 'Neger' (Negro) of which the Seehund type proved the most successful. Like all midgets they were only effective in fairly sheltered waters, and Allied counter-measures were sufficient to avoid serious losses. However they did prove one interesting point: they were so light that the blast from a depth-charge merely swept them aside without sinking them. The effect on the crew is not recorded.

Finally the first Type XXI U-Boats were finished, and four were commissioned early in 1945. But it is not possible to put a revolutionary type of submarine straight into service, and U2511 did not leave for her first operational patrol until a week before the German surrender. A smaller, cruder coastal version, known as the Type XXIII, had come into service a little earlier, and although the handful completed had a few successes they were also too late.

The end came on 7 May 1945, when Dönitz, by now Hitler's successor and also head of the German Navy, broadcast instructions to all U-Boats to cease hostilities and to comply with the Allies' conditions. They were told to surface, and to fly a black flag while making their way to the nearest warship to make a formal surrender. In this way hundreds of U-Boats made their way to Lisahally in Northern Ireland. There they lay in their melancholy lines, just as they had at Harwich in 1919. Twice in a generation U-Boats had taken on the world, twice they had nearly won a great victory, and now they had failed once again.

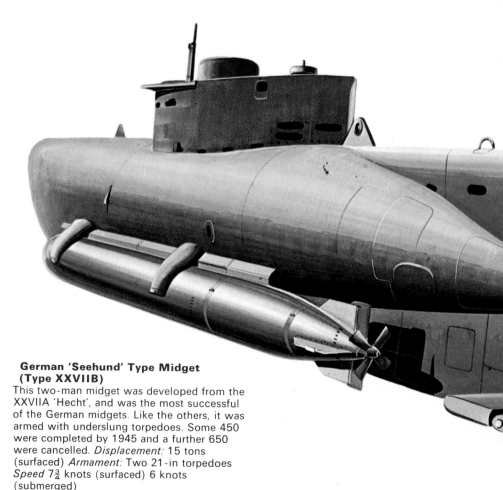

German 'Seehund' Type Midget (Type XXVIIB)
This two-man midget was developed from the XXVIIA 'Hecht', and was the most successful of the German midgets. Like the others, it was armed with underslung torpedoes. Some 450 were completed by 1945 and a further 650 were cancelled. *Displacement:* 15 tons (surfaced) *Armament:* Two 21-in torpedoes *Speed* 7¾ knots (surfaced) 6 knots (submerged)

German 'Molch' Type Midget
A third one-man type, from a different builder. Molch was similar to Biber, and nearly 400 were completed

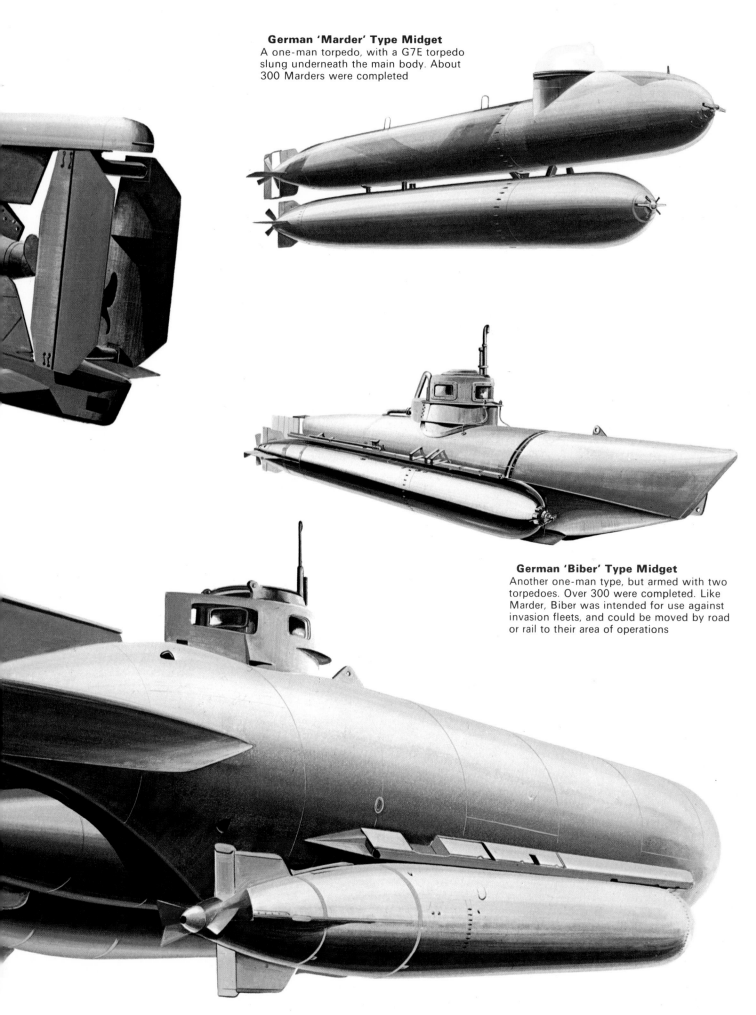

German 'Marder' Type Midget
A one-man torpedo, with a G7E torpedo slung underneath the main body. About 300 Marders were completed

German 'Biber' Type Midget
Another one-man type, but armed with two torpedoes. Over 300 were completed. Like Marder, Biber was intended for use against invasion fleets, and could be moved by road or rail to their area of operations

British Midget Submarines

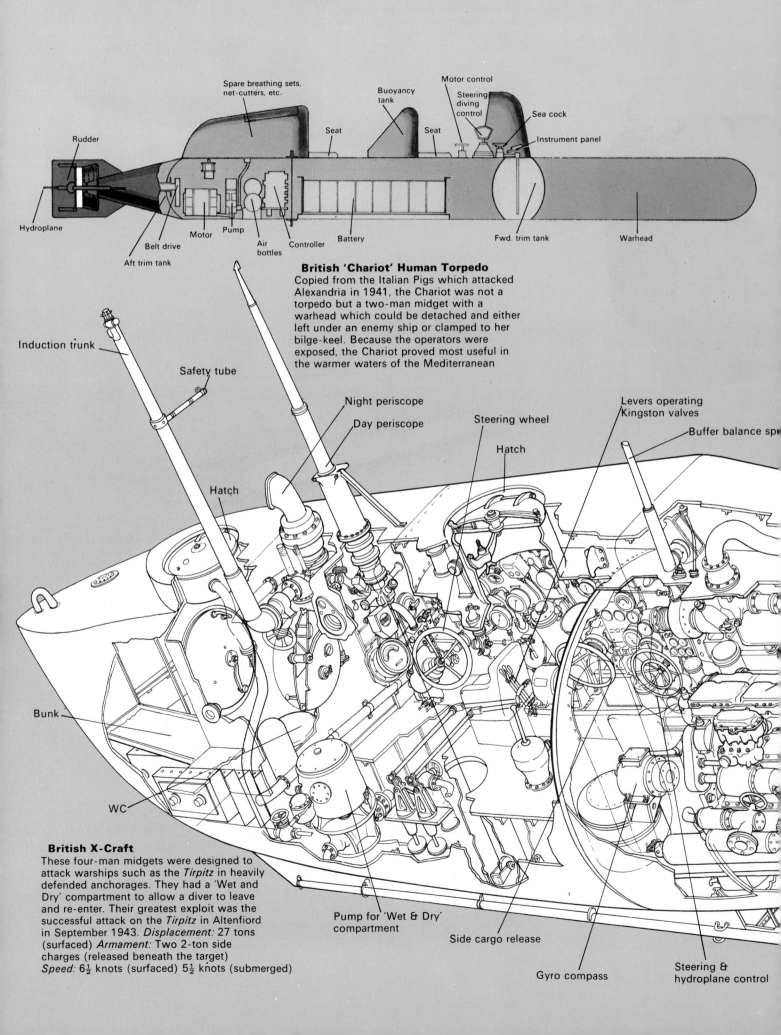

Spare breathing sets,
net-cutters, etc.

Buoyancy
tank

Motor control

Steering
diving
control

Sea cock

Instrument panel

Seat

Seat

Rudder

Hydroplane

Belt drive

Motor

Pump

Air
bottles

Controller

Battery

Fwd. trim tank

Warhead

Aft trim tank

British 'Chariot' Human Torpedo
Copied from the Italian Pigs which attacked
Alexandria in 1941, the Chariot was not a
torpedo but a two-man midget with a
warhead which could be detached and either
left under an enemy ship or clamped to her
bilge-keel. Because the operators were
exposed, the Chariot proved most useful in
the warmer waters of the Mediterranean

Induction trunk

Safety tube

Night periscope

Day periscope

Steering wheel

Hatch

Levers operating
Kingston valves

Buffer balance spr

Hatch

Bunk

WC

British X-Craft
These four-man midgets were designed to
attack warships such as the *Tirpitz* in heavily
defended anchorages. They had a 'Wet and
Dry' compartment to allow a diver to leave
and re-enter. Their greatest exploit was the
successful attack on the *Tirpitz* in Altenfiord
in September 1943. *Displacement:* 27 tons
(surfaced) *Armament:* Two 2-ton side
charges (released beneath the target)
Speed: 6½ knots (surfaced) 5½ knots (submerged)

Pump for 'Wet & Dry'
compartment

Side cargo release

Gyro compass

Steering &
hydroplane control

Although the last in the field, the British made the most impressive use of midget submarines. They copied the Italian 'pigs', calling them 'Chariots', and then designed a range of battery-driven midgets to penetrate the Norwegian anchorages which were sheltering German heavy units. In 1941/42 ships like the *Bismarck* and *Tirpitz* were beyond the range of heavy bombers, and there was no other way to penetrate a Norwegian fiord.

One of the leading advocates of midget submarines was Commander Varley, who had served in submarines in the First World War. His firm built the prototype *X3*, while Portsmouth Dockyard built *X4*. Six production models were begun in December 1942, and by September 1943 they and their hand-picked crews were ready to attack the battleship *Tirpitz* in Altenfiord. Unlike the Italian and Japanese midgets, these 'X-craft' did not have torpedoes, but carried side-charges, containing a half ton of explosive each, which were dropped underneath the target. Although fitted with a diesel engine as well as an electric motor, they were too small to undertake long passages and were always towed to their target area by full-sized submarines.

The attack on the *Tirpitz* on 22 September 1943 was a great success, for although the charges did not sink her, they inflicted such damage on her that she was eventually moved south for repairs. Here she was at last within range of bombers, and she was finally eliminated little more than a year later. All six of the X-craft were lost, including one which broke down on the way out, and the surviving one, *X10*, which was scuttled afterwards. A slightly enlarged version, the XE-craft, was built for the Far East. They had more stowage space and had the blessing of air-conditioning to reduce the strain on the four- or five-man crew. There was also an air-lock to allow a diver to leave the midget and place limpet mines on the target's hull, and spring-loaded legs to make it easier for the midget to rest on the bottom.

Before the Normandy invasion in June 1944 midgets were used to reconnoitre landing beaches, and to provide information on tides and obstructions. On D-Day itself several acted as navigation beacons well inshore to guide the first assault wave. In the Far East they revived Simon Lake's ideas of fifty years earlier by sending out divers to cut submarine cables. Chariots were used in Norway, but the water proved far too cold for the crews, and they proved better suited to the Mediterranean where they sank the Italian cruisers *Gorizia*, *Bolzano* and *Ulpio Traiano*.

British 'Welman' Type Midget
A one-man craft capable of fixing a 560-lb charge to its target by magnetic clips. It is not known how many Welmans were produced, but they proved unreliable

Access hatch
Aft instrument panel
Access hatch securing handle
Air bottles
Instrument panel
Lifting eye
Batteries
Compensating tank
Lifting eye
Charge release control
Battery
Charge
Motor
Drop keel
Comp. & bilge hand pump
Hydroplane & rudder control
Trim weight control
Trim weight
Silencer
Hydroplane & rudder

Lifting eye
4-cylinder Gardner engine
Propeller shaft
Rudder
Hydroplane

Oxygen cylinders

The Mediterranean

The submarine war that the British had feared in the Mediterranean when Italy entered the war in June 1940 did not take the form expected. This was partly due to the inertia of the Italian Navy, whose few energetic submariners were shortly to be sent to Bordeaux, but particularly because Admiral Dönitz was so reluctant to weaken the U-Boat offensive in the Atlantic by sending boats to the Mediterranean. For the British submarines, however, there were tempting targets in the form of Italian shipping taking supplies to the Italian and German troops fighting in North Africa. On the other hand the Mediterranean was dangerous for submarines: land-based aircraft were within a short flying distance at any time, and they could spot a submarine at a depth of up to 50 feet in calm weather, as against the North Sea, where a submarine is virtually invisible at periscope depth, or the Atlantic, where visibility extends only 30 feet down in ideal conditions.

Reverses to British fortunes, both on land and at sea, made it very hard to exploit the weakness of the Italians. The Luftwaffe had reinforced the Regia Aeronautica, which gave the Axis Powers air superiority over large areas of the Mediterranean and thus made the British submarines' job very difficult. Losses were heavy among the large submarines of the 'O', 'P' and 'R' Classes, not least because of their leaky external fuel tanks.

Nevertheless, in the early months of 1941 there were many successes. It is odd to note that British submarines were still forbidden to sink merchant ships without warning, and it was not until February 1941 that the Cabinet removed the restriction, on the assumption that all shipping found south of 35 46' N was hostile. By May over 100,000 tons of German and Italian shipping had been sunk by submarines operating out of Malta, Gibraltar and Alexandria.

In mid-1941 British submarine activity reached a new peak, when the three flotillas sank a further 150,000 tons of shipping. It was a repetition of the Sea of Marmora campaign of 1915, with the gun being used as much as the torpedo, and coastal targets such as bridges and railway lines coming under attack. Quite apart from the loss of supplies to the Italians and the German Africa Korps, which was described by the Germans as 'unendurable', these widespread activities strained a naval organisation which had never been very strong. Had this situation continued the British were heading for an impressive victory over their enemies at relatively small cost, but just as it seemed certain, disaster struck.

U-Boats in the Mediterranean

Once again, the submarine had taken a hand. At last the losses and demoralisation of Axis naval forces in the Mediterranean forced the Germans to allow some of their precious U-Boats to be transferred to the Mediterranean. When they arrived they found that the British anti-submarine tactics had grown rusty because of the poor performance of the Italians. The sequence of events was a grim lesson for the British, who had grown used to their freedom. The first important victim was the aircraft carrier *Ark Royal*, torpedoed in the Western Mediterranean by *U81* and *U205* on 13 November 1941. Next to go was the battleship *Barham*, torpedoed in the Eastern Mediterranean by *U331* on 25 November, and the light cruiser *Galatea*, sunk by *U557* on 15 December.

The exploits of Italian submarines were hardly notable for their vigour, but in one area the Italian Navy showed not only ingenuity but great personal courage. During in the First World War they had pioneered midget submarines as well as special assault craft for penetrating defended harbours. Profiting by this experience they developed the 'Maiali' or 'Pig', a torpedo-shaped small submersible craft which was controlled by two men wearing self-contained underwater

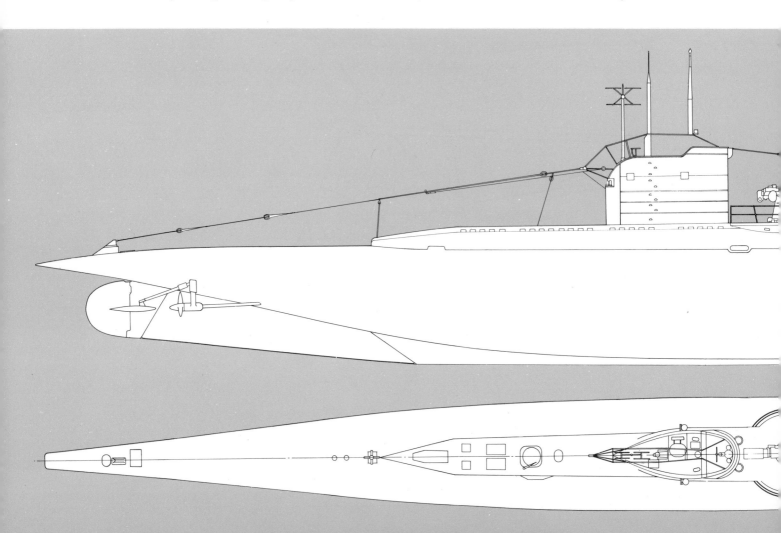

breathing apparatus (SCUBA gear). The operators rode the body of the craft, hence its nick-name of 'human torpedo', but it differed from a torpedo in that it was simply a slow-moving underwater vehicle to allow two frogmen to move about an anchorage. The 'warhead' was detached from the nose of the 'pig' and then attached to any convenient projection on the bottom of the target vessel, such as a bilge keel, by clamps.

The 'pigs' could not travel far, so the submarines *Scire* and *Gondar* were converted to carry three each in watertight containers on deck. After an abortive attempt against ships in Gibraltar in September 1941 the

Italian 'Pig' Human Torpedo
The best known of all midgets, these 'Maiale' (Pigs) immobilised two British battleships at Alexandria in 1941. The forward operator was the commander, who had to control the craft, while the diver was responsible for placing the explosive. *Speed:* 2·8 to 3 knots; *Endurance:* 5–6 hours at full speed; *Max diving depth:* 50 ft

Scire was sent to Alexandria two months later. On the night of 18 December she put her three crews over the side; as luck would have it, a British cruiser was entering the harbour and so the three 'pigs' were able to slip through the net defences without any difficulty. They found their targets, the battleships *Queen Elizabeth* and *Valiant* and an oiler, and duly placed their charges. Early the next morning the charges went off, causing heavy damage to the two battleships. Coming so soon after the other losses, it meant that the Royal Navy's heavy units in the Mediterranean had been wiped out, and that the initiative had passed to the Germans and Italians.

Other events in the Far East were to add to the Royal Navy's problems. For on 7 December the Japanese had launched their crippling attack on the American Pacific Fleet at Pearl Harbour, and had followed this by sinking the British capital ships *Prince of Wales* and *Repulse*. Aircraft, warships and shipping had to be switched to the Far East, stripping the Mediterranean to the bone. The only naval forces left to

harass the Axis supply lines were submarines, but now they had to operate in the face of enemy air superiority. Their base at Malta was under constant air attack, and it became necessary to submerge and lie on the bottom of the harbour by day, surfacing to recharge batteries at night.

As early as May 1941 Malta's position had been precarious, and so the minelaying submarine HMS *Rorqual* was sent on an experimental supply run. She took three weeks to convert at Alexandria, and finally sailed on 5 June with over 100 tons of urgently-needed stores, including high-octane fuel, kerosene and medical supplies. A second trip on 25 June showed that with careful attention to stowage even more fuel could be carried, and later in the year the fleet submarine *Clyde* took 1,200 tons of supplies, at a time when hardly any surface ships could get through. More runs were made by the *Osiris*, *Porpoise* and *Urge*, and by the middle of 1942 submarines had taken 65,000 tons into Grand Harbour, a staggering feat which was only matched by the efforts of the Japanese in the Pacific.

British *Vivid*
The 'V' Class was a development of the 'U' Class, but could dive deeper by virtue of having welded hulls. As the collapse of Italy in 1943 eliminated the need for small submarines many of this class were transferred to other Allied navies.
Displacement: 545 tons (surfaced)
Armament: Four 21-in torpedo-tubes; 8 torpedoes carried; one 3-in AA gun; 3 machine-guns; *Speed:* 12¾ knots (surfaced) 9 knots (submerged)

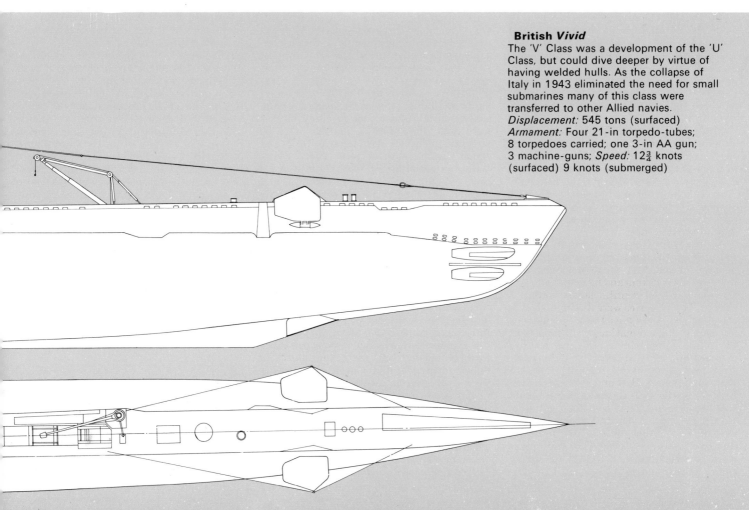

Submarines in the Pacific

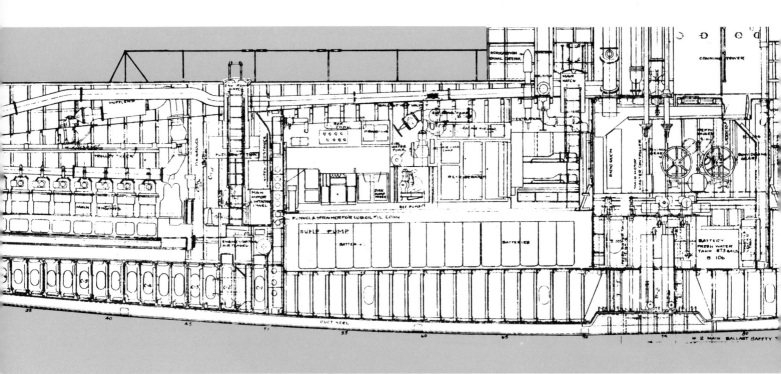

The destruction and immobilisation of the United States Navy's battleships at Pearl Harbour left it with only two ways of carrying the war to the Japanese: carrier-borne aircraft and submarines. By December 1941 the USN had 113 submarines, of which 64 were elderly boats built during the First World War and suitable only for training and coastal work, nine large cruiser-submarines which were not mechanically reliable, and 40 newer submarines. Fortunately Congress had authorised a further 73 boats, of which some 30 were actually under construction.

Although the number of builders had dwindled to three as a result of the Depression, American industry had little trouble in expanding the output of diesel engines and electric motors, so when the Bureau of Ships asked for three additional yards, two commercial builders and one Navy Yard to undertake submarine building, they were able to provide them.

At this point it is opportune to insert a note about the classification of US submarines. From 1911 all submarines were assigned class letters and hull numbers, and the old fish and reptile names were discarded. The 'V' series were distinguished by the numbers *V1–V9* as Fleet Submarines, but in 1920 the designations SS (Submarine), SF (Fleet Submarine), SC (Cruiser Submarine) and SM (Minelaying Submarine) were introduced as a temporary measure, with their own A, B, C and D pendant numbers. Thus the USS *Cachalot*, for example, was simultaneously known for a while as *SS170*, *C1* and *V8*, but in 1940 this multiple system was swept away, and only SS-numbers were retained. The fish names were reintroduced in 1931 with the *Barracuda* (*SS163*) and continued until the first

Polaris submarine was launched in 1959.

American standardisation
The Pacific was seen clearly as the area of any future conflict, so American designs emphasised high surface endurance, habitability and good torpedo capacity. After the unsatisfactory experiments with cruiser-submarines in the 1920s, the 'P' Group of 1933–1938 was developed through the 'S' and 'T' classes into the 1,500-ton 'G' Class of 1940. In view of the limited number of yards available, standardisation of design was essential, and although three classes were built, they were so similar as to be virtually identical, the famous *Gato* and *Balao* Classes, and the later *Tench* Class. With an overall length of 311 ft 9 in and a beam of 27 ft 3 in, they had welded hulls and diesel-electric drive, i.e. diesel generators driving electric motors coupled to the shafts through reduction gears. This method had also been introduced in contemporary British submarines, and replaced the former dual diesel or electric drive in older submarines.

All wartime US submarines had the same double hull divided into eight watertight compartments, with six ballast tanks and four fuel tanks, though stronger hulls were introduced in the *Balao* and *Tench* Classes. The armament was heavy, six torpedo-tubes forward and four aft, with stowage for 14 reload torpedoes, and a deck gun. During the war the gun changed from one 3-in/50 cal to 4-in or 5-in and a heavy battery of 40-mm or 20-mm AA guns, and the configuration of conning towers changed to accommodate them. But for all their heavy armament and generally excellent design, US submarines began the war with a serious disadvantage: like the German U-Boats they suffered

from defective torpedoes. The magnetic pistol was to blame as well, and for the first two years many attacks on Japanese targets were useless. It is strange that two countries with a high reputation for their engineering standards should have introduced a new weapon without spotting its weakness until long after it had entered service.

The Japanese, on the other hand, did not approach the submarine problem as systematically as the Americans. By 1940 there was a noticeable lack of medium-sized boats to supplement the large cruiser-types which seemed to fascinate their admirals unduly. The 1940 Additional Programme tried to rectify this with an order for more than 80 of the K6 Type, 1,100-tonners armed with four torpedo-tubes. Although rather small they had a theoretical range of 11,000 miles at 12 knots, about equal to an early *Gato*, and were considered to be a very successful design. Production problems resulted in only 18 being completed, *RO35–RO50* and *RO55* and *RO56*, and all but one were sunk.

The same programme saw the commencement of 9 'medium' 600-tonners of the KS Type, a strange decision in view of the distances involved in the Pacific, but under the 1941 Emergency War Programme there was an immediate return to giant aircraft-carrying submarines with the *I40* and *I46* Classes. The *I12* was a repeat of the 1937 A1

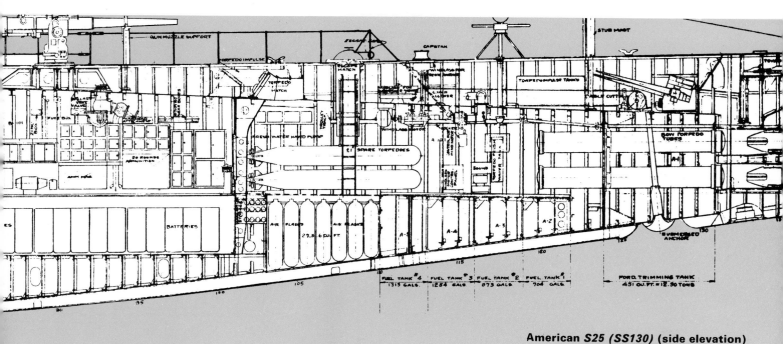

Labels on diagram: GUN MUZZLE SUPPORT, TORPEDO IMPULSE, BALLAST VENT VALVE, FUEL BOX, BATTERIES, TORPEDO HATCH, FRESH WATER HAND PUMP, SPARE TORPEDOES, AIR FLASKS, 29.3 6 CU FT, AIR BLASTS, 20 ROUNDS AMMUNITION, ESCAPE HATCH, CAPSTAN, WINDLASS MOTOR, SOUND, TORPEDO IMPULSE TANKS, CABLE CUTTER, BOW TORPEDO TUBES, SUBMERGED ANCHOR, FUEL TANK #4 1315 GALS, FUEL TANK #3 1284 GALS, FUEL TANK #2 873 GALS, FUEL TANK #1 704 GALS, FORD TRIMMING TANK 451 CU FT = 12.50 TONS, STUB MAST

American *S25 (SS130)* (side elevation)

Type, a long-range cruising submarine intended to act as the headquarters for hunting groups of smaller submarines. The surface displacement was nearly 3,000 tons, and aircraft were carried, but most of the additional displacement was used to increase endurance – to as much as 22,000 miles in the *I12*.

These submarines were meant to play their part in a grandiose plan to seek out and ambush American surface forces across the wide expanse of the Pacific, and they were supplemented by midgets to attack the enemy if he should refuse to leave his defended harbours. The aerial attack on Pearl Harbour was intended to be supported by a torpedo attack from some Type A midgets, and one of the minor mysteries of that debâcle is how the Americans sighted and sank one of them at the entrance to Pearl Harbour *before* the main attack without alerting the defences. The attack was not a

success, nor was a similar attack on Sydney Harbour in 1942, but in the same year the British battleship *Ramillies* was badly damaged by a midget launched from a parent submarine off Madagascar.

The nation that introduced the Kamikaze concept had little difficulty in applying it to naval warfare, and in 1943 the first of a range of suicide craft was developed, the *Kairyu*; it was a development of the Type A midget, but production did not start until early in 1945. A much better-known development was the *Kaiten*, basically a piloted version of the famous 24-in Type 93 'Long Lance' torpedo. The three later models of *Kaiten* used a high-speed hydrogen-peroxide engine, but suffered so many production problems that the Model 4 was fitted with a conventional torpedo motor and carried a much heavier warhead in compensation.

The main problem for the Japanese at the

beginning of the war was not one of design, but the question of how they intended to use their submarines. From the start the long-cherished aim of a general fleet action was paramount in the Imperial Japanese Navy's plans, and all submarine tactics had to be subordinated to that idea. Too much attention was paid to the need to maintain an offensive and aggressive outlook, which led to the grave error of assuming that warships were the only important targets for submarines. It also led to the equally serious error of neglecting the defence of merchant ships on the grounds that convoying was merely a defensive measure.

The lessons were painfully learned by the Japanese as American submarines proceeded to cut their lines of communication.

American *S25 (SS130)*
The 'S' Class was the last design produced for the USN in the First World War, and in 1941 a few units were stationed in the Far East. They proved to have too little endurance for the Pacific, and so they were withdrawn. *S25* was lent to the Royal Navy for training, and then became the Polish *Jastrzab*. She was sunk in error by friendly ships in 1942

Losses of vital tonnage went up, so that it became harder and harder to reinforce the perimeter of island bases, which were essential to the Japanese maritime strategy. Worse, the homeland depended on imports for 20 per cent of the food consumed, 24 per cent of its coal, 88 per cent of all iron ore, and 90 per cent of its oil.

In the light of these statistics it is hard to understand why the Imperial Navy did not complete any escort vessels until 1940. Apart from a handful of old destroyers converted, the only further effort made by 1941 was the construction of another 22 escorts, and even they were given a low priority. The Japanese High Command did not expect the American submarines would be able to penetrate the defensive perimeter, and it was not until late in 1943 that any sort of convoy system was introduced. Even then, it was a very reluctant gesture and it was hampered by the desperate shortage of escorts. Over 4 million tons of shipping was sunk by American submarines, and by mines laid by submarines and aircraft, and when the war ended in August 1945 the Japanese mercantile marine comprised only 231 ships – in 1939 *Lloyd's Register* listed 2,337 ships!

The American submarines in the Pacific were supported by a small number of British and Dutch submarines, and after the col-

lapse of Italy in 1943 the British were able to transfer reinforcements from the Mediterranean. By early 1944 there were three flotillas in the Far East, two at Trincomalee and a third at Fremantle in Australia, operating under American command. Because of their smaller size the British and Dutch boats were principally employed about the 10-fathom line west of Singapore where the big US submarines found it difficult to operate.

By comparison with the staggering losses inflicted by the American submarines, the tonnages sunk by the British and Dutch were modest, largely because the Japanese

had withdrawn many of their units. But many small coasters and junks were destroyed by gunfire. HMS *Tally Ho* sank the cruiser *Kuma* off Penang, however, while *Taurus* sank the submarine *I34* in the same locality. When the patrol was extended the losses went up, and HMS *Trenchant*'s CO was awarded the US Legion of Merit for sinking the cruiser *Ashigara*. The midget submarines *XE1* and *XE3* disabled the cruiser *Takao* in Singapore, and two 'Chariots' from HMS *Trenchant* attacked merchant shipping at Phuket in Thailand. Excluding minor vessels under 500 tons, British and Dutch submarines sank a total of 87,000 tons of shipping.

Japanese counter-measures were poor, and only 60 US submarines were sunk, with a much lower loss ratio than that suffered by the German U-Boats. When the war ended the Japanese authorities told the Americans that their anti-submarine forces had sunk 486 boats! American submarines were also able to sink eight aircraft carriers and 12 cruisers, the classic examples being the torpedoing of the 62,000-ton *Shinano* by the *Archerfish*, and an ambush by the *Dace* and *Darter* which sank two heavy cruisers and damaged a third. Such was the ascendancy of American submarines over the Japanese that they were able to tackle escorts with

American *Drum* (SS228)
The *Gato* Class was the standard wartime design for the USN, and proved a superb weapon for the Pacific. As the war progressed the AA armament was increased, because American submarines operated on the surface for much of the time. The *Drum* is preserved at Mobile, Alabama. *Displacement:* 1,526 tons (surfaced) *Armament:* Ten 21-in torpedo tubes (6 forward, 4 aft); 24 torpedoes carried; one 3-in gun; two ·5 and two ·3 machine-guns *Speed:* 20¼ knots (surfaced) 8¾ knots (submerged)

impunity. Their outstanding tactic was the 'down the throat shot', a full salvo fired at short range at an escort bearing down on the submarine. It required very fine judgment and an iron nerve, but it meant that US submarines sometimes sank escorts faster than they could sink submarines.

The German wolf pack system was introduced in the Pacific in 1943, but the Americans used groups of only three boats, with such exotic nicknames as 'Laughlin's Loopers', 'Ed's Eradicators' and 'Ben's Busters'. With the advantage of radar, which the Japanese escorts lacked, they were able to track their targets with ease and avoid any counter-attacks. Like the Germans, the Americans found that attacking on the surface at night was very profitable, but unlike the British the Japanese escorts could not stop submarines from racing ahead to a new attacking position, because of their lack of radar.

Triumph at Midway

By comparison the US Navy suffered relatively little from Japanese submarine attacks. The battleship *North Carolina* was torpedoed by *I15* in 1942 but survived, as did the carrier *Saratoga* when hit by *I26*. The greatest Japanese triumphs took place at Midway when *I168* put four torpedoes into the crippled carrier *Yorktown*, and the sinking of the carrier *Wasp* by *I19* south of the Solomons. The main reason for this was the high degree of skill shown by American anti-submarine forces, as underlined when the destroyer escort *England* sank six submarines in twelve days in May 1944. But the concentration on warship targets by the Japanese freed the Americans from having to organise a massive convoy system in the Pacific, and released escorts for more urgent duties with the front-line forces.

Japanese submarines were well aware of the need to attack American shipping, but failed to get a hearing from their superiors. When things began to go badly in 1942 the response was to hurl submarines into useless attacks on landing forces, or to use them to transport supplies to isolated Army garrisons. Not satisfied with this, the Army began to build transport submarines of its

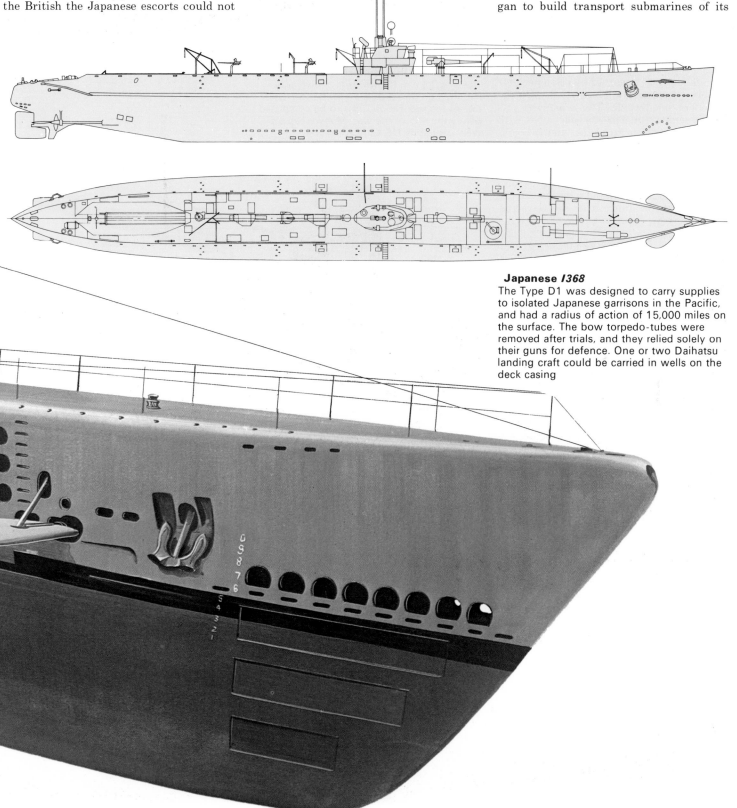

Japanese *I368*

The Type D1 was designed to carry supplies to isolated Japanese garrisons in the Pacific, and had a radius of action of 15,000 miles on the surface. The bow torpedo-tubes were removed after trials, and they relied solely on their guns for defence. One or two Daihatsu landing craft could be carried in wells on the deck casing

own, surely the most monumental dispersion of effort in the history of naval warfare; about 28 were built, and they were manned by Army personnel. When permission was given to attack communications it was too late, and in any case reliance was placed on the *Kaiten*, which were hardly suitable for extended operations. Like the Italian 'pigs' the *Kaiten* were transported on the decks of submarines, and were launched when close to the operational area.

The last flowering of Japanese submarine design was typically ambitious. In 1942 they ordered 17 of the Type STo, the largest submarines ever seen up to that time. These were the famous *I400* Class, an amalgamation of the Type A, B and C submarines, to produce an aircraft-carrying boat which could attack the Panama Canal. For this purpose they were meant to carry two seaplane bombers, but were altered to carry three in the hangar. In layout they followed the previous big submarines, but to keep the draught down as much as possible a peculiar double cylindrical hull was tried, with the cylinders side-by-side. The armament was heavy, eight 21-in bow torpedo-tubes with 20 reloads, and four torpedoes and 15 bombs carried for the seaplanes.

Only three of these giants were completed by August 1945, when Japan capitulated. When American technical experts examined them they found a lot of evidence of technical assistance from the Germans. Many German U-Boats had made trips out to the Far East to collect cargoes of rubber, tin and wolfram, and the Japanese had been very anxious to copy the features which made these boats so superior to their own. The *I400* Class had a schnorchel, and even had the same rubber coating on the hull which was being tried out in Germany as a means of absorbing Asdic pulses.

Costly failure

It would not be correct to suggest that the Japanese submarine effort was only directed towards large submarines, because in one way they anticipated the Germans in developing a boat with high underwater speed. In 1937/38 they built *No.71* in conditions of utmost secrecy, even to the point of launching her behind a smokescreen. She was small, only 140 ft long and displacing 213 tons on the surface, but she reached 21 knots under water. Although she never entered service, being nothing more than an experimental boat, she revived the ideas which had been tested and forgotten with the British 'R' Class twenty years earlier. During the war two operational classes were built to develop her ideas, the small *Ha201* Class and the larger *I201*s.

Despite these interesting developments the Japanese submarine effort during the

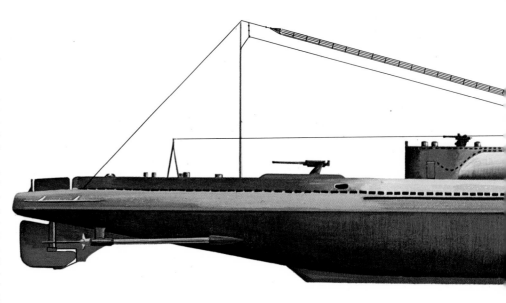

American 5-in Submarine Gun
The 5-in/25 cal. Mk XIII gun shown was mounted on board USS *Tigrone* (SS419), one of the few *Tench* Class to be completed before the end of the war. Many weapons were carried by US submarines, but this pattern was the most popular. *Weight:* 2·7 tons *Range:* 14,500 yards at 40° elevation *Weight of shell:* 53 lb

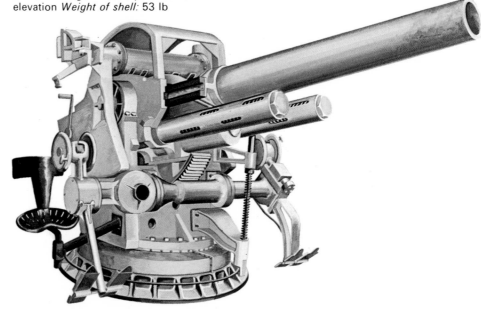

Japanese *I70*
The lack of numerical sequence makes Japanese submarine classes hard to follow; *I70*'s sisters were renumbered *I168–169* and *I171–172*. They were big ocean-going submarines with a range of 14,000 miles on the surface. *I70* was sunk by carrier aircraft only three days after the attack on Pearl Harbor. *Displacement:* 1,785 tons (surfaced) *Armament:* Six 21-in torpedo-tubes; 14 torpedoes carried; one 3·9-in AA gun; one 13-mm machine-gun *Speed:* 23 knots (surfaced) 8¼ knots (submerged)

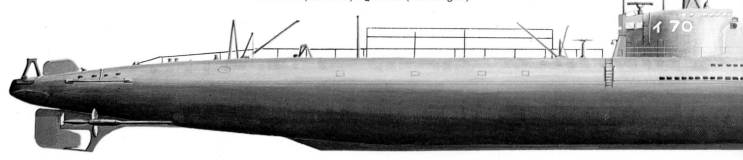

Japanese *I402*

The *I400* Class were ordered under the modified 1942 programme and were the largest submarines built up to that time. The intention was to provide them with three seaplane bombers in order to attack the Panama Canal, but the aircraft never reached production. Only three boats were completed by August 1945, and they were surrendered to the American occupying forces. *Displacement:* 5,223 tons (surfaced) *Armament:* Eight 21-in torpedo-tubes; 20 torpedoes carried; one 5·5-in gun; ten 25-mm AA guns

Second World War was a costly failure. Losses were extremely heavy; out of 245 submarines which served in the war (excluding ex-German and Italian boats taken over and midgets) 149 were sunk, a loss ratio of 60 per cent. There were few successes to match the exploits of the Germans, largely because the peacetime policy and training had proved totally wrong. The only successes of the aircraft-submarine tactics which the Japanese had developed so diligently came in 1942; a scout plane reconnoitred Diego Suarez harbour before a midget was sent in to torpedo a British battleship and another tried to set the Oregon pine forests alight with incendiary bombs. Otherwise this costly programme was entirely wasted.

Japanese 'Kairyu' Suicide Midget

The Type A midget was developed into a suicide boat, but production difficulties made it impossible to find engines or torpedoes for many of them. Over 200 were built. *Displacement:* 19¼ tons (submerged) *Armament:* Two 18-in torpedoes or a nose-charge of 600 Kg TNT *Speed:* 17½ knots (surfaced) 10 knots (submerged)

By the end of 1942 the first Japanese submarines had been converted to run supplies to beleaguered Army garrisons on outlying islands, and this was to be the fate of the majority of the larger boats. Armament was reduced and the casing was modified to carry a 'Daihatsu' landing craft or such items as amphibious tanks. Although the Imperial Japanese Navy prided itself on its aggressive attitude to sea power, it allowed the Army to dictate requirements to the extent that its powerful submarine force was reduced to a supply service. Had those same submarines been put to better use they might have had far more effect on the war to the benefit of both Army and Navy, but as it was they suffered heavy losses in running food and ammunition to garrisons who were already doomed. When the surviving submarines were converted back into *Kaiten* carriers it did at least bring them back to a fighting role, but by then it was too late.

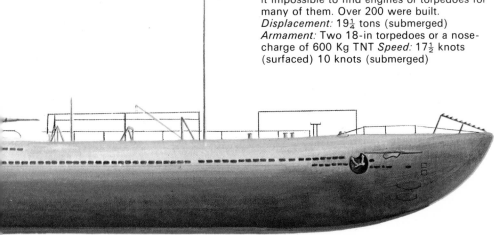

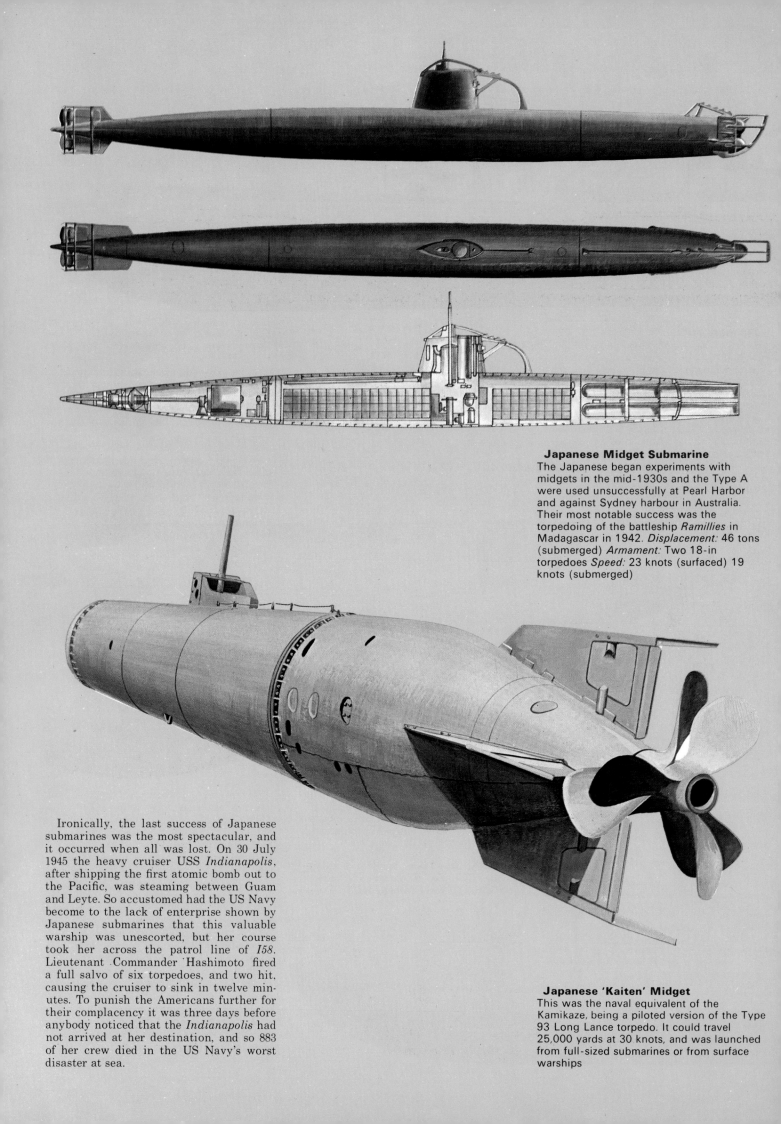

Japanese Midget Submarine
The Japanese began experiments with midgets in the mid-1930s and the Type A were used unsuccessfully at Pearl Harbor and against Sydney harbour in Australia. Their most notable success was the torpedoing of the battleship *Ramillies* in Madagascar in 1942. *Displacement:* 46 tons (submerged) *Armament:* Two 18-in torpedoes *Speed:* 23 knots (surfaced) 19 knots (submerged)

Ironically, the last success of Japanese submarines was the most spectacular, and it occurred when all was lost. On 30 July 1945 the heavy cruiser USS *Indianapolis*, after shipping the first atomic bomb out to the Pacific, was steaming between Guam and Leyte. So accustomed had the US Navy become to the lack of enterprise shown by Japanese submarines that this valuable warship was unescorted, but her course took her across the patrol line of *I58*. Lieutenant Commander Hashimoto fired a full salvo of six torpedoes, and two hit, causing the cruiser to sink in twelve minutes. To punish the Americans further for their complacency it was three days before anybody noticed that the *Indianapolis* had not arrived at her destination, and so 883 of her crew died in the US Navy's worst disaster at sea.

Japanese 'Kaiten' Midget
This was the naval equivalent of the Kamikaze, being a piloted version of the Type 93 Long Lance torpedo. It could travel 25,000 yards at 30 knots, and was launched from full-sized submarines or from surface warships

SUBMARINES SINCE THE WAR

Nuclear Submarines

The Blöhm und Voss shipyard at Hamburg after its capture by the British in 1945. Submarines are in various stages of construction.

As soon as Germany had surrendered to the victorious Allies, teams of intelligence officers and submarine experts moved into German shipyards and naval bases to seize as much as they could. Naturally there had been widespread sabotage and destruction of material by bombing, but the British, Americans and Russians were able to locate examples of the Type XXI, and even the few Walther boats which had been completed. In addition the British and Americans had the pick of all the U-Boats which had been interned at Lisahally in accordance with the surrender terms. Similarly when Japan capitulated in August 1945 large numbers of Japanese submarines fell into Allied hands.

Naturally, everybody was most interested in the Type XXI, as it proved to be a sound design. The Walther boats were treated with more reserve, mainly because it was going to take some time to find out how to work them. The Russians obtained some Walther hulls, and even went to the length

of loading the incomplete aircraft carrier *Graf Zeppelin* with U-Boat hull sections in her hangar; their enthusiasm over-reached itself, and the towed hulk sank after hitting a mine in the Gulf of Finland.

All navies knew how close the Allies had come to defeat at the hands of the U-Boats, and so the years immediately after 1945 were marked by prolonged experiments in submarine design, and also in anti-submarine warfare. The Type XXI features, the streamlined hull and large battery capacity, were immediately incorporated into new designs. The deck gun began to disappear, for it caused too much drag, and the former bulky conning tower with its platforms and periscope standards was streamlined into a fin, known in the USN as a 'sail'. The schnorchel became a standard fitting, known in American submarines as a 'snorkel' and by the

British it was referred to as a 'snort'.

Propulsion remained the tried and proven diesel-electric drive for the moment, but the Walther turbine promised the dream of a 'true submarine', independent of outside oxygen. The three major submarine powers, Great Britain, the United States and Soviet Russia all experimented with the idea, although the Americans soon decided to drop it because of its complexities. The Russian experiments remain shrouded in secrecy to this day, although it is known that Walther-engined boats were tested. The British ran the salvaged *U1407* as HMS *Meteorite* from 1946 to 1950. She was regarded as about 75 per cent safe, and her crew were doubtless thankful to see the last of her. But she spawned two improved versions, the 225-ft *Explorer* and *Excalibur*, which entered service in 1956–58.

These two submarines were not unnaturally known as the 'blonde' submarines because of their peroxide fuel. They served a useful purpose in as much as they gave the

Royal Navy's anti-submarine forces some valuable practice against fast targets. Their main use, however, was to prove finally that the Walther system was only a stopgap. There was more than one contemporary report of explosions in the two submarines, and at least one instance when the entire crew was forced to stand on the casing to avoid the noxious fumes which had suddenly filled the boat.

The reason the Americans had been so lukewarm towards the Walther system was that they had practical experience of nuclear energy. When the war ended the only use made of nuclear power had been in the form of bombs, but it was clear that a controlled reaction would be feasible. Nuclear energy provides a limitless source of heat, and makes no demands on oxygen for combustion. The disadvantage was merely that of weight and size, for a reactor needs thick lead shielding to prevent radiation, quite apart from its bulk. Therefore American nuclear physicists bent their research towards producing a reactor small enough to power a submarine.

While the designers were groping towards nuclear propulsion, the immediate problem for the US Navy was to modernise their

Russian 'W' Class

This class, like so many others, clearly owed much to the German Type XXI, and was probably begun as soon as Soviet designers had absorbed all the knowledge gained after the German surrender. The first units appeared in 1950 and about 200 were built by 1958. Many of these are now serving with satellite navies, and the class is obsolescent. *Displacement:* 1,030 tons (surfaced) *Armament:* Six 21-in torpedo-tubes (four forward, two aft) eighteen torpedoes carried *Speed:* 17 knots (surfaced) 15 knots (submerged)

submarine fleet to incorporate all the lessons of the war. A number of the *Tench* Class were completing to a slightly improved *Balao* design, and they were altered. The new design was known as the 'Guppy' type, standing for Greater Underwater Propulsive Power, and incorporated a lengthened and streamlined hull with larger batteries, as well as a modified sail and snorkel.

Many of the older *Gato* and *Balao* classes were converted in similar fashion, but even more were allocated to experimental duties.

British *Amphion*

For the Pacific, the Royal Navy needed a larger submarine with more endurance, and the 'A' Class resulted. They were not as large as the American boats, but they had air-conditioning and a radius of action of 10,000 miles. The early boats like *Amphion* had a low bow, but after trials this was raised

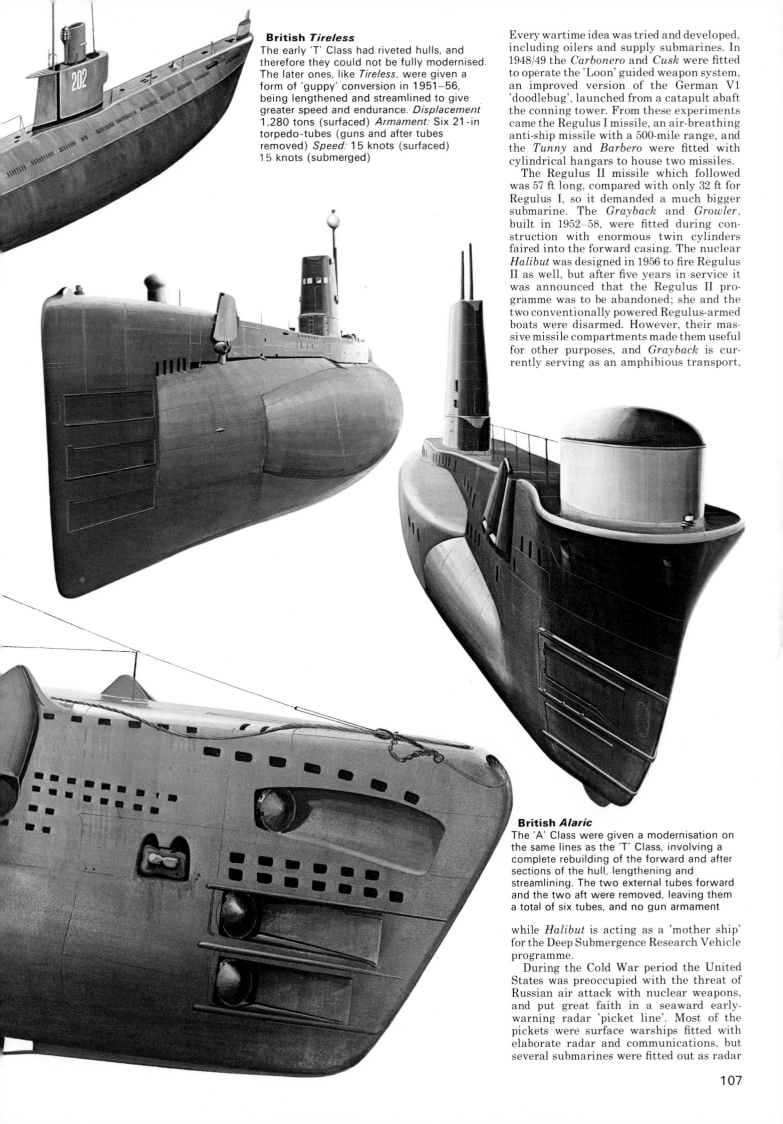

British _Tireless_
The early 'T' Class had riveted hulls, and therefore they could not be fully modernised. The later ones, like _Tireless_, were given a form of 'guppy' conversion in 1951–56, being lengthened and streamlined to give greater speed and endurance. _Displacement_ 1,280 tons (surfaced) _Armament:_ Six 21-in torpedo-tubes (guns and after tubes removed) _Speed:_ 15 knots (surfaced) 15 knots (submerged)

Every wartime idea was tried and developed, including oilers and supply submarines. In 1948/49 the _Carbonero_ and _Cusk_ were fitted to operate the 'Loon' guided weapon system, an improved version of the German V1 'doodlebug', launched from a catapult abaft the conning tower. From these experiments came the Regulus I missile, an air-breathing anti-ship missile with a 500-mile range, and the _Tunny_ and _Barbero_ were fitted with cylindrical hangars to house two missiles.

The Regulus II missile which followed was 57 ft long, compared with only 32 ft for Regulus I, so it demanded a much bigger submarine. The _Grayback_ and _Growler_, built in 1952–58, were fitted during construction with enormous twin cylinders faired into the forward casing. The nuclear _Halibut_ was designed in 1956 to fire Regulus II as well, but after five years in service it was announced that the Regulus II programme was to be abandoned; she and the two conventionally powered Regulus-armed boats were disarmed. However, their massive missile compartments made them useful for other purposes, and _Grayback_ is currently serving as an amphibious transport,

British _Alaric_
The 'A' Class were given a modernisation on the same lines as the 'T' Class, involving a complete rebuilding of the forward and after sections of the hull, lengthening and streamlining. The two external tubes forward and the two aft were removed, leaving them a total of six tubes, and no gun armament

while _Halibut_ is acting as a 'mother ship' for the Deep Submergence Research Vehicle programme.

During the Cold War period the United States was preoccupied with the threat of Russian air attack with nuclear weapons, and put great faith in a seaward early-warning radar 'picket line'. Most of the pickets were surface warships fitted with elaborate radar and communications, but several submarines were fitted out as radar

Russian Z-V Type

Between 1958 and 1961 seven of the conventional 'Z' Class were rebuilt to fire two ballistic missiles. This was part of a crash programme to counter the US Navy's sudden breakthrough in perfecting the Polaris system, but unlike the American boats these Russian conversions had to launch their missiles on the surface. None are now operational

Russian 'G' Class

This was an improved version of the Z-V Class, with three ballistic missiles. The 22 boats of this class now have the 650-mile range Serb (SS-N-5) missile in place of the older Sark, and an additional unit of the class was built in China

British *Oberon* Class

The thirteen *Oberons* are the Royal Navy's latest conventional submersibles, and also its most successful export design, as a number have been built for other navies. They embody many features of the German Type XXI, and have the reputation of being the most silent submarines in service.
Displacement: 1,610 tons (surfaced)
Armament: Eight 21-in torpedo-tubes (6 forward, 2 aft); 30 torpedoes carried *Speed:* 12 knots (surfaced) 17 knots (submerged)

pickets to provide more flexibility. This led to the construction of an enormous nuclear radar picket submarine, the *Triton*. She was the largest submarine ever built at the time (1959) and had two nuclear reactors; this power enabled her to circumnavigate the world submerged in 1960, a 41,500-mile voyage at an average speed of 18 knots.

All this time Russia's submarine force remained an enigma. Armed with as much information about German developments as her technicians could get, she worked hard

to modernise her fleet. By the early 1950s the first of the new 'W' Class were seen; although claimed to have been started in 1944 it is clear that they owed a lot to the Type XXI. They became the standard post-war type, and many were transferred to other navies. In 1961 work began on converting twelve to missile-firing submarines on the lines of the American *Tunny* and *Barbero*. One boat carried a single Shaddock surface-to-surface missile in a cylinder which elevated 20–25° for firing, but others

carried twin cylinders, and the third variant carried four Shaddock cylinders faired into a streamlined fin. There was also a radar picket version.

The next Russian submarine type to appear was the 'Z' Class, whose existence was doubted until 1952, when the first blurred photographs appeared in Western magazines. This was the class which was reputed to have tried the Walther propulsion system in the first few units, but the remainder quickly reverted to diesel-electric

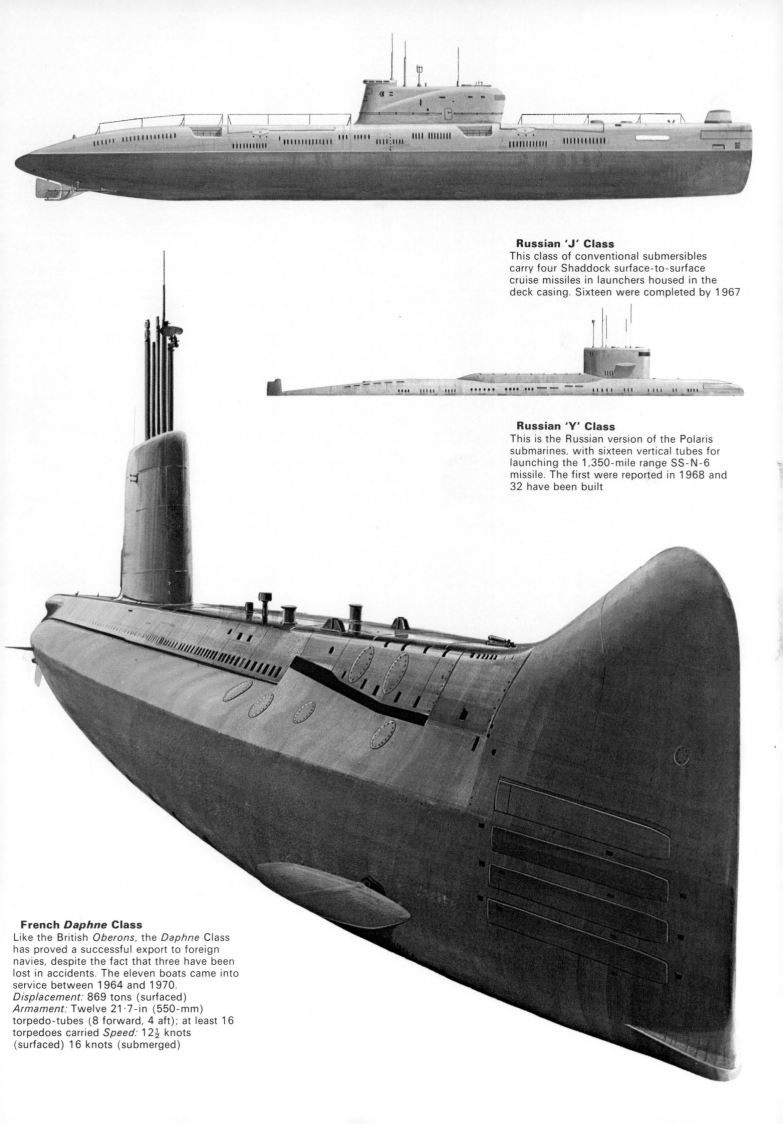

Russian 'J' Class
This class of conventional submersibles carry four Shaddock surface-to-surface cruise missiles in launchers housed in the deck casing. Sixteen were completed by 1967

Russian 'Y' Class
This is the Russian version of the Polaris submarines, with sixteen vertical tubes for launching the 1,350-mile range SS-N-6 missile. The first were reported in 1968 and 32 have been built

French *Daphne* Class
Like the British *Oberons*, the *Daphne* Class has proved a successful export to foreign navies, despite the fact that three have been lost in accidents. The eleven boats came into service between 1964 and 1970.
Displacement: 869 tons (surfaced)
Armament: Twelve 21·7-in (550-mm) torpedo-tubes (8 forward, 4 aft); at least 16 torpedoes carried *Speed:* 12½ knots (surfaced) 16 knots (submerged)

propulsion. They were more closely related to the Type XXI than the previous class, and at least 25 were built. A further ten were converted to fire two ballistic missiles from vertical tubes in the fin, and a slightly enlarged version called the 'G' Class was built at the same time to fire three missiles.

Great importance was attached in Western newspapers throughout the 1950s to the size of the Russian submarine fleet, but at the time its numbers were swollen by the large number of obsolescent 'M', 'S' and 'Shch' Class and other boats which had survived the Second World War. When the new construction came into service it was possible to pay off these old submarines, and by the end of the decade it is doubtful if any were still used for anything but training.

The best submersibles

The Royal Navy contented itself with modernising its 'T' and 'A' Class boats during the 1950s, along the lines of the American 'Guppy' programme. Unfortunately the earlier 'Ts' and the 'S' Class had riveted hulls, which made them unsuitable for modernisation, but several were modified for experimental work. At the same time a new class of submarines was built to incorporate the latest ideas. These were known as the *Porpoise* Class, and they were followed by the very similar *Oberon* Class, which acquired an enviable reputation for reliability and quietness. Since 1962 a total of 14 have been sold to foreign buyers, and they are regarded as the best conventional submersibles available.

The French had to rebuild their submarine force from scratch after the war. Apart from a handful of worn-out pre-war submarines, and some borrowed from the British, they had only five incomplete hulls which were worth rebuilding. Taking advantage of a British offer of four 'S' Class for training, they set to work to redesign the five *Creole* Class hulls which had survived the war. These came into service between 1946 and 1953, and lessons were incorporated in the six *Narval* Class built in 1951–5. Two more classes were designed in the 1950s, of which the later *Daphne* Class of 1957–67 proved as commercially successful as the British *Oberons*.

Holland found herself in a similar situation in 1945, with her fleet comprising worn-out or borrowed submarines. In 1954 the *Dolfijn*, first of a unique class, was laid down. She had a triple hull, with three separate cylinders disposed in a triangle. This novel idea had the advantage of making better use of the internal space available, and also gave great strength, but it has not been repeated in any other navy.

The Swedish Navy had not suffered any loss, being neutral in the Second World War, but to maintain that neutrality it was necessary to keep abreast of developments. The *Sjölojenet* Class was streamlined and modernised, and four new classes were built. Of these the *Sjöormen* Class is the latest. The other Scandinavian navies also continued the tradition of building submarines in their own yards. The exception was Finland, which had to pay a heavy price for being on the wrong side in the war, and was forbidden to possess submarines.

The other Baltic navy to get back into the submarine business was, inevitably, Germany. In 1956 two sunken Type XXIII boats were salvaged and reconditioned for training duties as the *Hai* and *Hecht*. A third boat, the former Type XXI *U2540*, was in 1960

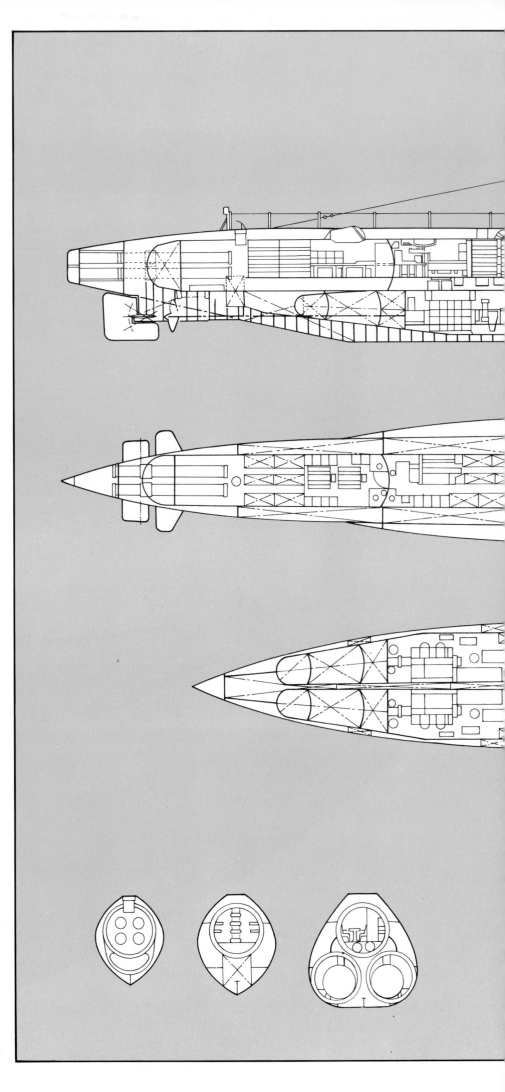

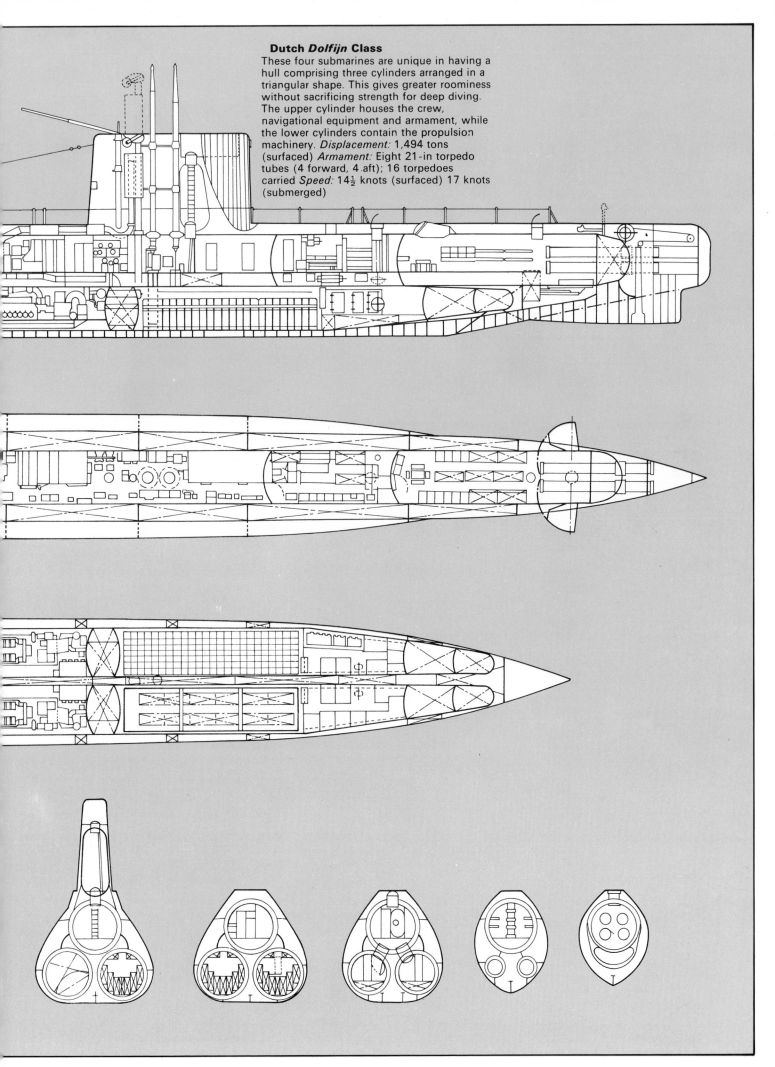

Dutch *Dolfijn* Class
These four submarines are unique in having a hull comprising three cylinders arranged in a triangular shape. This gives greater roominess without sacrificing strength for deep diving. The upper cylinder houses the crew, navigational equipment and armament, while the lower cylinders contain the propulsion machinery. *Displacement:* 1,494 tons (surfaced) *Armament:* Eight 21-in torpedo tubes (4 forward, 4 aft); 16 torpedoes carried *Speed:* $14\frac{1}{2}$ knots (surfaced) 17 knots (submerged)

recommissioned as the *Wilhelm Bauer*, and has been used for research purposes. The first indigenous design appeared in 1961, when *U1* was launched at Kiel but *U1* and *U2* had to be rebuilt to remedy structural weakness.

Meanwhile the Americans had been developing the concept of the 'hunter-killer' submarine, using ultra-sensitive listening gear and improved Asdic, known as Sonar in the USN. The submarine makes a good anti-submarine weapon, primarily because she is operating in the same medium as her quarry, but perfection of the techniques had to wait for new silent-running motors and efficient tracking gear. A serious disadvantage is that she has to operate virtually 'blind', without the rapid communication and readily accessible visual data available to surface ships. But the real weakness is that despite all the improvements in propulsion and streamlining, a 'fast' underwater submarine is only fast for a matter of

American *George Washington (SSBN598)*

This was the West's first submarine to be armed with ballistic missiles, and was a result of President Kennedy's acceleration of the Polaris development programme. She fired two of her sixteen missiles for the first time in July 1960. To bring Polaris into service as quickly as possible, five modified *Skipjack* type hulls were lengthened by 130 ft to accommodate the launching tubes. *Displacement:* 5,900 tons (surfaced) *Armament:* Sixteen Polaris intermediate range ballistic missiles; six 21-in torpedo-tubes *Speed:* 20 knots (surfaced) 25–30 knots (submerged)

hours, and must slow down before she exhausts her batteries. Until nuclear power was a reality, this was the obstacle to further progress.

The first water-cooled reactor was ready in 1952, when the USS *Nautilus* was begun. It took submarine propulsion back nearly 50 years to the days of the French and British steam-powered submarines, for the only way to use the heat of a nuclear reactor is to convert water to steam. Thus the *Nautilus* was driven by twin-shaft geared steam turbines, which developed 13,400 shaft horsepower and drove her at approximately 20 knots underwater. Her size inevitably made her clumsier than any wartime submarine, but it had its hidden advantages; only a large hull could provide the crew comfort necessary to support the high endurance provided by nuclear propulsion. In other words, the designers had come up against an old truism in submarine design: that crew efficiency is related to size, and even if a much smaller reactor could have been produced, the crew of a smaller submarine could not cruise submerged for extended periods.

Official US Navy Photograph

A rare picture of an American submarine in dry dock – the *Barbel (SS580)*

The size of the *Nautilus*, about 3,500 tons on the surface, and a three-decked hull over 300 ft long, allowed her 100 crew members a standard of accommodation which was better in some ways than surface ships of the same size. And they needed it, for in 1955, when *Nautilus* was completed, she made a run from New London to Puerto Rico fully submerged. This feat was eclipsed by her submerged crossing of the North Pole on 3 August 1958, when she proved to the world that a new era of submarine warfare had begun. Between 1955 and 1957 she steamed 62,562 miles on the original core of uranium, then logged 91,324 miles on her second core, and about 150,000 miles on the third.

In 1957 a second nuclear submarine was completed, the USS *Seawolf*. Slightly larger than the *Nautilus*, she was built to test another type of reactor using liquid sodium as a coolant in place of pressurised water. Although not as successful as the other prototype, she provided valuable experience for the first 'production models', the four *Skate* Class, which were completed in 1957–59. Their success convinced the US Navy that all future submarines should be nuclear-powered, and that decision marked a personal triumph for Admiral Hyman Rickover, who has been aptly named the 'Father of the Nuclear Submarine'.

Official US Navy photograph

The USS *Ray (SSN653)* shown here is an attack submarine of the *Sturgeon* Class, the largest group of nuclear submarines built to one design. They are intended to seek out and destroy other submarines and have their four torpedo-tubes amidships, to leave the bow position clear for a large sonar

In 1952 an experimental submarine had been ordered as a 'Hydro-dynamic test vehicle'. As the USS *Albacore* she entered service at the end of 1953. She revolutionised submarine design, because her 'teardrop' hull form gave more speed and manoeuvrability than any submarine had ever had. Her whale-shaped hull had no deck-casing, and the 'sail' was reduced to a thin dorsal fin. Since first commissioning, the *Albacore* has tested a variety of advanced equipment, but her main features have become the standard for later submarines; in particular the circular hull-sections and the single propeller shaft are a repetition of the British 'R' Class of 1918.

The next development of the nuclear submarine was a revival of a German project to launch a V2 ballistic missile from a pod towed by a submarine. Being a liquid-fuelled rocket, the V2 was ill-suited for use at sea, but postwar progress with solid fuels led to the Polaris missile system. This is a submarine-launched intermediate range ballistic missile (IRBM) capable of being fired from below the surface of the sea. It offers three main advantages over the big land-based inter-continental ballistic missiles (ICBM):

1 By moving the launching point out to sea the likelihood of a pre-emptive attack by enemy ICBMs is reduced.
2 Since the furthest point on land is only about 1,700 miles from the sea, the Polaris missile needs much less fuel than ICBMs, and can be smaller.
3 The difficulty of finding submarines in the oceans of the world means that in the foreseeable future there is no counter-measure.

Polaris works on a very simple principle of physics, the fact that water is incompressible; a missile is ejected from the submarine by gas or steam, its rocket motor ignites as it leaves the water, and the resulting downblast uses the 'hard' water underneath as a launching pad.

One major problem had to be solved before the Polaris system could be made to work, that of navigation. As a nuclear submarine dare not surface frequently to check her position by star-sights or radio-fixes, prolonged submarine voyages demand a much higher standard of navigation than ever before. The answer came in the SINS, the Ship's Inertial Navigation System, basically a computerised method of checking the vessel's actual movement from her point of departure by means of accelero-meters and gyroscopes. With SINS to track all drift and movement a nuclear submarine can dispense with magnetic compasses and dead reckoning errors, which makes a journey under the North Polar ice cap feasible. Furthermore, since a Polaris missile needs to know the distance to its target, it can be updated constantly by a fire control computer adjusting the firing trajectory from data provided by SINS.

Another problem created by Polaris and nuclear propulsion was habitability. If maximum benefit was to be gained from a submarine with virtually unlimited endurance, the human element had to be catered for. Intensive research into ventilation systems showed that it might be pos-

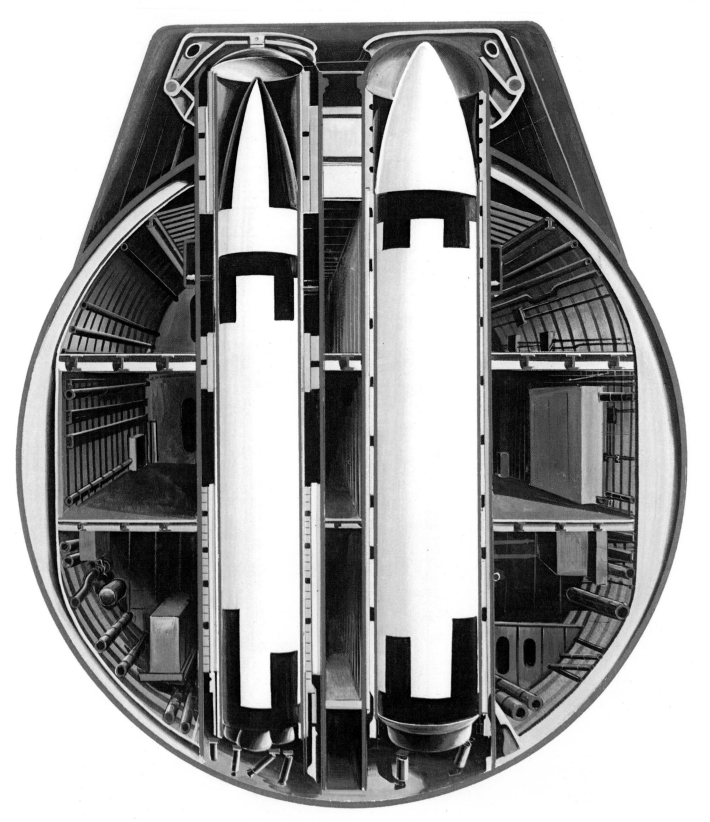

Diagram of Fleet Ballistic Missile System

Ship's Inertial Navigation System (SINS) maintains constant plot of ship's position for navigation and fire control

Fire Control computers receive information on ship's location and true north (from SINS), target locations and other information, and compute on a continuous basis trajectory information for rapid transmission to missile memory

Missile test and readiness equipment (MTRE) provides complete readiness checkout of all missiles and associated equipments

Launcher control prepares the 16 missile tubes for launch, including pressurization to insure that when the missile hatch is opened the tube remains free of water until missile is launched

Missile guidance 'memory' receives and stores trajectory data from the fire control system

Missile Control panel reflects status of all missiles. Sequence of missiles to be fired is selected here, and final launching circuit is closed here after captain has given permission to fire

Once all events have taken place to enable launch, closing firing key causes gas generator to ignite, whose exhaust forces missile out of tube

Only after it is safely out of the launch tube does missile ignite, to protect crew and ship. Once launched, the inertial guidance system in the missile directs the remainder of flight free of outside control

US Navy

Polaris and Poseidon Compared (left)
This section through a US nuclear submarine shows the installation of an A-3 Polaris on the left, and its successor Poseidon on the right. They would never be installed together

American *Skipjack*
In 1959 the *Skipjack* introduced the revolutionary 'teardrop' hull which gave much greater speed and manoeuvrability than the older type of hull. The rounded casing is reminiscent of a whale, and makes for bad handling on the surface, but once submerged the submarine performs far better

Russian *Leninskii Komsomol*
In 1963 the Russians reported that this submarine had crossed under the North Polar ice cap. She is one of the 'N' Class, the first Soviet nuclear fleet submarines to enter service. The small conning tower set far forward is a feature of this class and of the improved 'V' Class. *Displacement:* 3,500 tons (surfaced) *Armament:* Six 21-in; four 16-in torpedo-tubes *Speed:* 20 knots (surfaced) 25 knots (submerged)

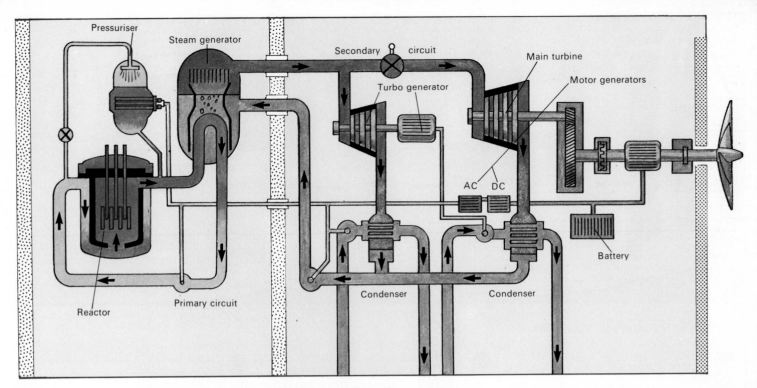

Nuclear Propulsion Power Plant
This diagram shows the basic components of the propulsion system of a nuclear submarine

sible to extend a submarine's submerged endurance to three months or more by re-cycling the air – in other words, making the crew breathe their own air after it had been refreshed with oxygen and 'scrubbed' to remove toxic gases. Many interesting points came to light, particularly the need to have paints which did not give off toxic vapours, but now nuclear submarines are limited only by the endurance of their crews. This gives the submarine the same advantage that used to be enjoyed by the sailing ship – independence of bases as long as the food and water last.

The accumulation of waste causes severe problems as a hundred men will account for a large amount of potato peelings: the latest submarines are big, but they do not have unlimited space, and it is not always safe to jettison rubbish. For the same reason modern submarines have self-contained sewage systems which are pumped out when they return to base; this is also necessary because the pressure at great depths makes flushing the 'head' too difficult. Because of the extended cruise period, colours of furniture and furnishings have to be brighter and more harmonious than they were, especially as they are always seen by artificial light.

Fortunately their great size allows nuclear submarines to have three decks, and so the accommodation can be made spacious. Crew comfort helps to reduce the strain of long patrols, but it is also necessary to provide films and gymnastic apparatus to fight boredom and lack of exercise.

As soon as the United States Government knew that the A-1 Polaris missile was workable, permission was given to build the first of a fleet of 41 submarines, each capable of launching 16 Polaris missiles. As each missile's H-Bomb warhead was equal in power to all the high-explosive bombs dropped in the Second World War, the deterrent effect of such a system was obvious. Before the end of 1957 two newly ordered attack submarines had been redesignated Polaris submarines. A further three followed in 1958, and the five became the *George Washington* Class, the first Fleet Ballistic Missile (FBM) submarines in the world. To mark their importance,

both in size and purpose, they were also the first USN submarines to be named after people rather than reptiles or fishes.

The next class, the five *Ethan Allen* Class, differed principally in being properly designed for their task, rather than hurriedly adapted from a smaller type. They and the 31 *Lafayette* Class which followed from 1960 onwards were better arranged internally than the original *George Washingtons*, and had improvements such as quieter machinery, but they retain the basic layout of two rows of eight missile tubes abaft the 'sail'.

The arms race begins
The news of the success of Polaris, after many pundits had said it would not be ready for another ten years, spurred the Soviet Navy on to develop a similar underwater deterrent. As we have seen, some of their conventional submersibles had been modified to fire two or three surface-to-surface missiles, but in 1958 work began on converting the first of ten 'Z' Class to fire IRBMs. The same system was used as before, two or three tubes housed in the fin, which opened like a clam shell to allow firing. Thirty 'G' Class were specially built for the job, and then came the nuclear powered 'H' Class, still using the same system. Not until 1968 did the first news leak out of a Russian version of the Polaris system, when the 'Y' Class appeared, with a very similar configuration to the American boats. Incidentally, all Russian class-designations are those assigned by NATO and bear no relation to what the Red Fleet may call them.

The first Russian nuclear hunter-killer submarines came into service between 1961 and 1963. Known in the West as the 'N' or 'November' Class, they numbered 15 units, and at least two were named. The *Leninskii Komsomol* emulated the *Nautilus* in the summer of 1962 by crossing the North Pole submerged, but in 1970 one of the class sank south-west of the British Isles. The 'V' or 'Victor' Class which followed were generally similar but greatly improved in detail, and

the 12 in service command a high reputation in Western intelligence circles.

The next country to build nuclear submarines was Great Britain, which had been experimenting with nuclear energy for some years. To save time a reactor was bought from the United States in 1958, to power HMS *Dreadnought*, the Royal Navy's first 'nuke', and the British reactor went into a second prototype, HMS *Valiant*, two years later. Since then a further two classes have been ordered, making a total of seven completed and four building. In 1963 it was announced that the Royal Navy would buy the A-3 Polaris weapon system from the United States and install it in their own hulls. These materialised in 1967–69 as the four *Resolution* Class, which replaced the

RAF's bomber force as Great Britain's strategic deterrent.

France was hardly likely to allow the British to have an 'independent' nuclear deterrent, but when the United States refused to supply Polaris missiles they went ahead with their own version, the MSBS M-1 (Mer-Sol-Balistique-Stratégique). A nuclear submarine had been laid down in 1958, but after being cancelled a year later she was redesigned as an experimental submarine to test the missiles and other equipment, and was appropriately named *Gymnote* after Gustave Zedé's prototype. She fired the first ballistic missiles, but the first operational FBM, *Le Redoutable*, did not come into service until 1971.

Apart from the People's Republic of China, whose intentions remain inscrutable, the only other country to contemplate the huge expense of nuclear propulsion was Holland. However, the two hulls planned in the early 1960s were replaced by conventional submarines, leaving only four navies with nuclear submarines. Red China certainly has the capability to build both nuclear submarines and Polaris-type missiles, but apart from a mysterious sighting of an *Albacore*-hulled submarine under construction in 1969, nothing is known.

The US Navy has improved the firepower of its later FBM submarines by arming them with the more powerful Poseidon missile. Very similar in appearance to the A-3 Polaris, Poseidon is two feet wider in diameter and three feet taller, but this modest increase in dimensions conceals many differences. Poseidon has twice the payload, which allows it to carry multiple warheads; this makes counter-measures even harder than before, since each missile can have three possible targets. The modifications include alterations to the missile tubes and replacement of the fire control system.

Despite the clear advantages of nuclear propulsion, conventional submersibles are still being designed and built. Nor are they confined to the smaller navies who cannot afford the cost of nuclear boats, for a new class of Russian diesel-electric submarines has been seen. One reason for this is that nuclear propulsion makes very heavy demands on skilled personnel, quite apart from its cost, and another is that the size of present-day nuclear submarines makes them unsuitable for coastal waters. There are areas in which small submersibles can function more effectively than the big fleet types, and so there are a number of French, British and German designs available for sale to foreign buyers.

Today the submarine represents the most potent naval weapon available. The nuclear submarine in particular represents a terrible threat to all surface warships, for her speed enables her to close in, attack with a variety of weapons such as guided torpedoes or even missiles, and then withdraw at high speed. The awesome destructive power of Polaris has already been described, but its value is enhanced because, unlike any other submarine weapon, it can be fired at a range of 2,000 miles or more. Even today the old convoy maxim holds good, that an attack submarine must sooner or later approach her target, and thus risk a counter-attack; a Polaris submarine, on the other hand, *avoids* all contact, and so she has the world's oceans in which to hide.

The future of the submarine could hardly be brighter. Advances in the design of nuclear reactors will probably reduce their size, and new weapons will increase their capabilities. But their great potential is also stimulating research on counter-measures. By the end of the 1970s we might well see a breakthrough similar in its effect to Asdic, such as a device to enable submarines to be tracked from satellites. Until then the submarine will continue to be the deadly weapon she has become in the last 30 years.

British *Resolution*
The *Resolution* was the first British Polaris or FBM (Fleet Ballistic Missile) submarine to be ordered in 1964. She was commissioned in 1967 as the most powerful warship ever to fly the White Ensign. She and her three sisters are armed with sixteen Polaris A-3 2,300-mile range missiles, with hydrogen bomb warheads. Although the missiles and their fire-control systems are American, the reactor and hull are British-designed, and they differ from the US Navy's submarines in having six bow torpedo-tubes. *Displacement:* 7,500 tons (surfaced)

The Ultimate Warship?

At the start of the Second World War the submarine had only one primary weapon, the thermal torpedo, which was kept on course only by gyroscopic stabilisation. She also carried a deck gun of 3-in to 6-in calibre for use against 'soft-skinned' targets such as merchant ships, but this was essentially an auxiliary weapon. Gyro-angling enabled the torpedo to change its angle during the run, and thus made it easier for a submarine to reach a good attacking position. Magnetic influence pistols were being introduced to make a torpedo explode within lethal distance under a target, like a proximity fuse, but these proved unreliable when first used.

During the war all operational submarines tended to have their anti-aircraft armament increased. This normally meant adding light automatic AA guns of 20-mm to 40-mm calibre on platforms on the conning tower, the most notable examples of this trend being the German U-Boats, which had a 'winter garden' crammed with Flak pieces. The need to reduce drag for high underwater speed put an end to this, and both AA guns and the original deck gun became redundant.

The greatest improvement in torpedo design was the provision of homing devices to enable the torpedo to 'seek' its own target. The German acoustic torpedoes showed the way, and by 1945 there were several patterns under development in both the US Navy and

A torpedo being loaded aboard a British submarine

the Royal Navy. After the war all navies developed similar weapons, but the limitations of acoustic homing (mainly the danger of a torpedo homing on its own submarine's noise) led to the development of wire guided torpedoes.

Wire guidance is very much older than it sounds, for it was the method by which the first Whitehead torpedo was controlled. The Brennan and Nordenfelt torpedoes of the 1880s also relied on a trailing wire paid out from a spool, but today's torpedoes are considerably more complex. Basically, fine wire is paid out from a spool inside the torpedo body, and instructions are sent from the fire control system by impulse down the wire. Even with older patterns of torpedo it has been possible to substitute an umbilical link for the hand-cranked spindles which were formerly used to set the torpedoes before firing.

American submarines have for some time been fitted with Subroc, an advanced weapon system which has no equivalent elsewhere. Briefly, Subroc is fired from a 21-in torpedo tube, and then a rocket motor is fired underwater to lift it clear of the surface and send it on a ballistic course; at the end of its trajectory it re-enters the water and acts as a depth-charge. The essential fire control data is provided by the Passive

Underwater Firecontrol Feasibility System (PUFFS), which takes bearings from propeller noises.

Aircraft, particularly the helicopter with its ability to hover overhead, remain the submarine's worst enemy. At first the only defence was the passive one of providing a sensor at the masthead to detect the noise of a helicopter's engine, but now Vickers Ltd have produced the Submarine Launched Airflight Missile (SLAM) to allow a submarine some means of retaliation. SLAM is an adaptation of the land-based Blowpipe missile, a light close-range ground-to-air weapon which can be fired from the shoulder. It comprises a compact launcher with six missiles, stowed in the fin but raised to fire, and controlled by television guidance from the submarine's control room. In recent trials in the old British submarine *Aeneas*, the system proved successful, and it could seriously reduce the effectiveness of anti-submarine helicopters.

The Polaris system for firing ballistic missiles has already been described, but the Russians are now the only submarine power to employ cruise missiles. The Americans dropped their Regulus I and Regulus II systems because they both involved operation on the surface, which has become too risky for submarines. One wonders, therefore, about the value of the Russian Shaddock and Sark missiles in the early missile submarines.

The ultimate in submarine firepower is the American Trident project, formerly known as the Underwater Long-Range Missile System (ULMS). The project calls for ten submarines of about 15,000 tons displacement (submerged), each one armed with 24 Trident missiles capable of travelling 6,000 miles. The size of missile would permit even more multiple warheads than the Poseidon, as well as decoys and jamming devices to enable its warheads to beat the most advanced defences. The cost is estimated to be $1,000 million per submarine, but the *détente* between Russia and the West will hopefully allow such a terrifying idea to be cancelled.

The depth-charge remained the principal weapon against the submarine throughout the Second World War, although it was supplemented by the aircraft bomb, and by specialised weapons such as Hedgehog. After 1945 a variety of launchers replaced the old-style depth-charge throwers and racks, in order to eliminate the need for an escort to pass over the submarine before dropping her charges.

Quick-reaction defence

The British favoured a three-barrelled mortar firing full-sized depth-charges. The first pattern was the Squid, but it was replaced by the Limbo, which had more range and could be trained over a wider arc. Limbo also had the advantage of being able to pre-set depth-charges with data supplied direct from the Sonar plot, and it remains in service today as a useful quick-reaction defence against a submarine which gets within a mile.

The US Navy and others favoured a rocket projectile to carry the explosive charge to the submarine. There are several versions of this type of weapon such as the now obsolete American Weapon Alfa, the Bofors quadruple launcher and the Norwegian Terne, but they all suffer from the basic weakness of carrying a small explosive charge, which reduces their chances of damaging a submarine.

The homing torpedo has been turned against the submarine, and it makes a

American Twin 20-mm Gun
Many wartime submarines in the Pacific used this twin hand-operated version of the 20-mm Oerlikon light AA gun. It was mounted on a platform on the conning tower or on deck, and was also used against small surface targets

potent weapon, especially when dropped by a helicopter. One way of destroying submarines by homing torpedoes is to programme the torpedo in a descending spiral; another is to use wire guidance. Significantly the three most advanced anti-submarine missile systems in existence today are merely delivery systems for homing torpedoes.

The American Asroc system works like Subroc, but in reverse. It fires a missile on a ballistic trajectory to the target area, and then parachutes a torpedo into the sea. The French Malafon is a 21-in torpedo with

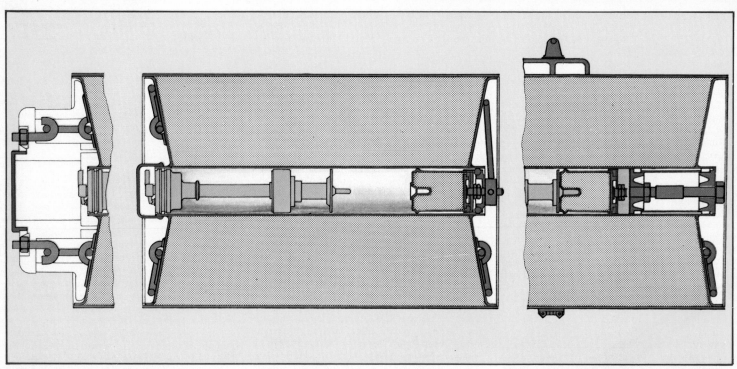

wings and tail, which is launched by rocket and then glides to its target area. The Anglo-Australian Ikara system differs from the earlier two in that the missile is actually a small delta-winged aircraft carrying a torpedo; its virtue is that it can be flown on a revised course to counteract evasive manoeuvres by the submarine, and when it reaches the area the carrier breaks up and releases the homing torpedo.

The original Asdic and hydrophones which were the only detection devices of the Second World War have been much improved and developed. These devices are now known as active and passive Sonar respectively, and the way in which they can be used has changed. Some U-Boats found that they could hide under 'thermal layers' of seawater of a different temperature, which made the Asdic beams bounce

British Depth-charges (above)
Left: The Mk VII (Heavy) was simply a charge with an added weight to make it sink rapidly. *Right:* The Mk VII (Aircraft Pattern) was the first airborne depth-charge. *Centre:* the Mk VII was the standard British depth-charge and differed little from the 'D' Type of the First World War

American Aircraft Depth-charge (below)
During the war considerable time was spent on re-designing the old 'ash-can' shape of the depth-charge to improve its flight-path and its rate of sinking. This was the US Navy's airborne depth-charge

Hedgehog Attack Pattern
The Hedgehog mortar could be fired while the U-Boat was still held in the Asdic beam. The elliptical spread of the bombs was intended to give the best chance of hitting a submarine, and a detonation meant a certain 'kill' except in very shallow water

American K-Gun Depth-charge Projector (right)
A later development of the British wartime depth-charge thrower. Two or three would be mounted on each side of a ship, and set to project a pattern of charges

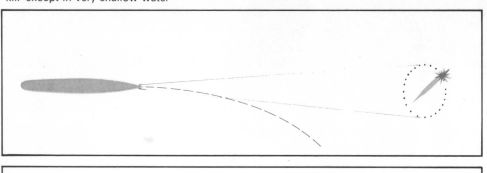

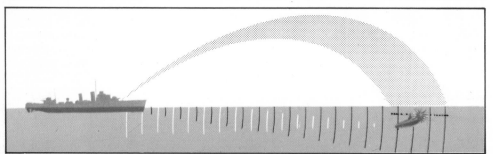

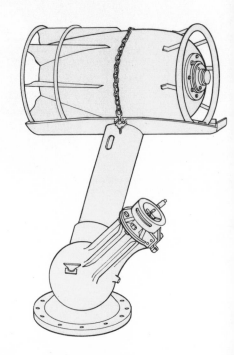

off. This has been countered by the Variable Depth Sonar (VDS), which is simply a Sonar transducer towed behind an escort and lowered to search beneath a thermal layer. The US Navy has developed very powerful Sonar sets, and they are frequently mounted under the bow, where the hull turbulence is at a minimum. Helicopters can use their dipping Sonars for the same purpose, and formidable machines like the Sikorsky Sea King have space for homing torpedoes as well.

However, the most potent anti-submarine weapon which has emerged is the submarine herself. She has many advantages, and they are multiplied by nuclear propulsion. Because she operates below the surface a nuclear hunter-killer suffers no reduction of speed from bad weather, and she can either use a thermal layer for her own protection or simply pass through it. She is her own sonar platform, with performance as good as her opponent's, and if she goes deep the pressure of water will reduce the noise of cavitation from her propeller. Her main problem is that she is operating in a semi-blind situation, and does not have the easy communication enjoyed by surface warships, but this is a small problem to set against her undoubted abilities as a submarine-killer. Here again, we should not be surprised to see a radical improvement within the next few years.

At this point we leave the submarine. She is at the height of her powers, having developed from a crude submersible torpedo-boat to a giant warship capable of cruising at will beneath the surface of the sea. History shows that every weapon is eventually displaced by a new one, but for the moment the submarine has no challenger.

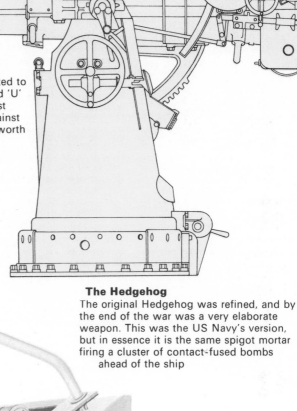

British 3-in Submarine Gun
The 3-in High-Angle gun was fitted to wartime submarines of the 'S' and 'U' Classes to provide defence against aircraft, but it was also useful against land targets or small vessels not worth a torpedo

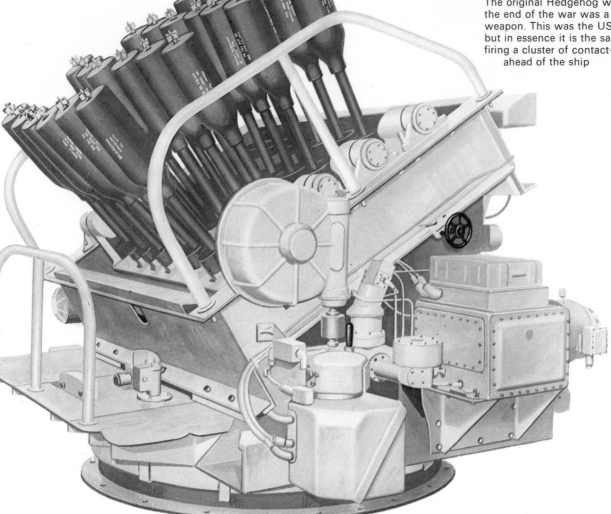

The Hedgehog
The original Hedgehog was refined, and by the end of the war was a very elaborate weapon. This was the US Navy's version, but in essence it is the same spigot mortar firing a cluster of contact-fused bombs ahead of the ship

Index

Acknowledgments

The author and the artist acknowledge their debt to the following institutions: The National Maritime Museum (Greenwich), The Imperial War Museum (Lambeth), The Ministry of Defence (Navy), Science Museum (South Kensington), the Submarine Museum (HMS *Dolphin*), the US Navy History Department, the US National Archives, The Museum of Space and Aeronautics and the Museum of History and Technology (Smithsonian Institution), the Glasgow Museum of Transport, the Musée de la Marine (Paris), ECPA and SIRPA (French Defence Ministry), the Austrian State Archives (Vienna), Norwegian Navy, Marinebund (Germany), Ufficio Storico della Marina Militare (Rome), The Washington Navy Yard Museum, the Bundesarchiv (Freiburg, West Germany), Bibliothek für Zeitgeschicte, the Central Naval Museum (Leningrad), and the Naval Records Club.

They also wish to thank the following people for their unstinting help in locating original material and photographs which would otherwise have been unobtainable: Geoffrey Edbrooke, David Lyon, George Osbon, John Lawson, David Brown, Rear-Admiral P. G. N. Buckley and Miss Riley (Naval Library), Gervais Frere-Cook, Basil Bathe, A. R. Browning, Samuel L. Morison, Arthur D. Baker, Christian Beilstein, Captain Pineau, Mr H. Schwartz, Dr Philip K. Lundeberg, Mr H. Hoffman, Dr Hervé Cras, Henri le Masson, Heinz Kurt Gast, Norbert Krüger, Bodo Herzog, Vice-Admiral H. R. Rousselot, Cdr W. H. Cracknell (USN), Cdr Eriksen (Royal Danish Navy), Cdr Brost (Bundesmarine), Dr Jurgen Rohwer (Bfz, Stuttgart), John Wingate DSC, Cdr D. W. Waters (Deputy Director, NMM), Kozo Izumi, Capt Julius Meyer (Royal Norwegian Navy), Frank Uhlig (US Naval Institute), Cdr Curt Borgenstam (Royal Swedish Navy), and Cdr Aldo Fraccaroli.

Bibliography

Colledge & Dittmar *Royal Navy 1914–1919*
Fraccaroli, Aldo *Italian Warships of World War I*
Fraccaroli, Aldo *Italian Warships of World War II*
Gibson & Prendergast *The U-Boat War*
Grant, Robert M. *U-Boats Sunk*
Grant, Robert M. *U-Boat Intelligence*
Gray, Edwin *Damned Un-English Weapon*
Greger, Rene *The Russian Fleet 1914–17*
Gretton, V-Adm Sir Peter *Crisis Convoy*
Herzog, Bodo *60 Jahre Deutsche U-Boote*
Herzog, Bodo *U-Boats in Action*
Jentschura, Jung & Mickel *Die Japanischen Kriegschiffe*
Le Masson, Henri *Du Nautilus au Redoutable*
Le Masson, Henri *The French Navy*
Lenton & Colledge *Warships of World War II*
Lenton, H. T. *British Submarines, German Submarines, American Submarines (part of series)*
Lipscomb, F. W. *The British Submarine*

Naval Records Club *Warship International* (periodical)
Morison & Rowe *Ships and Aircraft of the US Fleet*
Roskill, S. W. *The War at Sea*
Silverstone, Paul *US Warships of World War I*
Silverstone, Paul *US Warships of World War II*
Steensen, R. Steen *Vore Undervandsbade*
Sueter, Murray F. *Submarines, Mines & Torpedoes*
Techel, H. *Der Bau von U Booten auf der Germaniawerft*
Trusov *Povodnyi Lodki Russkom e Sovietkom*
US Naval Institute *Proceedings* (periodical)
Ufficio Storico della Marina Militare *I Sommergibili Italiane*
Van Quispel, H. *The Job and the Tools*
Watts & Gordon *The Imperial Japanese Navy*
Warship Profiles (series) *HMS Upholder*
    U107
    FS Rubis
    HMS Hesperus
    USS Barb